The Exile

by the same author

Lives and Letters 1906–1957

THE EXILE
A Life of Ivy Litvinov

JOHN CARSWELL

faber and faber
LONDON · BOSTON

First published in 1983
by Faber and Faber Limited
3 Queen Square London WC1N 3AU
Typeset by
Wyvern Typesetting Limited, Bristol
Printed in Great Britain by
The Thetford Press Limited, Thetford, Norfolk

British Library Cataloguing in Publication Data

Carswell, John
The exile: a life of Ivy Litvinov
1. Litvinov, Ivy
I. Title
947.084'2'0924   DK268.L/

ISBN 0-571-13135-2

Library of Congress Data has been applied for

Contents

Illustrations

For many years I was obsessed with the idea that God had sent me to Russia for the purpose of being the only English subject in the Soviet Union who could write. By writing I mean doing it so that people wanted to read it all the time they were reading it; they wanted to go on reading it simply for pleasure.

Note written in New York in 1943

TO TANYA

Preface

The main source for this book is Ivy Litvinov's own collection of papers, which her daughter Tanya has placed unreservedly at my disposal, and her own published writings. Next in importance is my own acquaintance with Ivy which, though intermittent, lasted throughout my life.

I have also had many conversations with those who knew her, notably, of course, her daughter Tanya, but also Mrs Marjorie Barnett, Mrs Yvette Stone, Dr and Mrs Solomon Jacobson, Mr Chaim Raphael, Dr and Mrs Iain Eliot, and Mr Roy Hudleston, FSA, who also provided me with valuable details about Ivy's ancestry. I owe thanks to all these and to Lady Leeper, for helpful recollections about her husband, Sir Rex, and Maxim Litvinov.

Help going beyond the line of duty, which I most gratefully acknowledge, has been given by the British Library, the Public Record Office, the Registrar's Department of London University, the authorities of Trinity College Cambridge and the Israel Academy of Arts and Sciences. Mrs Beryl Graves communicated to me Ivy's copious correspondence with her during the later years of Ivy's life, and provided other information. I owe her a deep debt of gratitude. I would also like to record my gratitude to Mrs Helen Rapp.

Though Maxim Litvinov is among the few Soviet politicians for whom there is abundant direct evidence about life and character, printed sources must be regarded with suspicion. The life by Arthur Upham Pope[1] is propagandist in tone, unreliable, and in some factual respects demonstrably incorrect. Murk surrounds *Notes for a*

---

[1] *Maxim Litvinov*, Secker and Warburg, 1943.

Journal,[2] which is attributed to Litvinov and has an appearance of verisimilitude. Ivy, on her husband's authority, always denied its authenticity and attributed it to a defecting Soviet diplomatist; and Mr E. H. Carr, under whose editorship it originally appeared, informed me that he now considered it a complete fabrication.

More reliable printed sources for Maxim in his later years are given in notes at the appropriate point. For his earlier life there is his own account of his escape from Kiev published in the Soviet magazine *Younost* (*Youth*) in 1946, which corresponds closely to what he himself used to relate to his family; and the portrait in his disciple Ivan Mikhailovich Maisky's *Journey Into the Past*[3] which also includes lively sketches of other revolutionaries in pre-war London.

But for Maxim, as for Ivy, I have depended mainly on the evidence of his daughter, and on Ivy herself.

I met Litvinov myself on only two occasions, both in 1936, when he was the principal Soviet mourner at the funeral of King George V. I was then eighteen. The first occasion was late in the evening when the French windows of our Hampstead drawing-room suddenly opened to reveal a pair of well-dined tubby men in full evening dress and top hats, with cigars in their hands: Litvinov and Maisky. My father greeted them by saying they should have gone on the halls. The second time was more of a conversation than a picture. I found myself sitting next to Maxim on the sofa (he had just come from lunch with the new King and said he had been favourably impressed by his earnestness) and having carefully read accounts of the funeral I made an enthusiastic remark about his fellow-mourner, Marshal Tukhachevsky. He suddenly looked grave, even anxious, and said, 'Yes: a very distinguished soldier' in a way that brought the conversation to an end. Tukhachevsky was shot the following year.

I have supplied such annotation as is practicable without a calendar of Ivy's unpublished manuscripts and the conversations I have referred to. Where no source is given for a quotation it belongs to either one or the other.

Many others have helped in various ways. To all of them my thanks.

Berins Hill   J.P.C.
12 August 1982

[2] André Deutsch, 1953.
[3] Hutchinson, 1962.

Introduction

The large and chaotic mass of papers which the subject of this memoir left behind her contains many essays in autobiography, some of them traversing the same ground in repeated versions. She longed to describe and unfold what she rightly thought was an unusual life story but she could not manage it. After a bit the unfolding got into creases and crumples and could be forced no further.

My attempt to do what the subject of this biography so much wanted to do for herself is due to the fact that I knew her as a close friend of my mother when I was a small child, and in her later years, when she came to England, saw a great deal of her. Between those epochs I often heard of her and even saw her occasionally. It was one of her characteristics that she did not lose touch with people, although the ends of her friendships were abrupt. So she remained a figure in my life. She was at first my mother's friend who had married a Commissar; then she was a woman endangered in a distant country who needed such reassurance as one could send in ignorance of her actual situation and from whom one received occasional scrawls on postcards asking for literary references and conveying her love. In the end she became a kind of domineering, eccentric, self-appointed great-aunt in Hove, burying herself deeper and deeper in auto-biographical typescripts.

These typescripts and papers seem to contain an active principle of disorder, peculiarly their own, and no amount of sorting will give them discipline. I have sometimes fancied aged, ghostly hands had been at work in the night to restore their disorder when I returned to them in the morning.

Included in the archive are large numbers of letters both to and from Ivy—for she was in the habit of recovering her correspondence and even went over it many years afterwards, inserting improvements to what she had originally written. In addition to the letters there are drafts of stories, published and unpublished; fragmentary diaries; many jottings and notes, mostly from reading or from observation of the world about her; and some transcripts of tapes she made during her visit to England in 1960, which are especially interesting because Manya Harari, with whom she made them, led the conversation on to topics and parts of Ivy's life that she did not otherwise write about.

Most of this material was created during Ivy's last years at Hove, but a great deal was brought by her out of the Soviet Union in 1972. Apart from a few very early papers, the earliest contemporary documents are the series of letters written to my mother, which begin in 1926 and continue until Ivy's self-imposed exile to Sverdlovsk in 1937. There were earlier and later letters in this series, but they have not survived.

After the move to Sverdlovsk comes correspondence with Ivy's daughter Tanya, together with a few letters from her husband Maxim. This series ends with Maxim's fall from office in 1939 and the reunion of the family in deadly danger. The contemporary record begins again with the Washington embassy of 1942–3, thins out thereafter, and becomes plentiful after 1947.

In examining and interpreting it one has always to remember that it was mostly written under an authoritarian regime by the wife (later the widow) of an important political figure, and that after Maxim's fall Ivy was in grave danger of the prison camp or worse. More than once she packed for such a journey. Veiled language is what one would expect and what one finds, and this book could never have been written, despite the copious documentation on which it is based, without the knowledge of her parents' actual behaviour and opinions which Tanya Litvinov has supplied in numerous conversations.

Ivy, then, learned to be obscure and allusive but in her nature she was the soul of indiscretion. Her letters to my mother, many of which were written outside the Soviet Union during fairly frequent visits to the West, especially Germany, in the 1930s and posted in street pillar-boxes, constitute a hair-raising hostage to fortune when one considers they were written by the wife of a Foreign Minister. And although she patchily grew more careful, her correspondence as wife of the Soviet ambassador in Washington was in many respects reckless. Even today I have had to disguise the names of one or two persons in the Soviet Union who might otherwise be embarrassed.[1] Different readers will assign different reasons for the strange turn Ivy's character took. I would describe her personality, fundamentally, as warm and affectionate, but delinquent. She admired her husband, and stood by him bravely in his most dangerous hours and in his long humiliation, even though she detested the official life to which he was entirely committed, and had herself no political convictions whatever. No woman could have loved her children and grandchildren more, or have given more of herself to them. She was unforgettable, overwhelming in her affection. She was unfaithful almost on principle and inconsiderate almost as a habit. For her the idea of guilt did not exist. Her heart went out with sudden enthusiasms to unlikely recipients and was often bruised as a result. So there was the side I have called delinquent, which developed as she grew older into moods of misanthropy and combativeness. Guilt she repudiated: but she was riddled with shame.

In all her perplexities her recourse was literature. She read and wrote as some people eat and drink, with a passion and persistence that overrode all other considerations. Like all addicts she often referred to her detestation of writing and to the pain of sitting for hours at the typewriter without being able to compose more than a few hundred words, and among her papers are many signs of the agony she went through. There is a page on which a paragraph appears as many as five times in almost the same words with each version struck out in favour of a fresh start. She would spend half an hour debating whether 'purse' or 'handbag' was the word she needed.

Her immense reading was dictated by the severity of her taste and the chances of what she could get hold of. Everything she read she annotated and criticized, and although she never mentions him, her attitude began to approximate to the positive, almost revealed standards associated with the name of Leavis. In poetry her tastes were conservative: Shakespeare above all, and Milton. Fiction, however, was her particular province. She adored Richardson (to whom she came late in her life), admitted Fielding, but rejected Smollett. Scott she detested, Dickens she came to admire, and she knew almost the whole of Trollope by heart. Jane Austen and Proust

---

[1] I have never substituted an alias for a true name, but have sometimes referred to a person by an initial which is not their true one, thus B—.

occupied special pedestals, and among more modern authors Gissing, Lawrence, Joyce (and even Bennett but certainly not Galsworthy) earned her respect. The most admired of her contemporaries were Adrian Bell and Henry Green, and though she read many others voraciously, few escaped censure. In her old age someone was so bold as to suggest she should read *The French Lieutenant's Woman* and after an interval for study received a withering rebuke. Her introduction to Saul Bellow when she was an old lady was not a success.

The total amount of her own published work is quite extensive, but much of it consists of translation from Russian into English, in which she attained facility and even distinction. Her original work is more modest: three novels—two of which were published when she was under thirty—some scattered autobiographical pieces, and a number of short stories, most of which were originally published in the *New Yorker*. On these her claims to literary recognition rest, and those with a Soviet setting could have been written by no one else. In them she made a small but unique contribution to English literature.

One must imagine someone who by upbringing and temperament was dedicated to participation in the literary life of her time but found herself carried from it into a special kind of isolation; her struggle against it goes far towards explaining her story and the strange development of her character.

This isolation was not created by her marriage, but was underlined by it, and in some ways her husband Maxim was its symbol. Yet in another way he was a source of reassurance and a lifeline to a world which he himself had abandoned. The picture of him which she endlessly tried to capture in words was not of a Commissar or a Bolshevik but of an older, slightly comic, rather reserved, but inwardly strong and resourceful lover: the man she had met in Hampstead and accepted in the Express Dairy.

Maxim must be a major figure in a book about Ivy, and with him it is impossible to leave out world affairs. At the same time such a book is not the place for an account—even if the materials were available—of his career as a statesman and its political background. Nevertheless, partly because of his marriage to Ivy, more is known about Litvinov's personal life and character than about most public figures in a country where the real characters and histories of notables are systematically suppressed and distorted. I have been able to add a good deal to what is generally known about Litvinov, and this has led me in some places—particularly as regards his early life—into events in which Ivy had no part, even though they formed the man she married.

The adventure of Ivy's marriage gives her story a significance it would not otherwise have. She knew this, and much resented it because it made people less interested in her than she felt she deserved, and her frustration was the stronger because she was never accepted, even in the social sense, into the Bolshevik aristocracy or the literary establishment which it had created. Lenin she never met. Stalin she met once, when he mistook her at a diplomatic dinner for the wife of the Finnish ambassador, and shook her warmly by the hand. The only two prominent Bolsheviks she knew well were Kollontai and Rothstein. She had the opportunity of meeting and talking to many other Kremlin figures and if her character had been different she could have provided vivid portraits of them, but she might not have survived in that case to make them known. It was the same with the literary figures. As it was, the reminiscences on which she lavished so much effort concentrated almost entirely on her younger days, and her experiences of the Soviet Union produced no accounts of high life. What they did yield are accounts of ordinary Soviet life.

She was an exile. Both by temperament and circumstances she was a foreigner to her surroundings, wherever they were, almost throughout her life. Exiled in the household created by her mother's second marriage, exiled in her husband's revolutionary Russia, and exiled in her native country when at last she returned to it, she had the exile's recklessness and the exile's caution—caution for the sake of survival, recklessness in having no responsibility except for her children.

As an exile whom it was impossible to overlook she drew many friends and admirers, some of them true and some merely interested in what she might have to tell. These last she treated with suspicion—indeed her wariness gradually became a barrier to almost any friend, and her story was never told as it might have been. This was partly because she had learned she should not tell stories, and partly because she wanted to tell different ones.

It is not easy to write about someone one has known well, especially if she has belonged to an earlier generation. Ivy was involved in so many movements of her time, yet was never touched by them, rather like a fakir crossing the hot coals unburned. She was a maddening woman, endlessly insistent, brave as a lion, incapable of being ignored, and in her strange way very loving.

Fate brought about her marriage to one of the leading men of her generation, so that she met most of the others on equal terms. Her youth had trained her for nothing of the kind. Vitality, strength of character, intelligence, wide reading, were her resources, and she had position, and was conscious of it. She could have made herself a celebrity on the model of the many celebrities she encountered, and the possibility of doing so lurked in her mind. Yet she resisted the idea. As an ambassador's wife she could publish an account of the fool she made of herself as a girl on her visit to D. H. Lawrence, and as the widow of a foreign minister reject all temptation to be famous at his expense.

I

An Amalgam of Ancestors

When Ivy Low was a liberated young woman early in this century, she had a dream she always remembered about her grandfather Maximilian Löwe:

> . . . if not a dream, a revelation: the round curve of the world and up it, rampant, jigs the beaky figure of grandpapa. His chest protrudes, his nostrils flare, he bears a naked scimitar in his hand. He jigs and jerks eternally up the curve of the world. And when I woke I told myself 'This is it!' and felt I had had the discovery of a lifetime.

Maximilian had died in 1905 soon after the time of this dream, and something of the ferocity of his grand-daughter's vision stares out of the whiskery portrait we have of him in old age. Most of his life was spent in the City of London, sometimes as a speculator, sometimes as an agent for the pioneers of electrical power, the Siemens and the di Ferrantis, who transformed the experiments of Faraday into the dynamo, the submarine cable, and the telegraph line from England to India. Like many other Victorian Jews—Marx among them—Löwe was carried to England as a result of the revolutionary struggles of Central Europe. He had been born at Eisenstadt in eastern Austria, about 1830, became a devotee of the Hungarian revolution of 1848, and after the defeat of Kossuth was a wanderer in Europe until, still a brisk and handsome young man, he followed his hero to England.

Victorian—and indeed Edwardian—society was far more open to continental exiles than the clichés of insularity might suggest, and this was true whether the exiles came to continue their political plans or, like Maximilian Löwe, to embark on more conventional careers with an enthusiasm for the land of stability and toleration which often exceeded that of the natives. Maximilian, it is true, took a wife from his native Austria. She was the daughter of a rabbi, but Löwe's family soon discarded all orthodox observances. His life was that of a businessman, first at Leyland Road, Blackheath, then at Westbourne Park on the fringes of Bayswater, where he and his wife Thérèse (whence came Ivy's second name) reared a family of five daughters and six sons, two of whom were knighted for services to conservative newspapers and the imperial ideal.

Maximilian's career had its ebbs and flows, but one of the more prosperous tides occurred about 1870. In that year his eldest son, Sidney, was sent to King's College School in the Strand, and in due course younger brothers followed him to that staunchly Anglican establishment after introductory duty as choirboys in mortar-board and Sunday best. But the former revolutionary had not entirely melted into his adopted country's conventions. His Anglicanism, and therefore by necessity his family's, was of a heterodox stamp, as a result of his falling under the influence of one of the clerical rebels who troubled the Victorian church in the age of Darwin.

In 1864 the Rev. Charles Annesley Voysey, a clergyman almost exactly the same age as Maximilian, was appointed to the north Yorkshire parish of Healaugh after successful service in the slums of the East End of London. Soon after his arrival in the Dales he published a book whose very title was calculated to cause dismay: *Is every Statement in the Bible about Our Heavenly Father Strictly True?* Demands for recantation were met by embittered resistance and judicial proceedings which were carried as far as the Privy Council in one of the last trials for heresy to come before that court. The controversy lasted for seven years as part of the ferment set up by the publication of *The Origin of Species.* In 1871, the year Darwin published *The Descent of Man,* Voysey was finally deprived of his benefice and formed a congregation of his own at St George's Hall, Langham Place, where, as he put it, his flock had to contemplate

the battlefield of two great parties, representing on the one side most of the earnest traditionalists, and on the other most of the not less earnest and religious men, whose thoughts are in harmony with the highest culture of the age, and the latest conclusions of science. It is a mere accident, so to speak, that I have anything to do with it.

'We are in open warfare', he told his hearers in his inaugural address in October 1871, 'against much of what goes by the name of Christianity.' The Fall of Man, everlasting punishment, the doctrine of atonement, the Devil, the Trinity, the Divinity of Christ, the Second Coming, the authority of the Church, the efficacy of the sacraments, the belief that religion was revealed in Scripture—all were rejected by this modern Pelagian as inconsistent with the over-arching idea of a loving Father and the right of the human intellect to free enquiry leading to ever-increasing understanding of the universe.

Among the subscribers who contributed nearly £3,000 to found Voysey's congregation were Samuel Courtauld, Charles Darwin, two members of the Wedgwood family, and Maximilian Low, Esq. of Theresa Villa, Leyland Road, Lea, SE. One of the singular features of the long list is the number of retired Indian army officers which it includes. In due course a 'Theistic Church' was built in Swallow Street, off Piccadilly, where every Sunday Voysey preached to packed congregations.

It is difficult now to recapture the terrible discipline enforced over the centuries by the doctrine of eternal punishment, and the transformation brought about by an effective challenge to it. Time out of mind it had been a potent sanction on conduct and a source of agonized foreboding not only to the simple-minded but to the highest intellects. From all this the Low family, with Voysey as their pastor, were emancipated, and they venerated him. Long after they grew up and in some cases moved away even from the comforting theism he taught, they corresponded with him, visited him, and in his old age helped him with money.

The early 1870s were years of prosperity for the Lows, but the later part of the decade brought disaster to Maximilian's finances and his larger ambitions for his eleven children had to be set aside. The second son, Frederick, was sent to America to seek his fortune at the age of seventeen, and the third, Maurice, at the age of fourteen, went to Austria to learn German with a family. Only Sidney, the eldest, was allowed at paternal expense to proceed to university because in 1875 he had gained a scholarship to Pembroke College, Oxford, which he managed to exchange, after only one year, for one at Balliol, then in its palmiest period under Jowett. Walter, the fourth brother, who was only eleven, and an even younger boy, Ernest, had little to look forward to in the way of prestigious education: nor had any of the six girls.

Walter Humboldt Low, to give the fourth son his full name, and a hint of his father's principles, was born on 9 May 1864. He did not follow Sidney and Maurice to King's in the Strand, but attended the City of London School, which he left in 1880, when he was only sixteen, for an office job in the City. But that was far from being the end of his education. Sidney said afterwards that Walter had the largest brain in the family, and no man could have worked his brain harder. In 1882 he matriculated into the University of London and by 1884—entirely by private study while earning his living—he graduated with honours in French. Only three years later, in 1887, he achieved the London MA in French and German, being placed third in that year's examination. In the meantime he held teaching posts (it seems simultaneously) at the Mercers' School and the struggling college for ambitious working men, Birkbeck. Nor was this enough. In October 1890, at the age of twenty-six, he went up to Cambridge as an undergraduate with a subsizarship at Trinity; and in 1893 was placed in the second class of the Mediaeval and Modern Languages Tripos.

This was not simply degree-chasing; other reasons besides that had taken him to Cambridge. At some time before attaining his London MA he had met a remarkable educational entrepreneur not much older than himself, named William Briggs, who had perceived the growing enthusiasm for academic qualification as a way to social advancement, and devised a system for passing examinations on lines which have now become familiar. The candidate, under careful drilling by a successful examinee, was equipped to answer a range of questions from which (as scrutiny of previous examination papers established) some were certain to appear. On this principle Briggs had founded the University Correspondence College, and was recruiting tutors to whom he paid 2s 2d, 2s 4d or 2s 6d an hour according to whether they possessed third-, second-, or first-class honours degrees. The headquarters of Briggs's organization was at Cambridge.

So all the time Walter Low was working for the Tripos he was slaving away for Briggs as well. Between 1887 and 1890 he produced no fewer than six numbers in Briggs's Tutorial Series, all on English language, literature and history; and in the last of these years, almost certainly at Briggs's establishment, he met a spindly, undernourished biology graduate of Imperial College named H. G. Wells, who had come to Cambridge to be interviewed as one of Briggs's tutors. A close friendship developed, in which Low, who was two years Wells's senior, was somewhat in the lead. 'Two passably respectable but not at all glossy young men,' Wells recalled in his autobiography, 'with hungry side glances at London's abounding prosperity, sharpening our wits with talk.' Low not only had an extensive knowledge of languages and literature, but also knew far more about current politics than Wells, who found him 'ambitious and not the acquisitive sort, mystical and deliberate'.

Low had already ranged outside the French and German literature in which he qualified, and had somehow taught himself Norwegian as well. The result was a translation, published in Bohn's endless series of classic novels, of two of Bjørnstjerne Bjørnsen's 'Folkslivnovelle', *Arne* and *The Fisher Lassie*, in 1890. Their author, who was still alive, had become one of the leaders of the Norwegian national struggle for independence from Sweden which nearly led to war before it triumphed in 1905. In their time these peasant tales from the fjords were advanced literature, and indeed were thought quite daring.

By this time Walter was married. How and when the dark Spanish-looking Jewish tutor met Alice, daughter of Lieutenant-Colonel Richard Aufrère Baker, late Madras Artillery in the East India Company's service, is not known: perhaps it was through membership of the Voysey congregation. But in September 1888, in a wood on the outskirts of Maidenhead, the colonel's daughter and the ex-revolutionary's clever son conceived a child, and early in 1889 they were married. Alice helped him with the lyrics in Bjørnsen's *Arne* and their first child, Ivy Thérèse, the subject of this book, was born on 4 June 1889. Two other daughters, Letty and Olive, followed at intervals of about a year. A series of green thoughts in a green shade.

Ivy as a little girl had vivid recollections of her contrasting grandfathers as they were entering old age. Maximilian 'had a hooked nose and bushy whiskers and small, watery eyes; tufts of white hair, yellow at the tips, straggled over the rubbed velvet collar of his overcoat, the ends of his muffler would not stay tucked in, and he bent over a tapping stick as he shuffled along.' The colonel on the other hand

strode over the pavement as if he were at the head of a regiment, and his crest of silvery white hair was never subdued by a hat in the coldest weather. . . . He too carried a stick, but not for support; he lifted it smartly from the ground in time to the jaunty rhythm of his steps, held it neatly under his arm, or raised it airily to greet an acquaintance on the opposite pavement. He too had a hooked nose, but it did not droop at the tip . . .

Maximilian seemed very much what he was: not so the colonel. Colonel Baker had his peculiarities and some style, but his career had been singularly lacking in distinction. He was the son of a clergyman, and at the age of twenty went out as an artillery subaltern to India where, after twenty-two years' service, he attained the rank of major, upon which his retirement with an honorific lieutenant-colonelcy followed less than a month later, in 1872. As a young officer his superior reported him as 'apathetic and careless in his duty, but of good character'. Though he served in India throughout the Mutiny he was retained at remote, untroubled bases in the south; and he does not seem to have taken part in any of the imperial campaigns in which the Indian army was engaged during the subsequent adventurous years. His one achievement in India was to marry the daughter of a real lieutenant-colonel who had covered himself with glory at the battles of Chillianwallah and Goojerat, became Military Secretary to the Governor General, and retired as a Lieutenant-General and a knight.[1]

Colonel Baker and his wife Louise had four children—three girls and a boy—all of whom, for reasons never disclosed, were baptized 'Katie', in addition to their other names. Ivy's mother Alice was the youngest. After Mrs Baker's death the colonel had a second family by a Miss Fox who had entered his service as a governess and became his mistress. The colonel did not marry Miss Fox, though there seems to have been no reason why he should not, and several why he should have done so. As he grew older he developed an unfortunate weakness for little girls. Ivy's mother Alice, therefore, grew up in a household where convention and irregularity were mingled. She had scarcely known her mother, who had died when she was only a year old, yet at intervals illegitimate younger half-brothers and sisters continued to arrive, while Miss Fox anxiously struggled to keep the older girls out of the way of their father.

[1] Lieutenant-General Sir Richard James Holwell Birch (1803–75) came of a family which served in India for several generations and there was a vague tradition in the family that some Indian blood had mingled with it in the eighteenth century. He fought in both Sikh Wars and played an important part as a staff officer during the Mutiny. His portrait haunted Ivy during her childhood as a detestable ghost crowding out the memory of her adored father.

All of this helps to explain why Ivy's mother Alice was far from being a typical Indian army daughter. She had the incisiveness of some of her forebears, and a good deal of their style, but she rather grandly explained to her eldest daughter, when she was quite a little girl, that Ivy had been a 'love-child'—along with an indication of what that term meant and an assurance that she should be proud of it as giving her a special warmth of nature in comparison with those conceived within the boundaries of wedlock.[2]

Walter Low had yet to graduate at Cambridge but he set up house with his new wife and daughter in Doughty Street, Bloomsbury, not far from the Foundling Hospital, to which the young mother said she would send baby if it wasn't good. It was while he was there that the translation of *Arne* came out, to enthusiastic reviews. But something more regular was necessary. He had his work from Briggs, and packaged courses continued to pour from his pen, but 2s 4d an hour was hardly enough. Soon after graduating, through the intermediacy of Briggs, he became editor of a weekly journal published by the College of Preceptors called the *Educational Times:* his salary was £50 a year, and there was £50 for contributors. As H. G. Wells put it, 'it was decided I should be the contributors' so between them they wrote the paper for the next few years. With one expedient and another Walter and his young family managed to establish themselves in 1890 at a house in Fairholme Road, West Kensington, just behind the Queen's Club.

But of Walter's many efforts and activities it can be said that the translation of *Arne* and *The Fisher Lassie* with which Alice helped him was the most important work in his short life. It was a small contribution to a vast movement towards the popularity of foreign literatures which was already gathering force in Britain and would sweep on for the next two or three decades. And it was reprinted with a preface by Sir Edmund Gosse more than twenty years after it first appeared.

The influence of foreign literature on the British public—what we might call the *reception* of foreign work into the canon of a particular generation of English readers—has perhaps never been more marked than in the years of Imperial consciousness between the Golden Jubilee and the War. The British romantics and Shakespeare had

---

[2] Alice rather liked to think that she herself was a love-child; and that her father was not Colonel Baker but the Hon. Aubrey Herbert, a minor poet, and at the material time Secretary to the Governor General of India.

established an influence abroad during the first decades of the century, and during the middle decades British readership had been dominated by great British names—Dickens, Thakeray, George Eliot, Browning, and Tennyson. Great French and German authors were of course read, but they were not naturalized, except perhaps for the political and the naughty. But by the 1880s Tolstoy and Ibsen, by the 1890s Turgenev, by the beginning of the following century Strindberg and Dostoyevsky, were not only translated but entered into English literature in a way that had never been accorded to Victor Hugo, Zola or Baudelaire.

Walter Low is a kind of paradigm of the progressiveness of his time: a zealot for education, a Fabian, a sympathizer with oppressed and obliterated nationalities, among them his own. The last was a subject on which he found Wells unsympathetic. 'I have always', Wells wrote long afterwards of their conversations, 'refused to be enlightened and sympathetic about the Jewish question.' What exactly was Low's position on it can only be guessed; but it is reasonable to suppose that he saw it not as a racial but as an international issue, and that with the stirring of nationalities that was already in progress he was suggesting that the Jews, as a nation, should somewhere in the world have a national home.

If life had followed its normal course Ivy would have been brought up in the coherent, Fabian, intellectual, mildly Zionist atmosphere which was gathering round her father, and an obsession about an unhappy childhood which cast a shadow over the rest of her life would have been avoided. But the winter of 1895 was exceptionally severe, and in February of that year her father died of pneumonia which followed on an attack of influenza. Walter was only thirty, but he had worn out his strength with unremitting work. He was not only editing the *Educational Times*, but had a post on the *Globe* as well; and in the past eight years had produced no fewer than twelve handbooks for Briggs's Tutorial Service, of which one, *Matric English*, was to run to fourteen editions—the last of them in 1931.

Ivy was only five when Walter died, and in later life could scarcely form a picture of her father, though she tried desperately to do so. He became for her the ideal no one could equal, but to which she herself had a duty to aspire. Her own intense application to literature and her high-mindedness on intellectual matters may have been partly hereditary; but they were also propitiations of the wonderful father she had never been old enough to know, or to please.

[An Amalgam of Ancestors]

Her childhood and her heredity became the constant themes of her later life, yet she never felt she had quite described them as they deserved. And certainly the genetic inheritance was remarkable: on the one side Hungarian-Jewish, on the other the long line of military Anglo-Indians, with or without the contribution of the aristocratic Aubrey Herbert, whose surname was curiously enough now to crop up again in her life.

2

The Unhappy Child

Walter's widow Alice, now left at 9 Fairholme Road with three small girls, was not totally without resources. Walter had been insured, and what was more had introduced her to the literary world, so that she had a column of fiction reviews in Frank Harris's *Saturday Review*. She was only twenty-five, lively and good-looking, and certainly intended to marry again, despite her encumbrances. Her two sisters moved in, partly as chaperones, partly, perhaps, as sponsors.

Two suitors soon presented themselves to Alice. Both were employed in that temple of learning, the British Museum Library, but otherwise were very different. One was in Printed Books and later went on to be Librarian of the War Office—a man of eminence and charm. He took Alice to restaurants in the Thames valley, where he toyed with a diamond ring in the presence of the five-year-old Ivy, for the benefit of the mother. The other, John Alexander Herbert (Sandy), was an expert in medieval illuminated manuscripts—a scholar, conventional, assiduous, loyal and dignified; but of narrow horizons.

Long afterwards Ivy wrote several extended accounts of her experience of her mother's brief widowhood and what followed its end; and from the care she lavished on them it is clear that this, together with her own marriage, mattered more in her own estimation of her life than anything else. For Alice's daughter, no other room would ever be like the drawing-room at Fairholme Road. Her accounts of this time vary and are sometimes overlaid with a veneer of fiction; but their total effect is the same. Ivy had been betrayed. Her mother's remarriage set a seal on the loss of her father, and whoever Alice had chosen to replace him would have been detestable to Ivy. She did not think about her father, or wish him back, but the light had gone out of her life; she began to dream about a stranger whom she met in the street and who took her back with him to his luxurious home.

Alice chose Sandy as the man Ivy was to spend a lifetime detesting. 'The mill belongs to Sandy still', the title of a song he had sung to Alice's accompaniment during the wooing, was the wire he received in Newcastle announcing her choice. It was to be a strange mill to manage.

Alice and Sandy Herbert were married in August 1896. Sandy was thirty-four, two years older than the predecessor whose instincts and energy had begun to undermine the fabric he stood by. He was indeed liberal and progressive, and did not believe in God, though his father was a clergyman in Newcastle; but he believed in things as they were, and he had the single-mindedness of a man who belonged to an institution in which he believed. In his eldest stepchild's eyes he became the very picture of a mediocre intellectual with a safe job—endlessly instructive, solemnly logical.

Ivy remembered, or thought she remembered, every detail about the wedding down to the dress she wore and the unexplained disappearance of the children's ploddy dog, Follow, who was there when the party set out for church and was never seen again. And as her awareness developed, all the worst passages of her life seemed to be concerned with her stepfather. Even the novels of Scott and Dickens which he read aloud to the children seemed a special kind of wickedness, and her hostility to Scott lasted for the rest of her life. Sandy's strict control of money (and after all, his salary was far from princely) seemed contemptible, and she sympathized with the servant who said crossly that Mr Herbert's income was 'quite enough to pay me for taking you on walks'.

Ivy was furious about the house they first went to live in at Harrow, although from her own description it was extremely commodious and boasted two servants—a quite considerable household for a man who was not yet even an Assistant Keeper, and would not attain that modest rank for another sixteen years. The steps to the temple in those days were slow. Before that Assistant Keepership was conferred Sandy had published four learned works, including his very important Catalogue of Illuminated Manuscripts.

Sandy read the children the New Testament as well as Scott and Dickens, but as became an agnostic and a Darwinian, he left the choice of opinions to them, including the question of confirmation. The problem was immediately resolved by Ivy in favour of emotional membership of the Church. As she put it in her early autobiographical novel, *Growing Pains:*[1]

> She heard the murmur of words, of which she only caught 'This thy child'; she felt the pressure of the Bishop's hands on her veiled head, and the sting of unexpected tears at the back of her eyes. In her seat once more I think she really did pray. She forgot to resume her ultra-devotional attitude, and a wave of compunction passed over her for her pitiful little pose.

Although Sandy was a progressive man, it was painful to him that his wife insisted on having what she called her 'personal life'. This, at the time they were married, consisted mainly in reviewing novels for the *Queen*, another connection she owed to Walter, for which she was paid rather less than the review copies fetched. But it also involved occasional expeditions to London for interviews with editors and other literary persons, and these were serious matters, as her diary showed:

> 2.30 Meet Jimmie at Achilles' statue. Fawn going-away dress, brown boa with brown chenille tassels, pansy toque, shot-silk parasol, brown gloves, fawn strap shoes.

She did not always return from these expeditions the same day, which resulted in outbursts when Sandy 'clenched and unclenched his fists' and referred to his wife as 'my lady fly-by-night'.

Alice seems to have confided deeply in Ivy; but she could also be severe, as Ivy writes:

> And so mother and daughter would mount the stairs to the bedroom in sinister silence. As they went up the short top flight the mother felt the small hand against her palm turn cold. But both were now in the grip of doom and even if released she would have trudged towards her own execution. Still holding her child's hand, the mother stopped in front of her dressing room table to grope in her middle drawer for her hair-brush. The moment Ivy was pinned face down on the bed the spell was broken, and she bawled and struggled with a plebeian lack of pride that humiliated her mother, who often told her children that she would rather have died than

[1] Heinemann, 1913.

make a sound when her father whipped her. Afterwards, ashamed, and afraid the neighbours would hear Ivy's yells and think she was killing the child, she half-carried the sobbing victim to the night-nursery next door and laid her on the bed with reproachful words, remorseful kisses. Then, drained and shaken, she went down the flight and a half to the drawing room there to sink into an arm-chair and smoke a cigarette from the silver box kept for male visitors.

Old Maximilian was sometimes among these visitors. The children saw their mother's face darken at the sound of the shuffling steps on the gravel, followed by the tap-tap of the stick on the three steps to the front door. They watched her summon a smile to her lips and run to the hall before grandfather had time to ring the bell. 'October the nineteenth,' the old man would say when he was comfortably settled and had reassured himself of the date, 'and we're in the year 1896 now. Forty-six years, one month, ten days ago, it was. London went mad, mad. Ladies fainted. Young men crowded to his side. Kossuth. England had a heart then.'

But on the whole Ivy saw very little of her father's numerous Jewish relations. Her mother, when the subject came up, as it sometimes did with her new husband's sisters, was steadfast, but slightly defensive. 'The Jews', she declared, 'are the most moral people in the world. Uncle Fred said he never came across a Jew dipsomaniac the whole time he was a Lunacy Commissioner in Wales.' 'Dada was a Jew, children, and you must always be proud of dada. If anyone asks you, you can say you have Jewish blood on your father's side.'

Walter's family was, however, a problem. The children spent a holiday with the Low sisters and came back accompanied by a letter that contained various criticisms about health and rearing. Then there was Sidney Low, now a successful leader-writer on the *Westminster Gazette*, noting, in the year old Maximilian maundered on about Kossuth, 'a new machine for producing moving photographs' and the fact that on 14 November 1896 motor cars had been allowed on the streets for the first time. It was not the world in which Sandy Herbert moved, nor indeed was it Alice's.

The reasons for Ivy's severance from her father's family were complex and not entirely attributable to their Jewishness. The Herberts were liberals, but the contemporary Lows were either socialists or, still worse, conservative imperialists, which Alice and

Sandy were united in regarding as vulgar and wrong. For the Diamond Jubilee Alice bought emblazoned mugs for her children, and on the relief of Ladysmith she even sent one of her daughters to school wrapped in a union jack like a pinafore. But she would not allow gossip about the royal family or pin-ups of princes and princesses, and when the children came back from school chanting 'We love the old flag with its red white and blue' she said it was a song fit only for board-school children.

Ivy was rebellious, difficult and censorious of her elders, who she suspected of being humbugs; and this, after a time, Sandy could not stand. He had introduced Ivy not only to Scott and Dickens, but to Trollope, with long-term personal consequences for her and political consequences that he cannot have imagined; and she was still impossible. He had a sister who ran a boarding-school at Tynemouth, and there he consigned Ivy, when she was about eleven, to be followed by her sisters Letty and Olive. It was a thriving establishment until the arrival of the Low sisters, but its reputation suffered severely from their stay—especially Ivy's.

She describes these schooldays in her novel *Growing Pains*. She was a theatrical, opinionated pupil, capable of intense attachments, but resentful and defiant. It was *Claudine à l'école* transposed to an English key, but happening at almost the same time, with the same jealousies, the same favouritisms between mistresses and adolescent girls, in which Ivy passionately took part. Her entire idea of education was emotional, and she was impatient of any regular systematic approach to a subject, even if it interested her. She felt she should either be able to capture it in a bound or it was not worth the effort:

> 'It's useless,' said the drawing mistress, 'your trying to draw the things you "feel you like", unless you get hold of some of the elementary principles of drawing. But of course if you won't believe someone of more experience than yourself it's a waste of breath talking to you.'

One of her hostile contemporaries informed her she was 'different', a charge Ivy countered by declaring everyone was different. 'Everybody's not different,' was the stolid reply. '*You're* different.'

It was a trouble that was to pursue Ivy through life. She felt there was a certain truth in what the girl had said. She might not have any particular outstanding gift, but she felt different. So unhappy, and indeed disruptive, did she become at Tynemouth that after four miserable years she was brought home, at the age of fifteen, and sent to day-school.

By then Alice and Sandy had moved to a flat in Portsdown Road, Kilburn, and the chosen school was Maida Vale High School, not far away. As she and Alice walked there for Ivy's first day Alice murmured, with a glance at the other pupils also making their way, 'They look rather Jewish.' 'I could see they were different from the girls at Tynemouth, and I began to wonder if it had been something mysteriously Jewish in my own face, and in myself, that had set me apart from my school-friends.' 'What's the point of handicapping a girl from the start?' demanded her mother suddenly, during this reflection. 'A man might not notice a girl being dark, with striking features, unless the address put ideas into his head. After all a pretty girl who's *not* Jewish does start with an advantage. Other things being equal.'

Perhaps without realizing what she was doing, Alice went on to place a heavy handicap on her daughter's self-confidence at a critical age. The motive may have been economy, or there may have been an element of subconscious jealousy in it. When Ivy was seventeen her mother arranged for all her teeth to be extracted, and Ivy went through life with dentures.

Alice's considerable shrewdness—at any rate in Ivy's picture of her —was concentrated entirely on externals, the main ones being, in her view, sexual success and the assertion of one's proper place in society. When, on a walk with Alice in St John's Wood, Ivy complained that her feet hurt, it became an object of instruction. 'You can say your *foot* hurts, but it's disgusting to say your *feet* hurt. It's middle-class.' The inevitable reply was that surely they were both middle-class. 'There is such a thing', said Alice after reflection, 'as being *in* the middle class without being *of* the middle class. If you know what I mean.' Ivy did: or at least her life shows that she did.

In old age she wrote a long and vivid, blow-by-blow manuscript account of her life with her mother at that time, full of comic, perceptive passages about the mixture of competition, rebellion, authority and maternal affection that lay between the pretty, pretentious Alice and the galumphing daughter she was trying to introduce to life and marriage. Ivy recoiled (and it was a permanent recoil) against the make-up and artifice her mother adored. 'To the pure', Alice would say, 'all things are impure'; and her private battery of aids to beauty was defended by describing anything she found in the bathroom as 'autobiographical'. Once, with unseasonable obedience to Alice's instruction about playful encouragement, Ivy placed a heavy hand on a young man's knee within minutes of being introduced, driving him into a state of panic. But the worst of it was that when it came to young men it was never clear whether Alice's example of how to encourage was merely illustrative. Certainly she very much disliked being addressed as 'mother' by her daughters when in mixed company.

Ivy made more friends at school than she did through her mother. One was a niece of Constance Garnett, called Speedwell Black. Another girl, Phyllis, was to cross Ivy's path in later years. Then there was Miss Brough, the maths mistress, for whom Ivy (to Alice's scorn) conceived a desperate devotion. 'I'd back myself to keep a man's attention against Broughy any day,' said her mother. 'Facts and maths aren't everything. I could grasp anything I wanted to, if I chose to give my mind to it. So could you.'

All Alice's efforts to get Ivy to concentrate on the one important thing were ludicrous failures, and Sandy grew increasingly irritated and sarcastic on the whole subject. It was clear to him that his eldest stepchild was not going to get married in the foreseeable future, and showed no aptitude for such feminine unmarried occupations as teaching or art. And there were three more girls to consider—Ivy's two sisters (one of whom had a tubercular hip) and his own child by Alice. His salary was modest and the prospect of promotion in the Museum remote. To be Keeper of the Manuscripts was beyond his horizon: Deputy Keeper he might in the end become. His wife was not exactly a help socially with his senior colleagues. On Primrose Hill, one day, he confronted Ivy with the unpleasant question of her future in such a way as to place a lasting stamp on her hatred of him. Soon afterwards he heard from a friend that the Prudential Assurance Company had launched a pioneer policy of employing middle-class girls as clerks at their newly built offices in Holborn, and procured the necessary personal recommendation that Ivy should be admitted as a 'Pru-girl'. At first she resisted, but in the end she gave in, and in 1908, at the age of eighteen, a 'Pru-girl' she became.

It was natural in the circumstances that she should see more of her father's relations, from whom she had been so long separated. The veteran of Kossuth's era was now dead, and his numerous children were widely dispersed, socially and geographically. Maurice was established permanently in Washington as the American correspondent of the *Morning Post*; two of the daughters kept house at Walberswick and had alienated themselves from Alice and Sandy by their criticisms of Ivy's upbringing after that fatal holiday. Another, Barbara, was in due course to become a distinguished Freudian psychologist. However, the most successful of all the family, Ivy's uncle Sidney, had remained on friendly terms with the Herberts and had taken them with Ivy to the first night of Pinero's *The Princess and the Butterfly*. Sidney had now risen to the highest flights of political journalism with the publication, in 1904, of a work on the practical operation of the British constitution called, with singular foresight of a title later adopted for a similar work by a Prime Minister, *The Governance of England*. It was praised by Rosebery and Curzon (the latter had reservations about Low's view that the Foreign Secretary-ship would never again be held by a peer), and was flung aside rather peevishly by H. G. Wells. In 1905 Sidney covered George V's Delhi Durbar, the grandest pageant ever mounted for the British imperial idea and was on conversational terms with many of the great men of the age—Spender, Milner, Morley, Rhodes, Stanley. He even composed verses on the great explorer's death, and was invited to write the last volume of *The Political History of England* which long remained the standard full-length history of this country. It appeared in 1907 and was the first systematic history of the Victorian period.

But Ivy did not seek to escape from her constricting life by applying herself to her uncle Sidney, whom she liked but regarded as silly and conventional. Her heart and enthusiasm went out to another member of that talented family, her aunt Edith, and to the man Edith had married, Dr David Eder.

It would hardly be an exaggeration to say David Eder was Ivy's second father, more real than Walter, and the very converse of Sandy. He must, indeed, have known Walter, for they were contemporaries and neighbours, and close to each other in sympathies, both as to socialism and the Jewish question. When Walter was struggling in the late 1880s as a London external student at Birkbeck College, David Eder was studying medicine at University College Medical School.

At the time Ivy first came under his influence Eder was a burly, genial man in his early forties with a house in Golders Green, consulting rooms in Charlotte Street, and a post as physician to the Margaret Macmillan Clinic in Bow. He was also an active member of the Fabian Society and of the London Labour Party, which he had helped to found in 1905. Among his friends was A. R. Orage, editor of the radical journal, the *New Age,* and he belonged to the inner circle of its contributors, so that he was to be seen from time to time at the weekly meetings held in the Chancery Lane ABC where Orage, Beatrice Hastings, A. E. Randall, John McFarland Kennedy, and Katherine Mansfield planned the next number.

Eder's earlier adventures had given a depth to his personality which would have been missing from a conventional doctor with a social conscience and progressive tendencies. He sprang from a family which had come to England in the mid-century and settled in St Pancras as manufacturing jewellers—a trade he followed himself for a short time, after a very sketchy education. In 1886, when he was twenty, his father's death provided him with a small inheritance which he used to send himself to University College Medical School.

He was not such a good examinee as Walter Low, and it took him nine years altogether to qualify—five to gain his B.Sc. and four more to complete clinical studies at Bart's. Part of the trouble was that he devoted a great deal of time to politics, especially those of the Bloomsbury Socialist Society[2] whose secretary he became in 1892. He emerged finally as a qualified practitioner in the year of Walter Low's death.

Although he was one of the earliest Fabians, Eder's socialism was not bureaucratic but romantic and warm-hearted. Doctrine had very limited appeal for him, and there was room for so many enthusiasms in his generous nature that a dogmatist could fairly accuse him of inconsistency. He believed in organized welfare, but was also an admirer of the veteran anarchist Kropotkin; and he was much preoccupied with the idea of a Jewish national home, though he saw it as being part of the British Empire, and it might be anywhere.

Like many of the early Zionists Eder saw the British Empire as a force for progress, for Hobson had not yet popularized the idea that imperialism was a baleful development of capitalism, and Lenin had not yet built that idea into Marxist theory, with consequences that have yet to run their course. Eder found socialism, imperialism and Zionism quite compatible. Indeed his Zion was coloured pink on the

---

[2] The society was founded by William Morris as part of his Socialist League, but developed ambitions of its own. At one time it included Edward Aveling and his wife Eleanor, Marx's daughter, in its membership. In 1889 it put forward a proposal for a federation of Socialist Societies which Morris considered to be 'nonsense . . . a mere symptom of faction', and soon afterwards the Bloomsbury Society was ejected from the League.

map. 'I am a Zionist,' Israel Zangwill once said to him, 'as much as you are an imperialist.'

As a young doctor Eder had acquired wide experience of the white man's burden, for after spending his little capital on qualifying he had had no money left to buy a practice; and as a Jew the number of salaried medical posts open to him in the England of those days was limited. Practice overseas was the obvious opening, and for eight years, from 1897 to 1905, he was almost continuously abroad, first in South Africa and then, for much longer, in South America. In 1898, as he proudly recorded later in *Who's Who*, he received a doctorate of medicine from the University of Bogota, whence he proceeded to act as medical officer for one of the belligerents in a civil war then being waged in Colombia. In 1901 he made a journey of exploration through the rain forests of the upper Amazon, and ministered for a time to the medical needs of a cannibal tribe. The collection of specimens he made on this expedition he later presented to the Natural History Museum.

A discouraging spell of general practice in the dreary industrial fringe of Cumberland followed these adventures, but in 1903 the young doctor was once more on his way to South America, this time as medical officer of the remote province of Acri in the north-west of Bolivia. On the voyage across the Atlantic his companions, who had represented themselves as agents of the Bolivian Government, revealed themselves as revolutionaries, and he found he had been taken on as chief medical officer of a revolutionary army. For nearly two years he was involved not only in treating the wounded, of whom there were not many, but in sieges and negotiations where his status as a doctor and an Englishman gave him a particular effectiveness.

These experiences formed Eder as a man of action as well as a doctor, and it was only with his return to England in about 1904 that his medical career really began. He took a partnership in an East End practice, and very soon became associated with the medical centre for elementary schoolchildren at Bow, the Margaret Macmillan Clinic. It was the first enterprise of its kind, and from it developed the whole network of the school health service. Eder was tireless in propagating the need to exploit the opportunity provided by compulsory primary education to reach schoolchildren as patients. In 1907 he read a paper to the Royal Society of Health on 'Diseases in the School Room' and founded another clinic in Devon Road, Poplar, which became the centre of an ambitious health and nursery school experiment. These ideas he ventilated in the *New Age*, and from 1910 onwards in a journal he founded himself, *School Hygiene*.

This pioneer work in welfare would itself have absorbed the energies of any ordinary man, but Eder was imbued with ideas of even greater import. He was one of the first English medical men to fall under the influence of Freud, whose work was then almost unknown in England. With Ernest Jones, whom he first met in 1904, Eder was the chief influence in introducing Freudianism into England. His attempts to do so in medical circles were deferred until later, but numerous articles in the *New Age* testify to his energy in explaining Freud to a lay audience.

To these activities his search for Israel remained for the time being subordinate. But it was never lost and in the end was to triumph over all his other interests. He was a member of the Jewish Territorial Association, which sought the national home which would not necessarily be in Palestine. Eder himself had looked for it in Cyrenaica, and had also considered Brazil and Colombia. It is not surprising that with so many and such wide-ranging activities, he suffered from insomnia, and that in 1908 he had a letter from so hard-working a man as Bernard Shaw urging him not to overwork.

It is almost impossible to overemphasize Eder's Englishness. His ideas, revolutionary though they were, could hardly have been held in their collectivity except by a man who had complete faith in the stability of the country and the society in which he lived and its power of adaptability to change without impairing its strength. In this sense he was anything but subversive, but as he wrote in 1916,[3] he saw in Britain and in British power throughout the world the main vehicle for his hopes as 'a socialist in economics and industrial organization . . . only because he thought socialism the essential basis of widely distributed individual freedom of expression and of opportunity for reasonable self-fulfilment'.

Eder's nature contradicted his doctrines. He revered Marx, but could not agree with him that the Jewish question (like all others) would be resolved automatically by the overthrow of capitalism. He declared himself to be an atheist, but had many of the attributes of a saint; and held that his mission was to 'cure people of their sense of duty' while preaching the gospel of the new welfare and devoting himself to all kinds of causes. Undoubtedly such a man, surrounded

[3] Quoted in *David Eder: Memoirs of a Modern Pioneer*, ed. J. B. Hobman, Gollancz, 1945.

with friends and bursting with unconventional ideas, 'brusque, kind, sardonic, sagacious', was likely to cast a spell over a rebellious poseuse of eighteen.

Ivy's life was thus determined not by her contemporaries but by certain members of the older generation; the primordial Walter, who had taught her to read; Alice, the closest link with him, yet at the same time someone who had betrayed him; the detested Sandy, for Ivy the Aegistheus of her story. The Eders, husband and wife, stood for all that the lost Walter could have offered his bounding daughter.

3

West and East

Ivy's aunt and her husband David Eder had both been married before: David, like his friend Walter Low, to the daughter of an Indian army officer; and Edith to another socialist doctor, Leslie Haden Guest, later a Labour MP and minister, by whom she had two children. That marriage had ended in 1908. The more mature union, though strong, was easy-going and elastic, and made room for others in both David's and Edith's lives.[1] Their house in Golders Green was a meeting-place for believers in many causes—Fabianism, welfare medicine, women's rights and Zionism. Bernard Shaw was a guest there, and so was Eder's contemporary and close friend Chaim Weizmann, then a reader in biochemistry at Manchester University. Edith was a vegetarian and wore a djibbah. 'Their flat heels', Ivy later wrote of Edith and her women friends, 'and the straight folds of their garments proclaimed them intelligent, just as much as their steady eyes and the uncompromising folds of their lips, so perhaps it is wrong to say they had no style, it just wasn't a very accomplished style.' Edith had an ivory skin which she considered should not be set next to ordinary white, so her collars were always carefully boiled in tea before being worn.

Ivy had been discouraged from seeing her Low aunts when she was a child, so it was not until her schooldays were over that she entered enthusiastically into the Eder circle. It had an immense and lasting effect on her. David Eder she adored, and Edith, she always

[1] Edith was one of H. G. Wells's conquests, but before her marriage to Eder. When, long afterwards, Tanya, Ivy's daughter, commented on Wells's overfriendliness towards her during one of his visits to the Soviet Union, Ivy commented: 'The old dog. That makes three generations.'

maintained, had a greater influence on her life than any other woman. It was all so different from the sprightly, rather shady, but superficially conventional world in which her mother lived.

There was more than a streak of Boswell in Ivy. Although she was very much her own heroine she had a need for heroes, and the Eders, though they came high, by no means satisfied this craving. Among her mother's review books Ivy had come across a novel by Viola Meynell, called *Second Marriage*, which captured her imagination. When her next appeared, it was seized by Ivy, who read it four times, and then wrote a fan letter to the author.

It was something she often did in her life, and was meant to lead to personal acquaintance. Addressed with some cunning not from her home address but from the Prudential, it ended:

> I wonder if you would meet me after 5 on any day and have tea. You take the tube to Chancery Lane and wait at the corner of Brooke Street, Holborn, while four or five hundred damsels issue forth from the Prudential Assurance Co., Ltd. You will know me because I don't wear spectacles. Any day but this Wednesday will greatly please. I know this is very bold of me; but after all, if you choose to snub me 'there is one shamed who was never gracious'.
>
> I hope you won't
> Yours sincerely,
> Ivy Low.

The detraction from the conventional apology is fundamental to Ivy's character.

Viola Meynell was then twenty-three, only two years older than Ivy, but already beginning to be well known as a novelist. She was one of a numerous family headed by Wilfred Meynell and his wife Alice, a poet of distinction. Wilfred had been a publisher until he retired to an estate at Greatham in Sussex, which is still the focus for the family life of many of his descendants today. The Meynells were literary, even to the extent of having a resident poet of their own in Francis Thompson, but unlike Ivy's other connections, they were well off. Their intensity—for they were very intense—was aesthetic, not, like the Eders, progressive. The Meynells were Roman Catholics, and very, very English.

Whether or not Viola succeeded in identifying Ivy coming out of the portals of the Prudential, an encounter did take place and developed into a friendship, with 'adoration bordering on infatuation' on Ivy's side and 'tolerant affection' on Viola's. Many letters were exchanged—hundreds according to Ivy—but only one or two have survived; and Viola's new friend became a visitor to Greatham. True, she did not feel quite comfortable with the aristocratic Meynells and their carefully regulated ways, and they may have felt she was too crude and gushing, and her admiration for Viola too ostentatious. But, reflected Ivy afterwards, 'Where *would* they have found anybody up to their high standards? I was aware of disapproval, but then I disapproved of myself; and behind the Meynell reserve there was a generous spark of *recognition* of that something that everyone longs to have recognized.' So she persevered with her new literary friendship, and began to write a novel herself. It had the rather good title *Growing Pains.*

It was a great age for self-expression through the novel. Some major practitioners of the larger canvas were still at work, but the new appetite was for briefer, thinly veiled self-portraits. Autobiography and direct experience were gaining ground at the expense of imagined narrative and fictitious character. D. H. Lawrence's first novel, *The White Peacock*, came out in the year Ivy met Viola, and *Sons and Lovers* would explode on the literary scene two years later. When, in due course, *Growing Pains* was published by Heinemann and brought Ivy's childhood and adolescence into print, its advertisement pages listed dozens of new novels, now all but forgotten.

The other literary influence to which Ivy, like many others of her time, was exposed was Russian. Considering how strong a tree English literature is, it is surprising how often the literature of a particular foreign country not only influences, but actually achieves a permanent place in the English literary tradition. There are some authors, such as Rabelais, Cervantes, Proust and Ibsen, who could be said to be part of English literature in the sense that no English reader who claims to be well read will be unacquainted with them, even though he will happily confess to total ignorance of Goethe and Racine. In Edwardian England this process of naturalization was going on in respect of the major works of Tolstoy, Dostoyevsky, and Chekhov, the first two of whom Ivy had found in the Constance Garnett translations on her mother's shelves—the former property of Walter Low.

Yet along with this adoption of Tolstoy and Dostoyevsky by the English reader went a profound repudiation of the Russian system of government. Throughout English society the belief was held that

Russia was a remote, sinister and brutal autocracy which rejected liberal values and threatened the British Empire. The charm of Russia's imperial ballet (which captivated London and Ivy in 1911), like the power of its literature, in no way compensated for these hateful qualities—if anything it emphasized them—but it would be nearer the truth to say that the artistic and political aspects of Russia were hardly thought of in the same context. Germany might be the more formidable rival politically but the Germans were more like us and one often went to Germany. Russia was vast, impenetrable, boorish, xenophobic, superstitious.

These views were strongly held in the Eder household. Zionism has its roots and its appeal in the endless persecutions of Eastern Europe. For generation after generation Russian, Baltic and Polish Jews had been harried, persecuted, and expelled by mobs and governments acting in the name of the Tsar, and in the reaction that followed the upheaval of 1905 fresh pogroms had added thousands to the tens of thousands of Jewish refugees from central Europe who had already found haven and refuge in Victorian England. Under King Edward VII the Russian refugee, especially if he were Jewish, found a place not unlike that offered by the Victorians to the Italian in flight from what Mr Gladstone had described as the negation of God erected into a system of government. The opponents of the Tsar, however extreme their views and however violent their methods, commanded widespread tolerance and sympathy.

Since then an even more massive system of government in Russia has succeeded over two generations in imposing a retrospectively purposeful and monolithic character on the pre-Revolutionary history of the Bolshevik party which it can hardly have seemed to possess at the time. So forcible was the personality of Lenin, such his opportunistic genius, that change of position could in his hands be made to seem loyalty to the purest of doctrine, and improvisation surround itself with an aura of complete inevitability. If his opponents did not deviate to the right, then they must have deviated to the left and, like Dr Johnson, if his pistol failed to go off he knocked you down with the butt end of it. The opponent who was not a garrulous, deluded intellectual could be eliminated as an ignorant, uneducated philistine. The small but ever-changing band round Lenin in exile gains, by his and his successors' efforts, a far more definite coherence than it possessed during the heroic years leading up to the Revolution.

The Russian exiles in London clustered round the Herzen Club in Charlotte Street, which was only a few doors away from Eder's consulting rooms.[2] Its membership ranged from the veteran anarchist Kropotkin to the Marxist Social Democrats and the inheritors of the older Russian terrorist tradition, the Social Revolutionaries. In the open life of London there was little pressure on the exiles to conform with any one set of doctrines, and the numerous groups were on the whole shadowy affairs with an ever-changing membership. The whole existed on a companionable basis of common origin and shared hostility to the Tsar. The amateur theatricals, choir-singing and discussion groups of Charlotte Street, drawing on the talents of the whole political spectrum, were celebrated.

There were, of course, similar colonies of Russian political exiles in other Western cities: Paris, Berlin, Zürich, Geneva. That of Paris was considered by many to be pre-eminent in its intellectual claims, and numbered among its members such notables as the littérateur Lunacharsky, who fitted happily into its bohemian society. But Lenin, though he lived in Paris for three years, detested the place, and would rather have lived in London if it had been central enough. Three of the first four substantive conferences of his party were held there and the great division between Bolshevik and Menshevik had been established, giving Lenin his primacy.[3] In London Marx had lived and died; and London held the British Museum where Lenin under the alias of Jacob Richter and sponsored by the secretary of the General Federation of Trade Unions, Isaac Mitchell, inscribed himself to 'study the land question' in April 1902.

The influence of the British Museum Library in the history of Bolshevism is often treated with a gentle smile as a kind of incidental British curiosity which put desperate conspirators and future men of destiny reading alongside earnest professors and seedy, forgotten literary men at the shiny black tables under Panizzi's overarching dome. This is insular astigmatism. To the Bolsheviks of that generation, and for long afterwards, the British Museum was far more than a glorious reference library open to all. Its accessibility, its comprehensiveness, its efficiency, the fact that it was free, the

[2] He had patients among the members of the Club, giving them among other things free access to salversan, which he was one of the first doctors in England to prescribe for venereal disease.
[3] The Second (1903, removed from Brussels), the Third (1905) and the Fifth (1907). The Fourth was held in Stockholm, in 1906. All the others have been held in Russia.

impressiveness of its structure, all combined to make it seem their forum, their university, almost their temple. It became a kind of symbol. Lenin himself venerated it. The more effusive Maisky rhapsodized:

> Had not this great room played an integral part in the intellectual history of our era ... Dozens of great leaders of popular movements in all quarters of the globe had gathered their materials and written their books there. Mighty shades from the past were all around me. I could hardly help asking myself whether I should prove in any way worthy of the great figures who had bent over these tables before me.[4]

Strange words from a dialectical materialist. It is even stranger that one of the priests of this temple should have been the unimaginative Sandy Herbert, travelling every day by the Metropolitan Railway with exemplary bourgeois regularity from his little house in Harrow.

In the Reading Room, in the summer of 1903, the man who was to count most in Ivy's life first met Lenin, who was then in the midst of that memorable controversy of the second Party Congress which led to the factions of Bolshevik and Menshevik, to the loss of Leninist control over the Party organ *Iskra*, and to the end of the first phase of his career as a revolutionary. The man in question was (or is best known as) Maxim Maximovich Litvinov.

He was at that time twenty-seven, and so six years younger than Lenin—a gap sufficient to produce deference in a junior but not enough to mark a difference of generation. He had just chased Lenin across Europe all the way from Kiev, first to Geneva, then to Brussels (where the Congress had originally assembled) and finally to London. He was already a committed revolutionary.

Litvinov's life down to that encounter under Panizzi's dome shows him to have had as many of the characteristics of a successful businessman as of a professional revolutionary. But there were also in him strong streaks of idealism and recklessness which, though not wholly absent in successful businessmen, fitted better with the career he had chosen. His original name was Meer Genokh Moiseevich Wallakh, to which he was born of orthodox Jewish parents in the modest town of Bialystok in the borderlands of Russia and Poland. Like Trotsky's Bronstein parents the Wallakhs belonged to the lower

[4] Ivan Maisky, *Journey into the Past*, p. 28.

middle class, but they were small bankers, not agriculturalists. Their sympathies, it seems, were mildly liberal, but in no way revolutionary.

In every layer of Russian society there was suffusion of dissidence—ubiquitous, multiform, fastening on no one doctrine but affecting every group: landowners and businessmen, lawyers and professors, Jews and orthodox priests, and even the direct props of the system, the civil service, the army and the police. Dissidents did not themselves necessarily become active revolutionaries, but the origins of the men who made the Revolution show that at most levels there was a revolutionary quota, and that at all levels the active revolutionary could find sympathy and protection.

Litvinov, absorbed a whiff of this climate while still at the *realschule*, or technical college, of Bialystok: the gymnasium, or grammar school, was not for him any more than it was for Trotsky, who also went to a *realschule*. 'You're clever', said his history teacher, 'but you could no more see the inside of a university than I could bite my elbow.' His father was taken briefly into the hands of the local police, and Litvinov told his mother he hoped there would some day be a Russia without prisons. It was a remark he reflectively reported to his children during the years of Stalin.

The narrow traditionalism of his parental home, isolated by its Jewishness in a town which in any case had few resources, oppressed Litvinov. He was enterprising and ambitious, and although short in stature, he was stocky and had considerable strength.[5] He does not seem to have quarrelled with his family, and maintained contact with them long afterwards when events had carried him into a different world from theirs,[6] but he left home at the age of seventeen to enlist in the 17th Caucasian Regiment as a regular soldier. He is among comparatively few prominent Bolsheviks to have served on a regular engagement in the Tsar's army. One other was Voroshilov, which may help to explain the friendship between these two very different men, both whom rose high in the service of the Soviet state.

Litvinov was robust and intelligent but as his eyesight was poor he was never likely to make much of a rifleman. It did not take long for

[5] He gave a demonstration of this on a walking tour in 1917, when he lifted my father two feet off the ground with both arms fully extended: a very difficult feat.
[6] During his conspiratorial period he would write a series of pre-dated letters to his family assuring them of his continued well-being, and entrust them in batches to friends who would post them at intervals.

the authorities to assign this educated Jewish recruit to the quartermaster's stores as a clerk, which gave him ample time to study. He thus became quite well-read and during his time at Baku, where the regiment was stationed, attracted the attention of a sympathetic superior, Captain Slugov, a Bulgarian who had joined the Russian army out of Pan-slav enthusiasm. Slugov introduced his protégé to the works of Turgenev,[7] and even offered him the chance of succeeding the regimental Quartermaster-Sergeant, who was shortly to retire. It was a post of dignity, comfort and profit, but Litvinov did not accept it, and at the end of his engagement, in 1898, he left the army.

The year 1898 is an important date in the history of Russian socialism, even if a certain dubiety hangs about some of the Party events it is supposed to mark. In that year, according to official accounts, the first Congress of the Russian Social Democratic Party was held at Minsk, and from then Lenin dated his own membership of the Party. So did Litvinov. The Congress was abortive, and most of the members were arrested a day or two after it began, but it shares with many other episodes in the early days of what became Lenin's Party a significance which was to be forged into current importance in the days of power; for once the Revolution had been achieved, behaviour in the pre-Revolutionary epoch was to be treated with the same solemnities as if it had occurred in the days of responsibility and office. The exact circumstances of Litvinov's becoming a social democrat he does not reveal; but that it was coeval with the Party itself and with Lenin's membership of it he always insisted.

He was now twenty-two, and got a job in Kiev as book-keeper in a sugar factory, after mugging up double entry and accounting practice on the train journey. Very soon he joined a socialist group which, like many others in the Russia of that time, was engaged in the production and circulation of unlawful pamphlets. He later described this as 'a cottage industry', meaning that its publications were not connected with any wider organization, but he was entitled to say that his membership of the Party was senior in the retrospectively created roll to that of Trotsky, Zinoviev, Kamenev or even Stalin.

Kiev, though an ancient capital, was not a particularly important place at that time, and had little to offer an agitator in the way of an

---

[7] While the name Litvinov occurs in Turgenev's novel *Smoke*, there is no evidence that Maxim adopted it on that account.

industrial proletariat. The socialist circle centred on a professor of chemistry at the local polytechnic named Tikhvinsky[8] and was divided, according to Litvinov's later accounts, between activists and doctrinaires who were earnest students of Nietzsche and of Avenarius's impenetrable *Kritik der Reinen Erfahrung.* Litvinov belonged to the activist group. In 1901 he was arrested.

The year of Litvinov's arrest was also the year in which Lenin launched from outside Russia, *Iskra (The Spark)*, a journal which was designed not only to propagate socialist revolution but by its very need for an organization to produce and distribute it to create a tightly-knit conspiratorial party. The preparation of the paper and its distribution would depend on a core of dedicated revolutionaries, and its contents would act as a detonator on the wider sympathetic but unorganized public by substituting precision and cogency for the eternal and futile disputations of the socialist sects. Litvinov was in prison before the first copies began to reach Russia, but Tikhvinsky was one of *Iskra*'s principal distributors in Kiev.

Litvinov was lodged in Kiev's principal gaol, the Lukianovka. Escape from it was considered impossible, but its regime was mild, even liberal. The governor was confident in his high walls, and many of the staff were either sympathetic to the prisoners, or biddable in various ways. Nevertheless, such was the strength of the place, that the main hope of most prisoners, including Litvinov, was to obtain an early trial and a sentence to the more open conditions of exile in Siberia.

The effect of the *Iskra* campaign, however, was beginning to be felt in Kiev, and copies of the paper even found their way into the prison. They were soon followed by some of the distributors, including at least one, named Blumenfeld, who had brought consignments from the West and had been in direct touch with Lenin. Contacts between the prisoners and the external *Iskra* organization were established, and a plan was formed for an escape: an escape which would in itself be a political demonstration. These events were followed with interest by Lenin in Zürich.

The first phase of the scheme was to extract from the authorities, apparently harmless concessions of a kind which could hardly be refused without oppressiveness: additional scope for recreation; the

---

[8] Tikhvinsky lived to see the Revolution of 1917, but opposed the *coup d'état* of October which brought Lenin to power, and was shot on the orders of Zinoviev in 1920.

formation of clubs among prisoners for debating and choir-singing; a measure of internal self-government in relation to the kitchens. Appointed representatives of the prisoners were allowed (accompanied, of course, by guards) to visit other parts of the prison. Special attention was directed at the head warder, and 'we managed to teach him not to examine bags and baskets too closely.' Several warders were prevailed upon to take messages out of and into the prison. Soon 'we enjoyed comparative freedom in our corridors and within the prison yard.'

The plan of escape was systematically co-ordinated with allies outside, and was not to be put into action until the signal from the *Iskra* organization was received. In February 1902 a large demonstration was mounted in the streets of Kiev and there was fighting in the Kreshchatik, the principal thoroughfare. More or less at the same time the prisoners received the signal to proceed with the escape, and a leader—or, in jocular Ukrainian terminology, adopted by the prisoners, a Hetman—was elected. When the first 'Hetman' proved unsatisfactory Litvinov was chosen in his place.

The escape took place in the early summer of 1902 on a dark, rainy evening. Litvinov was very proud of his elaborate plan, which had been carefully rehearsed and worked almost perfectly. The main obstacle was the external wall which, as so often, abutted on the exercise yard. Before exercise on the chosen night the supervising guards were invited to one of the cells by a prisoner on the pretext of a 'birthday drink' which had been laced with smuggled sleeping pills. These trusting guards were left stupefied on the floor. The sole armed sentry left in the exercise yard was then overwhelmed and disarmed by four men, and tied up. Seven others formed themselves into a pyramid against the wall, fastened a grapnel (also smuggled in from outside) to the top of it and, with the aid of a rope ladder, disappeared one after the other, followed by the four who had overpowered the guard. The officer of the watch had been temporarily diverted to another part of the prison by a false story of a prisoner taken ill. The whole thing took about five minutes; and the only failure was in a plan to divert attention to the other end of the courtyard by the singing of a choir composed of non-escaping (but collaborative) prisoners. Surprise and excitement left the choir temporarily mute, and they burst into song only as the last escaper vanished.

Their singing was interrupted by a pistol shot from the officer of the watch, who had now arrived on the scene. By this time the escapers

had scattered in the darkness but Litvinov found himself stuck in a
ditch beside Blumenfeld, who seemed to have suffered some kind of
seizure, physical or emotional, and was unable to move. The
searchers did not examine the ditch, perhaps because it was so close
to the wall, and when Blumenfeld recovered the two were able to
make their way gradually towards and over the frontier, first by
posing as apparently alcoholic vagrants, then as a surveyor and his
assistant, frequently helped by sympathizers. By way of Vilna, Berlin,
and Munich (where they were feted at a Social Democratic
conference) they reached Zürich, whence they sent a cheerful
telegram to the Russian authorities.[9]

This episode established Litvinov's qualifications as a revolutionary, and he often related it, dwelling particularly on the precise
planning, rather than the physical prowess, needed for its success. He
did not ignore the political implications of the escape, which he
counted as almost of greater significance than the personal freedom it
gave him and his companions. The impudent telegram and other
publicity designed to show the inefficiency of the Russian authorities
were the more important parts of the operation.

But above all the escape brought him into direct contact with Lenin
at an early stage of that extraordinary man's revolutionary career.
Lenin lived in Zürich, and it was from Zurich that *Iskra*, though
printed in London, was distributed. In the summer of 1902 Litvinov
not only became a member of the Russian Social Democrats Abroad:
he was appointed by Lenin as the distribution manager of *Iskra*. No
post could demand more resourcefulness. Packages containing copies
of *Iskra* were sent as unsolicited gifts to respectable unwatched
sympathizers, or trailed in waterproof bags behind ships docking in
Odessa, thence to be lifted at night from small boats. There was an
infinite variety of devices in Litvinov's fertile mind.

Litvinov did not, however, meet Lenin for nearly a year after his
escape. The encounter took place not in Zürich but in the Reading
Room of the British Museum, and Litvinov was accompanied by his
old companion Blumenfeld who was the secretary of the second
Social Democrat Congress then in progress. One of the most
important debates of this celebrated Congress concerned the control
of *Iskra*, which probably explains Lenin's wish for Litvinov's

[9] Both the riots and the escape were widely reported—not least in *Iskra*. In 1903 Lenin's
close colleague G. M. Krzhizhanovsky arrived in Kiev, and that summer there were
even more formidable riots in the town.

presence in London. The battle was won by the Mensheviks, despite negotiations, which came to a physical tussle between Litvinov, acting for Lenin, and Blumenfeld who had chosen the Menshevik side, *Iskra* remained in Menshevik hands and Lenin had to start another paper, *Vperyod* (*Forward*). Litvinov, now nicknamed by Lenin 'Papasha', was of course in charge of its distribution: 'There will always be transport [Lenin wrote to Krassin[10]] as long as we have Papasha. Let him take the most energetic measures for handing over his inheritance in case of failure.'

The convulsion of 1905 was now approaching, and Litvinov, under the code-name 'Felix', played a considerable part in assembling the Bolshevik third Congress, held in April that year in London, where he sat as the 'delegate' of the Russian Baltic Provinces. But despite his devotion to Lenin he was uneasy about the high-handed methods his leader had used to gather a body described as a Congress which consisted of delegates largely nominated by him.

Such doubts were drowned in the whirlpool of the revolt in Russia itself and the excitements of a totally new undertaking. In August 1905 Litvinov was summoned by Krassin to St Petersburg to organize what was this time to be an open revolutionary newspaper published in Russia's capital. For a brief dizzy six months the long-envisaged reunion of the external and internal revolutionaries was being celebrated on Russian soil. The new paper, *Novaya Zhizn*, was financed by Maxim Gorky, and his mistress, Andreyeva, was its official publisher. The manager was one Ludwig Wilhelmovich Nietz—actually Litvinov—and the first of its twenty-seven numbers appeared on 17 October 1905.

During its short life *Novaya Zhizn*, which had offices in the fashionable Nevsky Prospekt, was quite a success. It even carried its manager briefly into the chairmanship of the St Petersburg association of newspaper managers. Soon Lenin himself arrived to contribute political direction and massive leading articles. But in the general wave of counter-insurgency measures which ended that memorable year in Russian history *Novaya Zhizn* was suppressed and its manager, apprehensive that the police were beginning to penetrate his alias, left Russia. He was not to return there for thirteen years.

[10] Leonid Krassin, an engineer and manager of the Putilov works. Until the Revolution he was in effect the treasurer of Lenin's organization in Russia, and its most active fund-raiser. After the Revolution he entered diplomacy, and served for a time as Soviet emissary in both Paris and London. He became one of Litvinov's closest collaborators.

[West and East]

The years following 1905 were grievous for the Russian socialists, and especially for the Bolshevik faction. Bruised, rebuffed, and short of funds, the Bolsheviks slithered into heresies and internal dissension—'God-building' and 'empirio-criticism' belong to these years. Gorky set out for America on a fund-raising tour, and Litvinov was offered the post of road manager, but he declined. Whether that disastrous tour might have gone better had Litvinov been in charge of it is impossible now to guess. Instead he became a purchaser of arms in Western Europe for transmission to the remaining Bolsheviks in Russia.

Wealthy backers were now hard to find, and the millionaire Morozov, from whom Krassin had extracted so much for the Bolshevik cause, had committed suicide; so the money for these transactions came from banditry, politely termed 'expropriation'. Lenin officially repudiated it, as did Litvinov, but not all Bolsheviks did even that. Krassin, the cultivated engineer through whose hands the proceeds of 'expropriation' made their way out of Russia, endorsed violence as a principle, and so did the organizer of the Tiflis branch of the Party, a comparatively new recruit named Dzugashvili who later adopted the alias Stalin. Nor was Litvinov himself unacquainted with Kamo, otherwise Ter-Petrosian, the desperado who carried out the most spectacular of these raids.

In the autumn of 1906 Litvinov and Kamo acquired a consignment of arms in Belgium and set about shipping it from Varna in the yacht *Sarya* commanded by Ivanenko, a former member of the mutinous crew of the battleship *Potemkin*. The *Sarya* sailed from Varna on 25 September 1906 and soon afterwards was wrecked on the coast of Romania. The crew fled from the embarrassing scene, leaving behind the guns which had been purchased with so much trouble out of the proceeds of one of the biggest bank robberies in Russia.[11] Six months later Litvinov was in London to attend the fifth Congress of the Bolsheviks, which possibly marked the lowest point in their fortunes. It was also the first occasion on which Stalin, under the alias Ivenko, was present at a Bolshevik Congress.

The Congress, which was to have been at Copenhagen but was moved to London owing to the opposition of the Danish authorities, was held in the Brotherhood Church, Southgate Road, Hoxton. Severe economy had to be observed, and only two shillings a day was

[11] Litvinov published an account of this adventure in 1925 (see Fischer, pp. 87–90).

allowed to each delegate for subsistence. Even so it soon became apparent that the Congress would not be able to go on without more money, which was eventually obtained by an appeal made through Rothstein, one of the Congress members, and his journalist colleague H. N. Brailsford, to a philanthropic soap manufacturer named Joseph Fels, who, after consulting George Lansbury, offered a loan of £1,700 against a promissory note.[12]

One wonders what the pacific Lansbury would have made of the great 'expropriation' soon afterwards at Tiflis on 13 June 1907 by Kamo, acting under the orders of Stalin. Several people were killed, and the audacity of the raid sent reverberations throughout Europe. Parts of the huge booty were traced to various capitals, one of which was Paris, where a man calling himself Dethiarsk was arrested in possession of notes traceable to the robbery. Dethiarsk was Litvinov. He had not been concerned in the robbery itself, but he was undoubtedly trying to turn the proceeds into some less identifiable currency.

This was the occasion on which, as he later used to tell his family, he found a detective under his bed—an interesting reversal of roles. The Russians demanded his extradition, and the French press made much of his stylish *boulevardier* appearance; but since he had committed no crime in Russia he could not be sent back there, and eventually the French authorities took the easy way out by deporting him across the Channel to England, where he arrived in January 1908.

He had been in England, as we have seen, at least twice before, and already had some command of English. Moreover, he carried a letter of introduction from Maxim Gorky to a pillar of British intellectual life, Charles Hagberg Wright, Librarian of the London Library. Through Wright, who was knowledgeable about Central and Eastern Europe, he obtained a modest post as a clerk with the publishing firm of Williams and Norgate, under the name of Max Harrison, and so began a sojourn in England which lasted more than ten years, until well after the Revolution. Like many other refugees he worked hard at the office and gradually rose to greater responsibilities and a higher

---

[12] Fels insisted that the note should be signed by all members of the Congress, of whom there were two or three hundred, and the result was a remarkable document signed by, among others, Lenin, Stalin, Plekhanov, Krassin, and Lunacharsky. The loan was for only one year, and in 1908 Fels sought repayment, which Lenin was in no mood to make. But the sum was discharged to Fels's heirs in 1919 and the Bolsheviks recovered their note. The story is told by Maisky, pp. 134–7.

salary. One cannot wholly reject the idea—or, rather, he himself may at times not have wholly rejected it—that he might take permanently to English life as Maximilian Löwe and David Eder's father had done in an earlier generation.

Lenin's vision of impending revolution seemed to have vanished, and his schemes to have miscarried. The critical moment had come and gone, and to make matters still less bearable, the remaining Bolsheviks had to contemplate the prosperity of the main body of the social democratic movement embodied in the Second International, of which, of course, the Bolsheviks were still formally a part. It was a happy time for the democratic socialists of Western Europe, comfortably funded by the trade unions, acceptably represented in Parliament, the Reichstag, and the Chambre des Députés, yet not beset by the disagreeable realities of power. It was the time of Bebel, Kautsky, Bernstein, Jean-Jaurès; of Wells, Shaw, and the Webbs. Their books sold and their meetings were well attended, even exhilarating. Maisky, then a Menshevik, describes the almost carnival atmosphere of the Social Democratic Congress at Copenhagen in 1913, which was attended by, among many others, Kautsky, Ebert, Rosa Luxemburg, Jean-Jaurès, Keir Hardie, Ramsay MacDonald, Lenin, Plekhanov, Martov, Lunacharsky, and Alexandra Kollontai:

> For the sessions they had taken the fine big concert palace. . . . Nine hundred delegates, in addition to over a hundred press men, assembled in the great hall . . . There was a mass demonstration . . . a forest of red flags . . . thousands of young girls wearing red hats . . . fifteen bands . . . there must have been at least a hundred thousand people.

What a contrast to the Hoxton Congress of the Bolsheviks!

Lenin found the meetings of the Second International with their rhetoric, their logic-chopping, and their euphoria, hard to bear, and avoided them as much as he could. He designated Litvinov as the permanent Bolshevik delegate on its governing Bureau, and insisted that all communications with it by Bolsheviks should be by way of Litvinov, who accordingly attended most Second International meetings from 1908 onwards. Intellectual socialists deplored the presence of a man with no theoretical qualifications, and Rosa Luxemburg complained that at the Bureau meeting of 1913 the

Bolsheviks were represented by 'a complete idiot'.[13] 'But you are children,' the great Bebel remarked patronizingly.[14]

Bebel and Rosa Luxemburg were right in thinking Litvinov was no Marxist scholar or communist theoretician, and he never, throughout his life (which was perhaps longer on that account) made any claims to be so. Litvinov was a Leninist, not a controversialist, and though Maisky said he considered Lenin's outlook at this time was more German than Russian, Litvinov saw in him the man and the method by which alone the Revolution might be achieved. Litvinov was quite well-read in Russian and foreign literature, but not in philosophy or political science. His turn of mind was essentially practical. He was a shrewd judge of character, a skilful and painstaking organizer, physically courageous, resourceful and decisive. These gifts he put unreservedly at the disposal of the Party, and to Lenin such a man was precious. Lenin, though an intellectual man himself, rather despised and disliked self-styled intellectuals.

One should never forget that Litvinov had been a soldier, and that at an early age he had accepted both the necessity of discipline and the idea of putting his life at stake. He acquiesced in, and even enjoyed, the stringencies of the secret organization in which he had enlisted, and instinctively obeyed those whom he regarded as his superiors. But it was not an unthinking obedience, because it had in it the elements of professional pride; and these, as we shall see, could lead him into collision with superiors whose professional judgement he did not trust.

He was not a cold man, and his geniality and sociability were not superficial. His adherence to Bolshevism had sprung from resentment against a system of oppression, not from theoretical conviction. He assiduously planned for a revolution in Russia, but the notion of one in England seemed to him unimaginable because it would necessarily destroy the whole interlocking social texture, leaving nothing on which to build.

Precisely how Litvinov came to be acquainted with the Eders we do not know: it may have been through Eder's consulting room in Charlotte Street or through Fabian meetings; or through a Russian

[13] *Encounter*, September 1979. New letters from Rosa Luxemburg, s.d. 14 December 1913.
[14] A. Martynov, 'Recollections of a Revolutionary', in *The Proletarian Revolution*, II (November 1925), p. 281.

engineer friend of his named Klishko, who had married Ivy's schoolfellow Phyllis. However this may be, he was a visitor to the Eder circle in Golders Green in the years leading up to the First World War, and it was there that Ivy met him.

4

The Exiles

Litvinov had many more preoccupations in London than his work for Williams and Norgate or his duties as Lenin's delegate to the Bureau of the Second International. For six years after his escape he had worked in many parts of Europe, but from 1908 he became a regular resident in England, and as a senior member of the (then not very numerous) Russian Socialist Party Abroad, and the organizer of Russian exiles in London for the Leninist faction of it, he had now to become familiar with the society in which his flock had made their home, and his careful study made him the pre-eminent expert on British affairs among his colleagues. But he was not alone among them in having experience of the western world. Emigrés and exiles are often ineffectual in the histories of their countries; but this does not apply to the socialist émigrés from Russia during this period.

Russian socialism, to which Maxim Litvinov adhered for almost the whole of his life, and with which Ivy's life was to become involved through him, was peculiar among the socialist movements of that time, which were for the most part outcrops of the liberal, enlightened societies in which they flourished: opposed and detested by many in those societies, but tolerated at least as a comprehensible if unpleasant development of native growth. The focus of Russian socialism was created outside Russia, partly because the prophets of socialism had lived in Central or Western Europe, partly because an important part of the Russian intelligentsia had always looked westwards, and mainly because inside Russia active socialism was subject to a very effective system not only of repression but of extrusion. During the first twenty years of this century every stratum of Russian society was affected by the revolutionary tradition, but the numerous revolutionaries within Russia looked increasingly abroad for direction and sympathy; and by going abroad a Russian socialist made an almost dedicatory bid towards a leading place in the movement—not a gesture of abdication and despair. Inside Russia membership of the movement was necessarily dangerous, and abroad the direction of that conspiracy was in a strange land. The international character of Russian socialism, which at first sight seems inconsistent for a country so distinctive and peripheral, had its roots in Russian history and in the western origins of socialism. To the West, perhaps, this has given communism a special externality which has made it more acceptable to those attracted by the idea of fundamental change.

The deeply marked character of Russia made it certain that a difference would arise between the revolutionaries within Russia, who during the early years of the century became a subordinate echelon, and the exiled leadership from which they increasingly took their inspiration and their orders. When there was a convulsion in Russia, as in 1905 and 1917, the two streams would flow together, but with the external element carrying the prestige, almost the legitimacy, of the movement as a whole, and when the Revolution triumphed under the leadership of the most exiled of all the revolutionary factions, a tension was built into the new regime. The tension was not the less significant for being veiled under the slogans of international socialism and overarched by the magnetic personality of Lenin. But it was bound gradually to resolve itself by an eclipse of the émigrés, leaving behind only a vague but important shadow of sympathy in the West related to the place the émigré once held in Western society.

Those émigrés had spent many years in the West: Lenin seventeen, Trotsky fifteen, Zinoviev and Kamenev a considerable part of their adult lives. Lunacharsky and Kollontai fitted better into London or Paris than into Moscow. Plekhanov, the patriarch of Russian Marxism, spent almost his whole life abroad, as did the Menshevik leaders Akselrod and Martov. One must contrast with these the men who, in circumstances of great personal danger, carried out their directions on doctrine and strategy during the heroic days before the dawn, and had to accept leadership from abroad when it came. They lived with, and absorbed, the traditions of the autocracy they worked to overthrow.

The aberration by which Russian communism was nurtured by the

West and left the nurse's affection behind it, an aberration not allowed for by Marx, Lenin or the official teachers of communism, is significant for Litvinov's story. At first sight no European country is more foreign to a Western European than Russia, which was on the margin of European history until 300 years ago, underwent neither Renaissance nor Reformation, and looks more to Asia and Byzantium than to any country in Europe for its traditions. Yet Shaw and Wells, and the Webbs, made their pilgrimages there. It was only slowly that the gradual reassertion of the Russian identity within the communist system made itself felt, and the exiles, after their heady years of triumph, gave way to or were forced to adopt the interests of Russia expressed by the internal and originally subordinate representatives of Russian communism.

A general account of the exiles during the twenty years before the Revolution of 1917, together with their subsequent fates, would be of very great interest. Here, where we are mainly concerned with Ivy, we can only concentrate on those who came to England and were most active there. They were to be especially conspicuous in the diplomacy of the Soviet Union once it was established.

When Litvinov arrived in London in 1908, during the nadir of Bolshevik fortunes, the Russian revolutionary colony in London numbered perhaps three or four hundred. Some of them had been in London for many years and had been carried along by various streams of the revolutionary tradition before it had entered its socialist phase; and those who were socialists held different and changeable opinions. Some were, or had been, followers of Lenin, others were non-Leninists, in other words Mensheviks—a term which itself covered many opinions. Only hindsight gives coherence to their medley of opinion and character, seeking to affix labels of orthodoxy and dissidence to the inhabitants of seedy lodgings on the fringes of Bloomsbury and Camden Town as if they had then been the office-holders and diplomats they later became.

They did not form a systematic conspiratorial party but they played an important part, both in the London of that time, and as the embryo of the Soviet diplomatic service. They attracted sympathy and were welcomed as exotic allies in various progressive causes such as feminism and the crusade against imperial expansion. But the extent of their immediate influence on English life must not be exaggerated. Some of them barely spoke English. The worlds of high politics, of the civil service, of the universities, of successful literature, were hardly reached by them socially, though they studied them as outsiders. Their English acquaintance was drawn from the Labour movement, the trade unions and the more militant wings of such causes as women's suffrage. A few examples of the people among whom Litvinov now found himself, the heirs of Herzen, will make this clearer.

In the years immediately before the outbreak of the First World War one of the most prominent Russian exiles in London was George Vasilievich Chicherin, later the second holder of the office of Commissar for Foreign Affairs. (Trotsky was the first, but held the post for only a few important months before becoming Commissar for Defence in January 1918.[1])

Chicherin lived in a little attic on the fourth floor of 12 Oakley Square, only a few minutes' walk from the room Litvinov had found in 1908 at 33 Mornington Crescent. Already forty when he came to England. His extraction was gentlemanly, since he belonged to a family that traced its origins and name to an Italian courtier who came to Russia in the train of Zoë Palaeologue, last empress of Byzantium, on the occasion of her marriage to her second husband, Tsar Ivan III, which endowed the Romanovs with cloudy claims to her first husband's lost empire. A long line of Chicherin members of the official classes had followed—abbots, civil servants, generals and professors. George Vasilievich was the son of a diplomatist and had himself started a career in the Tsar's foreign office before becoming conscience-stricken, first as a disciple of Tolstoy, then as a revolutionary émigré.

He was a nervous, ascetic man, intensely sensitive and cultured, with marked homosexual tendencies. The ballet and the theatre he had long renounced, but he remained a passionate lover of music, and had actually written a successful book on Mozart. He wore the cheapest clothes, lived in squalor and abstained from meat and alcohol. As an aristocrat he remained a man of the night, a bohemian

---

[1] He objected on doctrinal grounds to the idea of negotiation between states, and said in accepting the Foreign Commissarship, that he would simply make some appeals to the peoples of the world, and close the office down. He did more than this, but it expresses his attitude. Chicherin then held the Foreign Commissarship until 1930, when he was succeeded by Litvinov. It is interesting that in more than sixty years history of the Soviet Union there have been only five Ministers of Foreign Affairs: Trotsky, Chicherin, Litvinov, Molotov and Gromyko. In this respect the tradition of the nineteenth century has been followed. Between 1816 and 1895 there were only three foreign ministers, though there were five Tsars.

whose mind worked best in the small hours, and was consequently a late riser. His long, loose, shabby overcoat with its capacious pockets full of papers, his untidy habits, his platonic attachment to a suffragette, Mrs Bridges Adams—all these are caught by Maisky, who came on the pair one evening:

> A freezing evening in the winter. In the streets outside the cold penetrated into your very bones. Damp gloom throughout the house. In the drawing room [it was Mrs Adams's house in Kensington] a feeble fire and near it a round table with a table-lamp burning brightly on it. It is the only decently lit spot in the surrounding gloom. At the table, huddled in their coats, sit Chicherin and Mrs Bridges Adams compiling a new leaflet against the Tsarist government.[2]

From 1915 onwards Chicherin found an outlet in Orage's radical paper the *New Age*, mainly on two themes he chose for his own: the sufferings of political prisoners in Russia and, later, the right of Russian exiles to be exempted from British military conscription.[3] But until the eve of the Revolution he played little part in the internal politics of the emigration, and could best be described as a Menshevik in the great division of Russian socialism. This did not prevent Lenin and Trotsky from seeing in him a potential Foreign Commissar and his signature would in due course appear on two of the most important treaties of the post-Revolutionary period, Brest-Litovsk and Rapallo. It is strange to think of this febrile, well-born insomniac, with his untidy habits, working for ten years in double harness with the punctual, businesslike, extrovert Litvinov, an obscure Jew with no intellectual pretensions.

More congenial to Litvinov was a man of much the same origins as himself, though a year or two older, Fedor Aronovich Rothstein: indeed they remained friends throughout their lives from the time they met. Rothstein had come westwards much sooner than Litvinov, having left Poltawa, where his father kept a small chemist's shop, in 1891, when he was only twenty. He had made straight for England.

[2] Maisky, *Journey into the Past*, p. 129.
[3] *New Age*, 16 December 1915 ('The inexpressible sufferings of the Russian people'); 23 March 1916 ('The internment of Peter Petrov in Edinburgh Castle'); 21 June 1917 ('The position of the Jews in Russia'). The *New Age* it should be noted, was anti-communist, though it happily egged on controversy. Its expert on Russia, with whom Chicherin was crossing swords in the 1915 correspondence, was Bechofer Roberts.

His reason for doing so was that England had produced John Stuart Mill, Buckle, and Herbert Spencer, and it was through studying their works that he had had his first brush with the Russian security authorities. He arrived to find successors to his heroes in Hyndman, the Webbs and Keir Hardie, and first set himself to compose a socialist successor to Gibbon's *Decline and Fall of the Roman Empire*, which he did not complete. Instead he supported himself by providing potted lives of Cicero, Socrates and Plotinus for an encyclopaedia of biography published in St Petersburg. From these uncertain beginnings he developed into an important and comparatively prosperous journalist specializing in Near Eastern subjects.

In the world of Russian socialism Rothstein was a senior figure, having reached the fountainheads of Marxism even before Lenin. His admission to the British Museum Reading Room bears the date 12 June 1895. He had never known Marx, it is true, but he had met Engels, and he naturally met Lenin during his celebrated visit to London in 1902–3. He took part in that now famous Congress on the Bolshevik side, as a man already established in British journalism who had been in England for nearly twelve years. By the time Litvinov knew him, Rothstein was living in a comfortable house on the lower slopes of Highgate Hill (53 Whitehall Park) with a wife and children and a steady job providing foreign press briefings for the *Daily News*. He was writing a book about modern Egypt and had a wide range of acquaintances among trade unionists and Labour politicians.

Rothstein returned to Russia in 1920 after nearly thirty years in England when he was in his fiftieth year. He was far more English than Russian and abandoned a well-established position in journalism for new adventures, taking with him his large and precious archive of press cuttings about the Near East. Almost at once he was appointed Soviet ambassador in Persia. His ambassadorial career lasted only two years,[4] but he remained an adviser in the Soviet Foreign Office until 1930 when he moved (on Litvinov's accession to the Commissarship) to be its official historian, and was crowned as such in 1939 (just before Litvinov fell) by membership of the Soviet Academy. Thereafter a gradual withdrawal into private life saved this thoroughly English Bolshevik from the worst consequences of the

---

[4] But it included the negotiation of the treaty of friendship between the Soviet Union and Persia which lasted until its denunciation by the Persian government in 1979, after a duration of fifty-eight years: a long time for a treaty.

1 *(above left) Maximilian Löwe, Ivy's grandfather, about 1880.*

2 *(above) Sidney and Frederick Low, about 1850.*

3 *(left) Ivy, aged 9, Harrow, 1899.*

4 *Ivy with Misha, 1917*

5 *Ivy, 1919.*

6 *Maxim reunited with his son, 1921.*

7 *Ivy in Oslo with Misha and Tanye*

bad times through which he had to live until extreme old age. Litvinov's family remember him as one of their father's and their mother's oldest friends in the period of disgrace.

In Rothstein we meet one of the most anglified of all the Bolsheviks, in Alexandra Mihailovna Kollontai one of the most cosmopolitan. She was repeatedly in London during the years leading up to the outbreak of the Great War and, soon after it, graduated into the Soviet diplomatic service. Maisky describes meeting Litvinov and other Russian exiles at her lodgings at 2 Russell Square in the winter of 1913, which must have been soon after the TUC Congress at Cardiff where she had been a fraternal delegate from the Russian Social Democratic Party.

Like Chicherin, she came from the upper classes; her father had been a general, though he was of liberal leanings. Her marriage to an engineer called Kollontai lasted only three years before ending in divorce, and in 1898, at the age of twenty-six, she launched herself on her international career by going to Zürich to study the then novel science of sociology under Herkner, whence she made her way to England to sit at the feet of the Webbs. By the time she returned to Russia in 1899 she had made herself known also to the chieftains of German socialism—Kautsky, Bebel, Liebknecht, and Rosa Luxemburg.

Alexandra Kollontai retained her husband's name but never again formed any permanent exclusive attachment, and once remarked cheerfully that sex should be like having a glass of water—evoking from Lenin the sour comment, 'Who wants to drink from a dirty glass?' The comment was a cruel one, because Kollontai's rule in these matters was the necessity of passion, which she demonstrated in her long association with Dybenko, the sailor hero, who, like so many others, perished in the Stalin purges. When Maxim was asked if he'd ever been in love with her he replied enigmatically, 'Who has not?' The rights of women as wives, mothers and workers, the endowment of motherhood, the protection of female workers, the formation of a radical women's movement in Russia, were at the centre of Kollontai's labours during her nine years with the internal revolutionary movement from 1899 to 1908. She had been a sympathizer of Lenin's in the years that led up to the convulsion of 1905; but after it she became—like many others—a Menshevik. Litvinov must have known of her long before they met in London, for she served as treasurer of the Russian Socialist Party in St Petersburg, and so was part of the financial network headed by Krassin in which Litvinov played such a conspicuous role.

Maisky thought Alexandra Mihailovna was 'emotional, perhaps too emotional,' and she was certainly flamboyant, whether it was sailing with billowing skirts down Parliament Hill against the sunset, with arms outstretched, after an émigrés' picnic; or glancing from under a fashionable hat in the direction of the press when she went to present her credentials as Soviet ambassador in Norway in 1923; the first woman ever to be an ambassador. Maxim approvingly said that 'she never dressed down to the masses', a remark which very much reflected his own style, which was conventional to the point of formality.

She eventually became one of the most loyal of Bolsheviks, and had the advantage (as well as the danger) of spending long periods in both the external and the internal apparatuses of the Party. Her career (marked especially by her association with Lenin during the years 1915–17) endured until 1945, three years after she had begun to suffer from a severe illness. She survived until 1952 when she died at the age of eighty, leaving behind her memoirs which remain unpublished. Maisky and Litvinov had both read them. One considered them interesting, and the other, privately, observed that they were mendacious in the interests of Stalinism.

Litvinov and Alexandra Kollontai must have met in St Petersburg in 1905, and from then on his work kept them in contact. His commission as Lenin's representative in the Second International, at whose Congresses she frequently appeared between 1907 and 1912, must also have caused their paths to cross; and her firm attachment to Lenin after the outbreak of the War probably owed something to Litvinov. She served as Lenin's adjutant in the preparation of the Zimmerwald meeting in 1915 (at which Litvinov was also a prominent figure), and in 1917 was entrusted with messages for the Petrograd Bolsheviks on the outbreak of the February Revolution. However, in the winter of 1913–14 she was reading in the British Museum for a book on the endowment of motherhood.

Kollontai, Rothstein, Chicherin and Litvinov were all close contemporaries, who had reached their forties by the outbreak of the War. Ivan Mikhailovich Maisky, who observed them all in the pre-Revolutionary years, and became one of Litvinov's closest diplomatic colleagues, was some ten years younger. He had been born in 1884, and was of partly Jewish descent, though he did not like it mentioned—like many other Russian socialists, he had changed his name; originally Lyakhovetsky, it suggests the same Polish-Jewish origins as Litvinov's family name, Wallakh. When he arrived in England, in November 1912, it was with a certificate signed by Chicherin as secretary of the Central Bureau of Russian Social Democratic exile groups; and he found that of the dozen or so fragments into which the exiles were split in London, 'the most powerful and best disciplined was the Bolshevik group under its leader and secretary, M. M. Litvinov'.

Maisky was then, and for nearly ten years remained, a Menshevik, but the debt he owed to Litvinov for his understanding of British life was great, and had very great consequences. For eleven years, from 1932 to 1943, he was to be Soviet ambassador in London, where his influence exceeded that of any of his predecessors since the days of Lieven, a hundred years earlier. Short and stubby, with a genial smile beneath his Tartar moustache and wispy goatee, Maisky was able to maintain relationships during periods of apparently devastating difficulty, and his buoyancy did not flag even in the worst days (though he was for a time imprisoned), and in extreme old age, for he survived as an Academician, memorialist, and even letter-writer to *The Times*, until he was ninety-one. He died in 1973. If ever Litvinov had a disciple it was Maisky, and the admiration felt by the disciple for the master was lasting and genuine.

Such was not the fate of one of Litvinov's other close friends in London during those pre-War and pre-Revolutionary years when the embryonic Soviet diplomatic service was being formed. The name of Klishko certifies Litvinov as a suitable person to use the British Museum Reading Room in 1914, but otherwise plays little part in history. He was a Ukrainian and an engineer, and had shown his identification with England by marrying an English wife, Phyllis, who, as we have seen, had been at school with Ivy in Maida Vale. The Klishkos lived in Golders Green, not far from the Eders, and it seems probable that Ivy met Litvinov through this connection. Certainly Klishko and Litvinov were colleagues in the London Bolshevik underground at this time, and for many years afterwards the Klishkos and the Litvinovs remained close to each other, though Klishko, who had returned to Russia after the Revolution, occupied only modest posts in the official hierarchy. In the early 1920s we find him in the Russian Trade Mission in London, which in those days of partial recognition played an important diplomatic role, and he was among those expelled after the Arcos raid. In 1937 he was shot, and his wife consigned to prison, from which she only emerged seventeen years later, in one of Khrushchev's amnesties.

Litvinov's life as an underground socialist lasted altogether nearly twenty years from his first conversion to revolutionary politics, and during them he must have met many hundreds of revolutionaries, many of whom played important parts in the Revolution and what followed. But he made comparatively few close friends or allies among them. His letters to Lenin, of which a number survive, are distant and respectful, and entirely concerned with current business. The four persons whose careers have been sketched here were the closest to him, and were to remain so: Chicherin as a detested superior, and the other three as life-long friends and colleagues who, like him, had developed in Western Europe. The denizens of the revolutionary world inside Russia—apart from Kamo—he barely knew, and was even to regard as ignoramuses. So strong was this feeling that Stalin's presence at a Congress in London was something he could not later recall, so unimportant had it seemed to him at the time.

Among English socialists, on the other hand, Litvinov had many friends, and soon understood that while they would be happy enough to sympathize with a real Revolution in Russia, gradual reform with full compensation was the approach they favoured in England. He was a voracious reader of the newspapers, as well as a regular attender at Fabian meetings and left-wing political gatherings, and saw in them all more of the romantic attachment to revolution elsewhere than to the proletarian victory which Marx had foretold as due in the most advanced of capitalist countries. Like many refugees before and since, Litvinov came to like England and even, as he came to know it, to exaggerate the strength of its social system. And against principles which dictated an almost monastic existence he was drawn into the orbit of an undisciplined English girl, stagestruck by literature, eager to marry, and brimming with vitality.

5

Ivy in Hampstead

So much is needed to outline the shape of the force swimming in obscure depths which rose like Leviathan and took Ivy to a different and dangerous world with no more agreement from her than she always gave to adventure. In these years leading up to the First World War she was in her early twenties, a black-eyed, raven-haired, tall, plump, and above all vigorous young woman, eager for modernity. She had read deeply and widely, especially in fiction, and was already as censorious about style as any Fowler. That she was a kind of heroine she did not doubt—an improper heroine perhaps, but only on the way to being a heroine of letters. She had written a few pieces already for the *Manchester Guardian*, which had been printed, and in 1912, when she was only twenty-three, her first novel, *Growing Pains*, was accepted by Heinemann. It came out in 1913, and was devoutly dedicated to 'the memory of Walter Low by his eldest daughter'.

Many influences were playing on her. There were the Eders, Patriarchal, progressive and Freudian. There was her mother, who was developing a career in increasing independence of Sandy with a first novel—to be followed by many more—called *The Measure of Our Youth* (1909). There were the Meynells, although, despite her friendship with Viola, the family daunted her. Then there was a young man—'my first young man'—Edmond Kapp, at that time an undergraduate at Cambridge, and later a caricaturist and artist of distinction.

Ivy also formed a friendship with a woman somewhat older than herself. This was my mother, Catherine Carswell, then Catherine

Jackson.[1] She was some ten years older than Ivy, and had already survived an unhappy marriage which had nearly cost her her life. Altogether she was in strong contrast to Ivy, being tall, slender, aquiline and fair. Her disastrous marriage had left her with a little girl, and since she had finally quit her native Glasgow for London, she had been writing reviews of novels and metropolitan drama for the *Glasgow Herald*, from which she moved in 1912 to be assistant dramatic critic of the *Observer*. Perhaps because of her experience of marriage most of her close friends were women. One was a singer, another a sculptress, a third a doctor working for the LCC; a fourth, Athene Seyler, was just starting a career on the stage that was to make her celebrated, and another was being courted by a lively young Spaniard who was technical adviser to the superintendent of the line of the Northern Spanish Railway, Salvador de Madariaga.

Ivy's friendship with Catherine had arisen from a cordial review of *Growing Pains* in the *Glasgow Herald*, and it lasted, though not without its frictions, as long as Catherine lived. But it was far from being a union of temperaments. At the time they met, Ivy was passing through an incense-laden phase of High Anglicanism verging, under Catholic influence perhaps exerted by the Meynells, towards Rome; while Catherine, brought up among the austerities of the United Free Church of Scotland, never wholly shed a kind of puritan sternness, even in the most bohemian surroundings. She loved and respected her Glaswegian parents, with all their strange habits, because in their direct way they had loved her and had never claimed to be anything but the believing Scots bourgeois they were. She was to have her part in crusading against Scottish humbug, but her relations with her own parents were uncomplicated, in contrast to Ivy's attachment to a father she could scarcely remember and her contemptuous hostility to his successor. For the time being Ivy felt a sense of subordination to the older, and apparently better established, woman.

Catherine lived in Hampstead and there Ivy soon moved to be near her. 'Everything about Catherine's house [it was a cottage in The Grove] enchanted me—for the first time I had come into contact with trained taste, I thought, forgetting the chaste aesthetic of the Meynell flat, and their country house.' Her two friends had to meet, but it was not a success—Catherine thought Viola 'quaint'. But 'my friendship with Catherine Jackson did not merely change my life—it made it

[1] She had married H. P. M. Jackson in 1903. The marriage had been annulled in 1908.

over anew, it gave me a new aesthetic, and a new approach to the external world.' It was a great trouble that Catherine was so tidy, and, Ivy sometimes felt, disapproving.

Ivy's new quarters, her first and most-loved independence, were in Golden Square, a few steps from Catherine in The Grove, and next door to a policeman. There were still outside privies in some of the neighbouring cottages, and the rent was only 6s a week for the two small rooms on the second floor. Catherine helped her to furnish them, but Ivy never quite got over a sense that the older woman was covertly criticizing her, subjecting her perhaps to some kind of puritan discipline which it was her duty to repudiate.

Ivy's sense of subordination often took the form of vigorous criticism, and few, even her dearest, were spared. Thus we find her writing in January 1914 to Viola Meynell about Viola's latest novel, *Modern Lovers:*

> Dear Viola, this is the most mature work you have produced—as of course it ought to be. One or two little crudities, such as Effie saying to her mother 'how pretty you look!' and something else (I am at home and haven't the book beside me) seemed a pity. The whole book produces an impression of great distinction, humour, and above all, sympathy. I am not in a position to say I'm proud of it, but if I were, I would. But positive or not I'm sorry you didn't let me save you two mistakes in grammar, both of which I pointed out to you. Spr*u*ng instead of spr*a*ng and 'there *were* a quantity of shops' (I quote from memory). And, Viola, you have twice used the word *tireless. Never* do that again. Lots of versifiers do it—but really there's nothing to say for it. *Unwearied* is what you mean. At least I think so. Ask your mother . . . .

The letter ends by assuring Viola how important Ivy feels religion is. 'I am going to be quite different, I believe. (By the way as a beginning of the new leaf I stayed in bed till it was too late (1) for the 9 Mass, (2) for the 11 (3) for the 12.15. Just managed to get home for lunch by 1.45.)'

Catherine and Ivy were now setting out as literary crusaders. In the same year, 1913, as Catherine reviewed *Growing Pains* and helped to establish its author in Golden Square, she informed the readers of the *Glasgow Herald* that she had been 'deeply impressed' by *The White Peacock*, D. H. Lawrence's first novel. The following year the unwearying Ivy completed and placed, this time with Secker, a second novel. It was far less proper than the first, and daringly entitled *The Questing Beast*. Since it drew heavily on her experience at the Prudential it can claim to be one of the earliest novels about women in office life. The trouble was a passage about the seduction of the heroine by an articled clerk, and a scandalized W. H. Smith & Son refused to handle it, so that its circulation was restricted and its author delighted. Though the novel suffers from too much use of the flashback technique, and has two heroines, both secretaries—one mousy and virtuous, the other raven-haired and bold—it is a far more vivid and original book than *Growing Pains*. The need to work, the fines for lateness, the camaraderie and spitefulness of the clerks, the wages of £55 a year, are extracted in sharp detail.

In 1913 Lawrence's *Sons and Lovers* had burst on the public. Ivy read it with wild enthusiasm and wrote postcards to all her friends and acquaintances urging them to do the same. 'Discovered a genius,' she scribbled to one; 'I've found a classic by a living author' to another; to a third, 'Don't talk to me about Joseph Conrad.' And she did more. Having read the celebrated series of articles in *The Times Literary Supplement* entitled 'The Younger Generation', in which the author (actually Henry James) magisterially surveyed the latest novelists and placed Lawrence 'in the dusty rear', she wrote to Lawrence in the name of 'the younger generation'.

He replied from Fiascherino in Tuscany, where he was living with Frieda. As the correspondence developed Lawrence's answers were read with increasing excitement at Golden Square. Then in the spring of 1914, came an invitation, in terms now lost, to visit them in Italy, which the impetuous Ivy resolved to accept. 'She was rigged out', wrote Catherine afterwards, 'in my only "tailor made" (so as to make a neat impression if possible) and seen off by me with best wishes.'

Ivy wrote her own account of this adventure thirty years afterwards. She conceded Frieda was handsome, but thought she had a limp handshake, and was 'a bit sloppy and arty'. 'Embroidered Rumanian blouses were just up her alley.' Ivy's embroidered blouse, on the other hand, along with her self-confidence and ready smile, was bound (she thought) to make an impression. 'Lawrence was from the people himself, and however neatly and nicely his sisters dressed, the one thing they would never have had at that time was peasant embroidery. That was the monopoly of the intelligentsia.'

When Lawrence greeted her by asking whether she thought he looked like a working man, she said enthusiastically that 'he reminded her of a man in a third class compartment—tired, you know, but still full of life.' Reflecting, perhaps, on Henry James's sentence about the dusty rear, he seemed less than pleased.

Things improved for a bit, but as the visit went on they grew steadily worse again. Ivy was taking Lawrence's preaching about 'truth to one's feelings' rather too seriously. 'The Lawrences slept in a bedroom just across the hall from mine and truth to my feelings at the time would have made me suggest to Frieda that we should change places.' When Lawrence invited Ivy to go for a walk Frieda pressed her with poisoned heartiness to agree: 'Lawrence can't bear walking alone! He'd ask the dullest person in the world, just so's not to walk alone!' Nor did Lawrence himself spare Ivy, and he demolished her claims to musicality and religious feeling with savage sarcasm. She lacked rhythm, he declared, she was *unmusically* musical. As for religion, about which she was so serious, 'You are not a child or a peasant. You get on perfectly well without it.' Poor Ivy: 'Instead of being charming and original, it seemed I was fidgety, garrulous, clumsy and absurd.'

Yet the weeks she spent with the Lawrences were not wasted. She formed a just appreciation of that remarkable man who, she confessed, despite his dogmatism, had the gift of 'just saying what other people didn't even know they were thinking'. And she listened to his discussions with various visitors, among them Sturge Moore, the poet, and Peshkov, Gorky's adopted son, who came to submit his short stories for Lawrence's comments.[2] Ivy felt confused by Lawrence's comments, for they seemed to be aimed at the man and his relations with his wife, rather than at the merits of what he had written. Indeed that went to the root of Lawrence's attitude to literature.

In early June 1914, after about a month of excitement and subterranean warfare, Ivy was more or less politely escorted to a distant railway station. It was a Sunday, on which day, as Frieda sympathetically explained on the road, the trains would be very crowded. Ivy thought of asking why Sunday had been chosen, since any other day would have suited her just as well, but decided against it. She swore later that bystanders had seen both her and Lawrence in tears at the parting.

Certainly the friendship did not end there, and it had very important consequences. When, a few weeks later, Lawrence and

2 Gorky himself was living in Italy at this time, but he and Lawrence seem never to have met.

Frieda themselves made the journey to England and were married, the acquaintance was resumed. Our only actual sight of it is in a vivid passage of Middleton Murry's which describes Ivy, her kimono billowing round her, rushing down to greet the Lawrences, Murry and Katherine Mansfield as they mounted Holly Hill from Hampstead tube station—a sight which caused Katherine to turn back with the declaration that she wouldn't have that sort of thing (Lawrence trudged on to his appointment with a lame explanation that Katherine had not been feeling well). It was through Ivy's adventure that my mother formed her lasting (and to Ivy enviable) friendship with Lawrence; and Lawrence was also introduced to Dr Eder.

In the immense literature devoted to D. H. Lawrence the influence of David Eder and of Ivy's Freudian aunt Barbara Low has been neglected. Eder gave Lawrence medical advice and examined him in 1915; and it was through Eder and Barbara that Lawrence was exposed to the views of Freud and set on the path that led to *Psychoanalysis and the Unconscious.* 'At this particular moment', wrote Murry of July 1914, 'Lawrence's novel *Sons and Lovers* had been discovered by some of the Freudian psycho-analysts, who were enthusiastic about it because it exemplified some of Freud's main theses: and Dr. Eder called more than once on Lawrence to discuss the doctrine. . . .'

Eder had read *Sons and Lovers* as a result of one of Ivy's excited postcards, and found in it confirmation of the theories which he was one of the few men in England at that time to espouse. In the same year (1913) he had travelled to Vienna to meet Freud himself and came back charged with energy for a Freudian campaign. In August 1913 he wrote an article called 'Doctors and Dreams' for the *Manchester Evening Despatch* in which he declared that 'Dr. Freud has deposed the consciousness from its high place in psychology. . . . Psychoanalysis, as the new method is called, differs from hypnotism and suggestion chiefly in this: that the physician does not suggest to the patient what he shall do, but he helps the patient to discover what he can and must do.' Early in 1914, just before Lawrence returned to England, Eder delivered a paper to the North of England Educational Conference entitled 'The Unconscious Mind of the Child' which was afterwards reprinted in *Child Studies.* So great was the indignation that the issue was withdrawn.[3]

[3] Eder was used to this kind of thing. When he lectured in 1911 on hysteria and obsession to the neurological section of the BMA, the whole audience left the hall.

[Ivy in Hampstead]

Lawrence later put Eder into his Australian novel *Kangaroo* as the benevolent leader of a semi-fascist secret society for national renewal:

... a smallish head carried rather forward on his large but sensitive, almost shy body. He leaned forward in his walk, and seemed as if his hands didn't quite belong to him. But he shook hands with a firm grip. He was really tall, but his way of dropping his head, and his sloping shoulders, took away from his height. He seemed not much taller than Somers, towards whom he seemed to lean the sensitive tip of his long nose, hanging over him as he scrutinized him sharply through his eye-glasses, and approaching him with the front of his stomach.

Psychoanalysis was not the only doctrine that Eder introduced to Lawrence. The idea of a pure, untrammelled community far removed from the poisonous society of industrialized Europe first appears in Lawrence's history during his walking tour in the Lakes in July 1914, when he misheard his companion Koteliansky's chanted Hebrew, and baptized the projected utopia 'Rananim'.[4] Eder also had a Rananim. Once it might have been anywhere—perhaps the upper Amazon or Cyrenaica—but by 1914 his mind had been made up. The National Home of the Jews must be in Palestine. Lawrence's correspondence with Eder, even though only a few fragments of it survive, continued for the rest of Lawrence's life and from it emerges a sympathy with Zionism on the part of Lawrence which the stereotype of his character does not allow for.

In 1915 Eder visited the Lawrences in Cornwall and at the end of that year Lawrence was writing to Mrs Eder about plans, in which the Eders were included, for a community in Florida. In 1917, clearly irritated with Eder's commitment to Zion, Lawrence was writing from Zennor demanding his doctor should 'drop Jewishness' and asking him to read 'a little book of philosophy' which he had written.[5] But by then Eder was deeply engaged in other affairs. He had returned from military service in Malta, was soon to become Political Officer of the Zionist Federation, and shortly after that the Jewish

[4] See John Carswell, *Lives and Letters*, Faber and Faber, 1978, p. 97.
[5] Ultimately *Psychoanalysis and the Unconscious*. The letter is dated 25 August 1917. At almost the same time Lawrence was writing to Waldo Frank about the same 'tiny book of philosophy'. The quotations from Lawrence's letters to Eder, the only source I have traced from them, come from J. B. Hobman's *David Eder: Memoirs of a Modern Pioneer*.

Commissioner in Palestine under the Balfour Declaration. Again and again Lawrence wrote to Edith Eder asking for news of her husband, and by January 1919 was beginning to be captivated with the idea of emigrating to Palestine himself: 'I want to know about Palestine, if there is any hope in it for us. . . . I want to seek Eder.' A little later, to Eder himself:

> Oh, do take me to Palestine, and I will love you for ever. Let me come and spy out the land with you—it would rejoice my heart into the heavens. And I will write you such a beautiful little book, 'The Entry of the Blessed into Palestine'. Can't I come and do the writing up? . . . I wish you would take me to Palestine. I don't believe you'll pull it off, as a vital reality, without me.

Even if the idea of Lawrence as a propagandist of Zionism seems bizarre, the thought did not leave him. 'I suppose you wouldn't like me to come', he was writing in March 1921, 'to Palestine for a couple of months, and do a Sketch Book of Zion.' It is a pity it was never written. Though Lawrence and Eder never met again, so far as can be discovered, the last letter in the series came from Wiesbaden in 1929, only a few months before Lawrence's death.

Lawrence was deeply suspicious of those who sought to influence him—any hint of it could quickly turn initial friendship into unrelenting hostility; and although he had many Jewish friends—Koteliansky being the most notable—wounding remarks about Jews came readily enough to him when in a waspish mood. Eder's sister-in-law, Ivy's aunt Barbara Low, he once characterized as 'a chattering Jewish magpie' whom he did not wish to have settle on his roof. Yet even in his lecturings on the subject to Koteliansky (who was not spared in this respect) it is clear he had thought about it a great deal, and something of Eder's Zionism shines through:

> With them [the Jews] the conscious ego is the absolute, and God is a name they flatter themselves with.—When they have learned again pure reverence to the Holy Spirit, then they will be free, and not slaves before men. Now, a Jew cringes before men, and takes God as a Christian takes whiskey, for his own self-indulgence.

Lawrence was not the only improbable individual Eder reached with his blend of energetic benevolence, Freudianism and Zion. The historian Lewis Namier was, it is true, of undoubted Jewish origin but had been brought up as a Roman Catholic and throughout his life remained a devout Christian. What is more, from the time he came to study at the London School of Economics, and still more after he was adopted by Balliol just before the outbreak of the First World War, he was a passionate worshipper of all things British (though also, at that time, a Fabian). It was to be many years before he finally committed himself as a Zionist, and even then it was only as a practising Christian, and for a Zionism within the ambit of the British Empire in which he so deeply believed. But his interest in Freudianism came far earlier, and had much influence on his enduring historical work. His references to Eder at the time of his recruitment to the Zionist Organization in 1928 suggest that he fell for his charm against his better judgement, and there seems no doubt that he had know Eder from a much earlier period.

The Eder salon in the years before the War when Ivy became a junior member of it must have been a most interesting group, mingling the known, such as Wells, Orage and Shaw, with obscure and even seedy persons like Klishko and Litvinov. And very soon Ivy was beginning to use the typing she had learned at the Pru to work for Klishko on a strange machine with alternative typefaces of English and Russian. She did not use the Russian, of course, but it was the only typewriter he had, and he shared it with his friend Maxim.

Ivy described the coming of the War in a short piece she wrote long afterwards for the *Guardian*. She was standing outside Hampstead tube station with Catherine on the evening of the August Bank Holiday, surrounded by the crowd returning from the roundabouts and coconut shies on the Heath. Half an hour earlier—before she had looked at the evening paper—their cockney holiday clothes had looked cheerful and quaint:

> Now, massed together in the street the gaudy attributes looked menacing, looked like war-paint. It was we, the two arty young women confronting them . . . in our bonnetty looking close hats and ankle-length skirts, who looked quaint, trivial, irrelevant. Tired of staring at the headlines, Catherine turned to the Woman's Page at the back of the paper, and glanced at a drawing of a girl in just such another close-over-the-ears hat as ours, but a shorter skirt. 'I'm glad hems are lifting a little.'

Ivy met Maxim Litvinov just after the War broke out. She was twenty-five, he thirty-nine, and 'his stoutness and a certain gravity made him look considerably older. His manners were abrupt, his shoes were shabby, and his clothes, besides being "all wrong" were creased and shapeless from the newspapers and maps with which his pockets were always stuffed.' Nevertheless the Eders, particularly Edith, were taken with him; and the fact that in Ivy's view Maxim had 'much in common' with Eder was one of the things that drew her to him. 'Both men were abrupt and inarticulate except under sudden emotional stress, both had expressions ranging from the grave to the jovial, and both loved children.'

Edith Eder admired Maxim as a man who 'had won all hearts at the Fabian Summer School in Derbyshire.' '"Fat and well-liking" she called him, and said the very way he sat in an armchair was reassuring.' But she deplored what she called his 'absurd doctrinaire politics'—so remote from the benevolent humanitarian socialism of Matlock. This did not prevent her from taking Ivy to a Fabian Society meeting one evening (J. C. Squire was the orator) and not only leaving her protégée to converse with Maxim, but inviting him to dinner afterwards, and getting him, over the meal, to describe his escape from Kiev. As he left, he offered a hopeful invitation to tea, but Ivy was for not going. 'For Heaven's sake,' said her aunt, 'I'm only doing it for your sake. I thought it was the young man for you. And now you don't want to go.'

Ivy soon moved her typing services from Klishko to Maxim—not, of course, to help with his political work, of which as yet she knew nothing, but with his publishing and teaching of Russian. He was a shy, cautious suitor, who on his first visit to her cottage in Hampstead was almost deterred by seeing her neighbour, the policeman, emerge from the house next door, putting on his helmet to go on duty. 'We are perhaps too ready', he explained to Ivy, who had dashed out to meet him when she heard the gate opening and caught him before he turned away, 'to see everywhere surveillance. Our life makes us suspectful.'

They drank endless tea together, and she talked excitedly with her women friends about the strange English of the man she called 'the Slav'. 'But why is sheep she, not it?' he had asked. 'Sheep aren't inanimate, they eat grass and have lambs.' 'But I mean sheep on the sea, not ship that have lambs and eat grass.' But his English was by this time very fluent and wholly adequate not only for business purposes but for teaching Russian to English pupils. His clients included Messrs Vickers, who then, as later, were developing their business in Russia and sent him their employees; and a young

Australian called Rex Leeper, who had just come down from Cambridge and hoped to go into the Foreign Office.

Over tea in the Express Dairy in Heath Street where they often met, Ivy helped Maxim to improve his English—throughout her life she adored improving people's English—and she did more: she guided him in reading English literature. In later life the Foreign Commissar observed with an unconscious echo of Gibbon,[6] that Trollope had been of greater help to him in understanding English society than any number of text-books. She also introduced him to her uncle Sidney Low, who after initial disapproval was delighted to find that his niece's curious Russian friend had read *The Governance of England* and had things to say which were worth the professional attention of a journalist.

Maxim was also introduced to Ivy's mother and stepfather, Alice and Sandy, and was not slow to recognize the experienced siren in Alice. When asked by Ivy afterwards if he could believe her mother was nearly fifty his stolid reply was, 'easily I could'. Sandy he seems rather to have liked as a conventional uncomplicated Englishman, and also perhaps as a servant of the Bloomsbury temple. As for Alice and Sandy, they were now resigned to Ivy's independent ways and strange friends.

She made him read *Sons and Lovers* as well as Jane Austen, and he offered her the history of the French Revolution along with Shaw's *Intelligent Woman's Guide to Socialism*, commenting that Shaw did not know much about the subject. They bicycled all over the home counties—he was an enthusiastic cyclist—and he took her to the cinema, which she had always thought was 'low' but he adored. They were harmless new amusements which industrialization had opened to the masses, though neither he nor she would have put it that way. By the beginning of 1915 they were lovers. Ivy commented afterwards that she was sure it had cured his spots: 'He used to be terribly spotty . . . and he so sweetly said that the doctor had said it was lack of sex life. And it was, I think, because after a few weeks it had absolutely cleared up. Absolutely.'

'I nearly didn't marry him, you know,' says one of Ivy's tapes, made long afterwards. But when they were married at Hampstead Town Hall on 22 February 1916, by a registrar with the appropriate

[6] Cf. Gibbon's remarks that *Tom Jones* would be read long after the Austrian Empire had been forgotten and that the Captain of the Hampshire Grenadiers had not been unserviceable to the historian of the Roman Empire.

name of Bridger, it had been more her doing than his. The bridegroom was described as a 'literary translator' of Savernake Road, NW3, son of a bank manager—all true—and the bride as a spinster of Golden Square. Ivy's mother insisted on being present, which meant that the Eders could not be, because Alice and Edith so disapproved of each other. Catherine and her recently married second husband Donald completed the party, which after the brief ceremony made its way by tube to Soho for a celebratory lunch in a small restaurant. The occasion, according to Ivy, was 'distinguished by a kind of hard gaiety' and the bridegroom made 'a solicitous but faintly intimidating host'. When they were alone together in their new lodgings in Parliament Hill, looking down on the ponds, he asked her if she would be his good and faithful wife, and she said she would try. 'Don't you feel we have burned our sheeps?' he said. 'Boats,' she could not help saying.

Neither her family nor his friends can have been happy about it. Ivy's mother, though she had always wanted her daughter to marry as soon as possible, resented her following her example by marrying a Jew. Sandy, though he quite liked Maxim, was unable to regard him as an acceptable husband for a young British woman. What Maxim's political associates thought about their comrade marrying a woman of no political convictions and a member of a bourgeois family containing two leading conservative journalists is obviously unknown. True, Lenin did not disapprove of marriage, even for leading revolutionaries, and was himself married. But as a man following a doctrine and imbued with the need for security he must have been uneasy about his veteran supporter's choice. The dedicated should marry the dedicated, and Ivy was not dedicated, and never would be, in any political sense.

From most points of view Ivy could hardly have chosen a less eligible man. He was thirteen years older than she was, and verging on middle age. Literature, which was her abiding passion, lay on the edge of his interests. He had no money, profession or apparent prospects, and was affiliated, in ways he had not fully explained, to a secret revolutionary movement. She was untidy, unpunctual, talkative and defiant. He was exact, punctilious, disciplined and taciturn. Moreover he was a man for whom any alliance was potentially dangerous, and to a man of his experience the embarrassments to which she might expose him must have been only too clear.

[Ivy in Hampstead]

Maxim was deeply attracted to Ivy—and not least perhaps by her contrasting qualities, her openness, her vitality, her absence of calculation. One of his favourite pet names for her was 'Gipsy'. She must have offered all that he was not, a kind of release or at least an opening in the solitary life to which he had committed himself. Yet he had so committed himself, and more is needed to explain why he was willing to bind himself to so unexpected a wife, and to family responsibilities which, as he told Ivy, he would find it his duty to abandon if the cause required it.

Her uncalculating nature can have made little of this solemn warning, but perhaps she saw more clearly than someone better informed that he was a man imbued with the idea of commitment, and that pledges once entered into by him, even if they were inconsistent, would not be discarded. So a marriage was established in Hampstead Town Hall which, though battered in normal and abnormal ways as few have been, lasted until the death of one and was defended to the day of her death by the survivor. Despite his renunciation of Judaism there was embedded in Maxim the instinct of a Jewish family man. He could not resist children, especially when they were small, and although he denied the fact, he longed for them.

For Ivy her marriage was the great event of her life, and she wrote many accounts of the wooing—as many as she wrote about her early childhood and her father's death. These two concentrations of her later years confirm that emotionally the two episodes were connected and that in this older man who had faced responsibility and danger, who could be so comfortable, genial and reassuring, her adored but half-remembered father lived again, and crowded out her detested stepfather. 'Much money', Maxim once told her early in their marriage, 'and the lives of comrades have been entrusted to me.' She had felt shy and clumsy with the young men she met, but there was a curious flattery in the way this older, rather comic ugly Russian, with his secret commitments and his air of authority, was willing to take her. When, long afterwards, she worked the best of her accounts of her marriage into a short story she gave it the title 'Call It Love'.[7]

[7] Ivy published two English accounts of this part of her life: one, heavily fictionalized and omitting all reference to the Eders, is the short story 'Call it Love' (*New Yorker*, 1969); the other, 'Early Days', is a fragment of autobiography published in *Blackwood's Magazine* in 1973. Extensively corrected manuscripts of both are among her papers, and there are other fragments on the same subject, which she obviously loved to relive. I have relied heavily on both published sources, but more on 'Early Days'. The account of their first meeting in 'Call it Love' is wholly fictional.

6

The Revolution

'The difference in age, culture, and tradition,' wrote Ivy in one of her autobiographical pieces, 'his inflexible puritanism, my devotion to impulse, made heavy weather for our frail barque.' He was precise and orderly—'as neat as a monk in his cell'—and her wild untidiness was hard for him to bear. Even worse than her rumpled piles of clothes and papers were her outbursts of opinion. 'After all,' she exclaimed at one of the little parties of exiles held in his flat, 'Who did most for socialism—Tolstoy or Marx?' I can picture her flashing eye and thrown-back head in the stony silence that followed. 'I confess,' she records, 'the question remains in my mind unanswered to this day.'

She tried to cheer her husband up by quoting Johnson's opinion that marriage has many pains but celibacy no pleasures, and he patiently agreed, but they shared few tastes. He read for information and amusement, not literary enjoyment. Style, which mattered so much to Ivy, did not interest him at all, and when she was so bold as to criticize the language of some of the Party's propaganda leaflets he was quite cross. Ivy had little success in persuading him to like her favourite authors. Heny James, even in the form of 'carefully selected' volumes, made no appeal, and he rejected D. H. Lawrence with horror for what he called 'his intimacies'. He wearied of her talking about books; and was passionately addicted to newspapers. The same was true with nature and the visual arts. He was not interested in pictures and positively disliked modern painting. The only flower whose name he knew was a rose. For him a tree was a tree, be it ash, oak or willow. She brought him a fascinating beetle she had found on Hampstead Heath and even pointed out to him the charm and skill of a spider working on its web in the corner of their sitting-room, but he hardly looked up. While he liked country walks, and delighted in routes that led by lanes and by-roads so as never to touch a highway or a town, his greatest pleasure in them was the planning and then following them with maps. 'All through our lives together,' Ivy wrote, 'in whatever country we found ourselves, his happiest hours were spent in drawing up itineraries.'

The only fine art he truly enjoyed was music, and he was an inveterate concert-goer. But unfortunately Ivy, who later became passionately interested in music, was, in the early days of their marriage, still under the influence of having had it dinned into her at school, and hated being dragged off to the Queen's Hall for Beethoven and Mozart, in whose music Maxim found refuge and relaxation from his revolutionary preoccupations.

Yet in spite of all these differences the crossgrained timbers held together. He had a twinkle and a sparkle noticed by many besides his wife—men as well as women—which redeemed or seemed to redeem his orderliness and austerity; and she had a generosity and valour that rescued her disorganization and tactlessness. She respected him, and he admired her. Very soon their marriage was cemented into an unbreakable alliance by the arrival of two children within eighteen months of each other.

Misha was born to a father who was still an obscure conspirator, Tanya to a man already a public figure. In less than two years he both saw the fulfilment of his political dreams and became a family man. Misha was born in March 1917, in the wake of the Revolution that overthrew the Tsar (Ivy was still in the nursing home when the news of that first Revolution arrived). By the time Tanya was born in August 1918 a second revolution had carried Lenin and the Bolshevik faction of the social democrats to power.

Maxim's fellow-exiles in London had expected that if there was a revolution in Russia he would emerge as the London representative of the revolutionary government. For the New Year of 1917 he gave them a party for which he had prepared the borsch, salt herrings and roast turkey with his own hands. Much vodka was drunk to the health of the future 'ambassador', and a very pregnant Ivy managed a carefully rehearsed piece of phrase-book Russian—'Where are the skates of the ambassador?' He was to need them sooner than he expected.

In March 1917, as soon as she came out of the nursing home with

[The Revolution]

Misha, Maxim took her to see *The Cherry Orchard*. It was not just a family celebration. For the first time she found herself partner to a public figure. The reporters were at the theatre, and as he came out Maxim was able to give them a few words about the Bolshevik attitude to the great change in Russia, including the news that Lenin was at that moment on his way to Petrograd. Soon afterwards he began to dictate to Ivy a journal[1] of which only a fragment, perhaps the beginning, remains.

> 17 March 1917. London. I went to bed more excited than I knew. The news seemed to have let loose a flood of thoughts in my mind, keeping me awake the whole night. I was much too alive to lie in bed, and got up at six, seething with excitement to see the paper. So it is a real people's revolution . . . the type jumped in front of me as I ran through the paper. I could hardly make myself read consecutively, in my eagerness to read to the end of the column, now to glance at the middle of another, as if I would make one mouthful of the whole paper. I can't remember how I spent the morning; I went about the daily routine almost unconsciously. I tried to shave with the toothpaste and got into the bath without turning on the tap. A curious sensation. Did I have breakfast at all? What joy! Is there no way of getting to Russia immediately? I rushed to the Russian Consulate to ask for a passport and asked them why they hadn't taken down the portraits of the Tsar and his family in the hall. The despondent officials said they had received no instructions, that I must apply to the Home Office, etc. etc. What shall I do? Shall I wire to the Provisional Government for facilities? They have more to think of than my return to Russia. I remember how I pitied my exiled friends who could not share with me the joyful spectacle of the revolutionary scenes in 1905. Now I have to pity myself. I feel unsurpassed joy and unsurpassed pain at the same time. What a tragedy! To have spent half my life in the . . .

The rest is missing.

From all over the Western world the Russian revolutionary exiles,

[1] The extract given shows that at some points in his life Litvinov felt the urge to put his private thoughts on paper, and if Sir Robert Bruce Lockhart is to be believed (*Diaries of Sir Robert Bruce Lockhart*, Macmillan, 1973, p. 102), Litvinov told Sir Rex Leeper in 1933 that he was keeping a journal. He also dictated some memoirs to Ivy when he was in the United States; and after his first fall from office he devoted a great deal of time to a composition which he typed himself. The story of this, however, will be told in its proper place.

whatever their sect, were responding to the same call and no barrier of power or war was able to stop them, like salmon battling upstream, from making their way home. Alexandra Kollontai had gone ahead of Lenin. The aged Kropotkin gave up his flat in Brighton and embarked for Petrograd. The Menshevik leaders Martov and Akselrod set out from Switzerland, and Trotsky sailed from New York. Gorky made his way from Italy. For a time the revolutionaries of the interior were to be dominated by the men of the diaspora returning.

One wonders if Ivy had ever bargained for a husband whose chief resolve was now to return to Russia in the certainty that he was destined to play an important part in its Revolution. She believed in freedom and progress, she was glad the Tsar was overthrown, but she had no deeply rooted political convictions. Her ambitions were literary. Yet if she wanted to keep the stability Maxim represented for her, with his maps, his neatness, his caution about money, his devotion to their children, she would have to follow him into the fearful adventure of the Revolution.

She begged him to stay in England, at any rate for a time, and told him the Bible required a newly married man to stay at home for a year to comfort his wife. His response was a demand for chapter and verse, which she could not give; and that evening he silently handed her a slip of paper which said 'Deuteronomy XXIV:5. When a man hath taken a new wife he shall not go out to war, neither shall he be charged with any business: but he shall be free at home one year and shall cheer up the wife which he hath taken.'

Ivy and Deuteronomy combined would not have kept him in England if Lenin had ordered otherwise; but Lenin's instructions, which were now reaching him, were to stay where he was. Lenin seems to have decided that if the Bolsheviks should come to power their Foreign Minister should be the well-born former Menshevik, Chicherin, and not Litvinov, despite his impeccable Party history. Litvinov should remain in England as a propagandist, organize the revolutionary exiles for their return to Russia, and agitate for the release of those of them who, like Chicherin, were for the time being interned by the British government.

These, therefore, were his main activities during the spring and summer of 1917, though there were breaks. Maxim and Ivy went for a walking tour in the Forest of Dean carrying the infant Misha in a bag strapped to their backs; and there was more than one visit to Ivy's old friends the Meynells at Greatham, where 'all the younger members of the family took to Maxim.' Francis Meynell, the youngest of them all, was already launched on his career as a Labour journalist and was soon to become a resolute conscientious objector; but political discussions at Greatham were confined to the afternoon walks of the younger generation. The evenings, presided over by the Meynell parents, were set aside for readings from the works of Francis Thompson and playing 'words out of a word'. The upper-class literary Catholicism of Greatham can hardly have appealed to Maxim much, but 'words out of a word' captivated them both. The game remained with Ivy until her dying day, and dozens of samples survive among her papers. Maxim used to play it during sessions of the Supreme Soviet (of which he was long a member) to while away the overwhelmingly tedious proceedings.

Towards the end of 1917 they moved from Parliament Hill to a flat on the verge of Cricklewood, 50 Hillfield Road NW6, and it must have been there that they read the news of what *The Times* described as 'Maximalist Sedition in Petrograd': the Bolshevik Revolution. Trotsky became Commissar for Foreign Affairs, and the policy of a settlement with Germany was initiated. For the Western allies the darkest winter of the War began. At this grim moment Litvinov was appointed Soviet Plenipotentiary in Britain.[2]

Destiny had intended Maxim to be a diplomat. He assumed his professional status with extraordinary rapidity together with a complete repertoire of protocol in all its potentialities, and a large fund of courteous yet tiresome persistence. Within a day or two of his appointment the Foreign Office was being bombarded with polite letters from him (badly typed by Ivy) demanding recognition and all sorts of privileges chosen with mischievous skill: possession of the Russian Embassy, chairmanship of the Russian Chamber of Trade in London, interviews with officials, the right to use cipher, a formal call on the Foreign Secretary, who was then Lord Balfour.

'It will be a little difficult', reflected a Foreign Office official on 5 January 1918, 'for us to boycott Mr Litvinoff.' The negotiations between the Germans and the Bolsheviks, recently reinforced by

[2] He seems to have learned of his appointment from the newspapers, though it was officially made by Trotsky in a telegram dated 1 January 1918. It is possible that he was not the first choice for the post. A Foreign Office minute of 5 January 1918 speaks of information that the post had first been offered to Rothstein, who refused it. Rothstein, oddly enough, was at the time working at the War Office as a translator of Russian.

Chicherin's return from internment in Britain, had begun at Brest-Litovsk. However unattractive the Bolsheviks might be, no chance of keeping Russia in the war could be thrown away. Lord Robert Cecil, the Parliamentary Under-Secretary, suggested that the way out might be to appoint 'a temporary unofficial agent' to maintain contact with Hillfield Road, and the Office was equal to the occasion. 'Fortunately,' wrote the recipient of this suggestion, 'we have in London a person who seems in every way qualified . . . Mr. R. Leeper, who has been doing valuable work under Colonel Buchan,[3] knows the Russian problem well, and is intimately acquainted with Mr Litvinoff and Mr Rothstein.'

Rex Leeper, whose distinguished diplomatic career thus began,[4] had come from Melbourne to New College, Oxford, just before the First World War, and soon after coming down had met Litvinov at a party given by Salvador de Madariaga and his new Scots wife Connie, who was a friend of both Ivy and my mother. That meeting had started Leeper on a study of the Russian exiles in London, partly through becoming a pupil of Litvinov for Russian conversation, and partly by eliciting a certain degree of interest from Ivy. He came to like Litvinov, as most professional diplomats did, and for many years the two men, though normally opposed officially, were on cordial terms.

Lord Robert Cecil had at first thought of assigning Hagberg Wright, Librarian of the London Library, to the post of keeping in touch with Litvinov, but after seeing Leeper he decided that the Australian was the right man; and very soon afterwards Leeper was appointed a temporary clerk in the Foreign Office. In this capacity he presented himself one morning at Hillfield Road and was admitted by Ivy in her dressing-gown. Later meetings with Litvinov were held on a bench in St James's Park and then (when they both complained about the winter weather) in a waiting-room inside the Foreign Office itself—a decision only reached after earnest consideration at the most senior levels.

So long as negotiations were still in progress at Brest-Litovsk, Litvinov was in a position to extract a surprising number of

---

[3] The novelist and biographer, then in charge of the Intelligence Bureau of the Department of Information.

[4] Sir Rex Leeper (as he later became) rose to be one of the Foreign Office's principal experts on Eastern Europe, and served in Warsaw, Riga and Constantinople. During the 1930s he was head of the Office's public relations. At the beginning of the Second World War he organized PID, the Political Intelligence Department.

concessions from the Foreign Office. 'I suppose', wrote a War Office official wearily, 'that the next time I send a messenger through to Russia I shall have to get Mr Litvinoff's visa. Do you know if Mr Litvinoff has an office anywhere or will it mean sending the passport to Hampstead?' 'This is very awkward,' wrote the recipient in the Foreign Office, 'but there is no way out of this either. Mr Leeper should arrange this.' And Mr Leeper did. Litvinov had acquired the right to issue visas, simply by asserting it; and in its wake was conceded the right to receive unexamined mail and to use cipher.

Soon he moved his office from Hillfield Road to Victoria Street, at the same time loudly demanding possession of the Russian Embassy, which was still occupied by the crestfallen diplomats of the former regime. Their chief, Nabokov, protested against the countenance being given to their competitor, but to no effect. 'The situation of Mr Nabokoff', wrote Lord Hardinge, the Permanent Undersecretary unfeelingly, 'and the Embassy staff, is really pitiable, but they must recognize that they represent nothing, and that it is impossible for us to withhold recognition from the *de facto* government.'

The decision to concede informal recognition to Litvinov was by now part of a more ambitious plan to obtain the equivalent for a British emissary to the Bolsheviks, and on 11 January the scheme was set on foot over the famous lunch at Lyons in the Strand, in which the participants were Litvinov, Rothstein, Leeper and the British agent-designate, Bruce Lockhart. Lockhart thought Rothstein was the more lively of the two Russians until the end of the meal, when Litvinov called for 'pouding diplomate' (which he had found on the menu) and was told by the waitress that it was off. Commenting that he was not recognized even by Lyons, he scribbled for Lockhart a letter of introduction to Trotsky, in which he included a report on the efforts he was making to publicize the Bolshevik cause in England.

These were indeed as vociferous as his dealings with the Foreign Office were polite. Only the day before the lunch at Lyons he had published an 'Open Letter to the Workers of Great Britain' in the socialist paper *The Call*. He had written to J. H. Thomas seeking an interview (Thomas sent it to the police) and was in touch with Lansbury, whose pacifist socialism and early Marxist training under Hyndman made him a far readier sympathizer. He received a deputation from the Irish TUC, and assured them that the Bolsheviks had long been students of the writings of James Connolly; and on 18 February addressed an enthusiastic meeting at the Central Hall

Westminster under the chairmanship of the Labour MP William Anderson, who declared that 'men like Lenin, Trotsky, and Kameneff [applause] were being held up to us by the newspapers as German agents with their pockets bulging with German gold [cries of 'shame'] and it is time lies of this sort were nailed down.' Litvinov's speech more or less repeated one he had already made at the Labour Party Conference held at Nottingham in mid-January, to which he had managed to get himself invited as a fraternal delegate. If peace was achieved at Brest-Litovsk, he declared, the Revolution would spread to Germany, so bringing an end to the German autocracy and to the War itself.

Questions were asked in Parliament about this energetic propaganda, and the Special Branch was deeply worried. Its chief, Basil Thomson, submitted a file on Litvinov's past to the Foreign Secretary, which ended with a triumphant suggestion that he might be prosecuted for marrying under false pretences, since his real name was Wallach (sic). Lord Balfour was not impressed, and scrawled underneath in red pencil:

All the above seems to me nonsense. L has been in this country for years. His wife is I believe a niece of Sir Sidney Low. If he ought to be arrested for marrying under a false name why did not the police do it before? L is a diplomatic personage.

Ivy was necessarily caught up in all this publicity and the social life that went with it. She took to it with considerable aplomb. She might defer to literary men, but politicians and public figures held no terrors for her, and she rather enjoyed showing it. At one party, in the spring of 1918, the former Pru Girl found herself sitting next to Ramsay MacDonald and opposite Bertrand Russell, of whom she cheerfully demanded to know what he thought of Freud. 'He fixed his eagle eye on me for a moment, but hardly troubled to answer my brash questions'; so she turned to the Labour lady who had politely enquired what it felt like to be an ambassadress. Maxim's lectures on protocol had not been wasted. 'It was what we were expecting, only we don't call it being an ambassador when your government is not recognized.'

But in March came the abject peace terms of Brest-Litovsk and the devastating German offensive in the West which it only too obviously made possible. Far from being weakened by the socialist revolution in the East, the German autocracy seemed for a few months to have victory within its grasp.

What Litvinov may privately have thought of the peace treaty can never be known. Under it his native town of Bialystok was severed from the new Russia which he served, and one must not forget that although he had little cause to love the old Russian Empire, he had been a Russian soldier. Even after the capitulation he was saying privately to Leeper that the Bolsheviks were anxious to offer resistance to the Germans 'as soon as they were in a position to do so'; and in a pamphlet published in April[5] he deplored 'the disastrous Brest-Litovsk Treaty' into which the Bolsheviks had been forced by events. What is certain is that the treaty destroyed his (and Bruce Lockhart's) diplomatic significance. Whichever way the War went, Russia would be among the defeated powers.

Peace with Germany at Brest-Litovsk in March 1918 marked a critical point in Litvinov's career as the Revolution's representative in Britain, very much as the understanding with Germany twenty-one years later was to mark the end of his influence over Soviet foreign policy. Until Brest-Litovsk he had commanded respect, even sympathy. Lord Balfour himself had said (admittedly in private) that he was 'a diplomatic personage', and he had been invited, along with Ivy and the revolutionary Kamenev (who was then on a curious expedition to the West) to dinner with the Webbs. He could rely on the old British suspicion of Russian autocracy and a widespread willingness to tolerate, and even welcome, a perhaps liberal successor to it. As yet that successor had little blood on its hands, and in the prevailing chaos it could hardly be reproached with systematic repression. Litvinov, in his pamphlet, could justifiably say that 'in point of mere numbers of persons arrested or papers suppressed the Soviet Government will compare very favourably even with Kerensky's regime.'

The only trouble with that quotation was the word 'will'. Very soon after it was published the series of events began which produced the wave of revulsion against the Bolsheviks throughout British society. The separate peace with the Germans was followed in July by the murder of the Tsar and his family; and on 31 August, only a few days after the birth of Ivy's second child, Tanya, Kaplan tried to kill Lenin,

[5] *The Bolshevik Revolution: Its Rise and Meaning*, by Maxim Litvinov, with a preface by E. C. Fairchild, 1918. The preface is dated April but indicates that the pamphlet was written 'some little time ago'.

and unlocked the terror which will always be associated with the name of the Cheka and set Russia once more on the railroad of oppression.

On 4 September Bruce Lockhart was arrested in Moscow[6] and Maxim had only just time to register the birth of his new daughter before he was arrested in retaliation and lodged in Brixton along with Bertrand Russell who was serving six months there for pamphleteering against the War, which by that time was almost won. Ivy's charwoman, Charlotte, gave notice. 'She was not going to be seen going in and out of a house where there was always a policeman hanging round. She did not know what Mr Litvinoff could have done; he always seemed a quiet, pleasant-spoken gentleman. But whatever it was she did not want to get mixed up with the police.'

Maxim was, as always, calm and self-controlled. Much later he commented that he always knew when he was being watched in England—the watchers even used to say goodnight when they had seen him to his door—but that never happened in Russia. He was respectfully treated during his weeks in Brixton, which lasted only for as long as it took to arrange his exchange for Bruce Lockhart. Rex Leeper collected him and took him to Aberdeen, whence he was to sail for Stockholm.

It must have been a strange trip. They were still friends, but now plainly adversaries also. That spring and summer Leeper had written a series of penetrating criticisms of Bolshevism for the War Cabinet which Balfour minuted as 'interesting and valuable'. He had drawn heavily on earlier conversations with Litvinov and Rothstein, but his conclusion was embodied in a note headed 'The Growing Menace of Bolshevism in Russia'. 'As the military power of Germany is gradually being crushed Germany ceases to be the greatest danger to European civilization, while a new danger—no less deadly—looms up in the near future.' But on no account, warned Leeper, must Germany be allowed to regain her strength by claiming to be the bulwark against that menace. That task should be undertaken by the victorious West, through the proposed League of Nations. As the two men parted at the gangway Leeper said he was sure Litvinov would be back within ten years.

[6] In her last years Ivy recorded that Maxim had told her that the arrest of Bruce Lockhart (as was alleged at the time) was due to 'provocation'—i.e. due to the activity of an agent who deliberately involved him in a counter-revolutionary contact in order to contrive his arrest.

Ivy was not allowed to go with her husband—indeed it would hardly have been practicable that she should voyage into chaos with two small children, one of them only a month old. Maxim had been ruthless on the subject. 'You would just be a burden to me,' he said. 'I would have to waste days getting you settled.' So he departed to become adviser to Chicherin, Foreign Minister of a bizarre government, under siege from numerous disputing armies, native and foreign. Maxim's family was not to see him for two years; and Leeper got a wire from him in Moscow saying he seemed to have lost his return ticket.

7

To Moscow

Ivy's two years' separation from Maxim after his enforced departure from England, were, she afterwards wrote, 'the most meaningless of my life'. Many thought she had shipwrecked herself by marrying a man who had vanished into the chaos and terror of an uncharted Bolshevik Russia. 'I always said that man would desert her,' said Sir Sidney Low. Even D. H. Lawrence had regarded the alliance as temporary . 'A good thing Ivy is married,' he had written in 1916. 'She will be able to get unmarried when she wants to.' She was still well under thirty.

But unmarried was just what she never intended to be. It would be wrong to say that even at the very beginning she had a romantic passion for her husband, but there was an element of the Othello relationship in it and she loved him for the perils he had passed, just as she was taken with the twinkle in his eye. She was taken, too, by his strange destiny and by the fact that in the England of that time he was the best-known Bolshevik except Lenin and Trotsky, and the only one anybody had met. She certainly intended to follow him.

It was not that she felt any particular enthusiasm to rush and help in the great new Soviet experiment. She was interested in neither the theory nor the practice of politics. But there was a streak of defiance and iconoclasm in her, a sense of rebellion against conventional life to which Bolshevism, at that particular moment in its history, made a strong appeal. It was a feeling not so much of cynicism and disillusionment as of an inner need—common enough at the time—to challenge the world about her and refuse to accept the restraints and pressures which produce order and conformity. If she had been able to foresee how rigorous those very forces would become in the country to which her husband had gone, perhaps she would have hesitated, just as she might have hesitated if she had reflected about what a conventional man her husband really was. But very few people in England at that time saw the Soviet Union in that perspective. Lansbury did not. Wells did not. Of the early British visitors to the Soviet Union only one, Bertrand Russell, recorded the underlying prospect.

> I was stifled and oppressed by the weight of the machine as by a cope of lead. . . . Imagine yourself governed in every detail by a mixture of Sidney Webb and Rufus Isaacs, and you will have a picture of modern Russia. I went hoping to find the promised land.

The others found far more to praise and were heard with interest on their return. H. G. Wells was depressed by the evidence of poverty but convinced that the Bolsheviks were the only people who could govern Russia. George Lansbury 'almost shouted for joy' on seeing the Red Flag over the Soviet border post, and considered 'that if there is such a thing embodied in humanity as the spirit of religion, then Lenin has got it to a larger extent than any man I ever met'. He was sure the Labour Party should join the Third International. It would be no exaggeration to say that during Ivy's two years of separation from her husband there was a greater degree of sympathy for the Soviet Union among trade unionists and progressively minded persons in Britain than at any time until 1941.[1]

The most important reason determining Ivy to rejoin Maxim as soon as she could, whatever the dangers and hardships, was the children. It was unthinkable that they should grow up without their father, as Ivy herself had had to do. She rejoiced when her Russian friends called her Ivy Walterovna after the father she so revered but could scarcely remember in the flesh. For her children the patronymic should be a reality. Their father showed his tenderest side in paternity: his children, he declared, with simple force, were part of him.

---

[1] Wells, Russell and Lansbury all visited Russia in 1920 and all three had interviews with Lenin, of which they provide vivid accounts. The interviews have a remarkable similarity of pattern and setting. Lenin was always unaccompanied and left on his hearer a strong impression of austerity and realism. He was clearly willing to devote considerable time and trouble to foreign visitors at this particular period.

[To Moscow]

Ivy's resolution was strongly supported by her mother. Alice
Herbert's second marriage had survived in a rather desiccated way,
despite a series of adventures with 'Me-en' (including Wells), and she
was now launched on a not unsuccessful career as a popular novelist
under the imprint of John Lane. Her works were light and daring
without being improper. *The Measure of Our Youth* had come out in
1909, *Garden Oats* in 1914. She was now working on *Heaven and
Charing Cross* which was to have some vogue in 1922. Alice's advice
to her daughter was to stick to her husband—Alice rather liked
Maxim—but not to avoid adventures.

Ivy pictured herself later as a woebegone wanderer during these
two years, drifting with her little family from one place of shelter to
another; but she did not actually lack friends who were willing to
help, and her natural high spirits were not always damped down. Dr
Eder, it is true, was now in Palestine furthering the Zionist cause but
she saw much of Rothstein, who had succeeded to Maxim's
responsibilities as the unofficial Soviet agent in London until he too
returned to Russia in 1920, and through him must have received
much of her husband's news. However, her chief friend at this time
was my mother, who had now married, in 1916, Donald Carswell.

My parents were then living at Hollybush House in Holly Hill at the
top of Hampstead, where I had recently been born, and Ivy was often
there with her two children. My mother and father had both liked
Maxim, though the philosophy of communism was very far from
theirs. My father had passionately rejected the Hegelianism which
had been fashionable in Scotland when he was young, and had
become an earnest Asquithian Liberal. So earnest were his
convictions in this respect that he had recently given up his post on
The Times and been called to the Bar in the vague hope of using it as a
stepping-stone to a political career. Alas, his contribution to the
sinking Liberal cause got no further than speaking for unsuccessful
Liberal candidates. He was a mild, scholarly Scot, ill-fitted for the cut
and thrust of politics or even of advocacy. But what he did bring from
his legal studies was a considerable expertise in the law of nationality,
and on that subject he was able to offer Maxim and Ivy some advice
which they did not forget, and was later to be important. Under the
law as it then stood (though it has been subsequently changed) Ivy
lost her British nationality on marriage, and acquired that of her
husband; but Misha and Tanya were irrevocably British subjects
since they had been born in Britain. The only thing that could have

negatived this would have been the formal diplomatic status which Maxim, for all his efforts, had failed to achieve.[2]

Ivy's link with England was not so much legal as personal; and among her many English friends the most lasting was my mother Catherine—a contrast in temperament and principles, but notwithstanding loyal and affectionate.

Catherine, as Ivy often commented, had her austere, critical, Scottish side. She tended to distrust as pretentious any claim to artistic feelings which was not accompanied by hard work and professionalism, and she had had ten years' experience of producing regular reviews of batches of novels of varying quality. She had now married a man whose slow pace and gentleness made it certain he would not achieve the ambitions he rather amiably nourished, a man who could not have been more different from Ivy's precise, energetic Maxim.

Ivy had been earlier in the field of publication, but Catherine was now the more seasoned writer. True, she had so far published no book, but she had been working on one for some years, and in 1920, under the title *Open the Door!*, it won a literary prize and temporary popularity. Her work for the *Glasgow Herald* had come to an end when the editor detected a favourable review of D. H. Lawrence's *The Rainbow* which had not been submitted for his earlier scrutiny, but she was now working regularly on theatre notices for the *Observer* instead.

Catherine had also become a very close friend of D. H. Lawrence, who had commented on the early manuscript of *Open the Door!*, and in 1919 sketched an outline of a novel in which they might collaborate. Until he left for Italy in 1920 Ivy often met him at Hollybush House, and it must have been thence that she had rushed as a billowing apparition to greet Lawrence as he trudged up the hill from the tube station accompanied by Murry and Katherine Mansfield.

Katherine Mansfield and Ivy did not match well. Ivy was exuberant, extroverted and overconfident, Katherine was watchful, guarded, tortured by doubts about herself and others. Katherine was not a lady, though she sometimes fancied the idea of behaving as one: Ivy had no such aspiration, but always behaved with no effort and complete conviction as a slightly eccentric member of the English upper classes. Yet as women who had dedicated themselves to

[2] The suggestion that Maxim himself at one time sought, or even obtained, naturalization as British appears to be without foundation.

8 Ivy with Misha and Tanya, 1928–9.

9 The Litvinov family at home, Moscow, 1931.

10 Litvinov and Salvador de Madariaga, Geneva, 1934.
And *how* M. loves people who touch him!

11 Tanya in the early 1930s.

12 Misha in the early 1930s.

authorship both Katherine and Ivy mastered a particular form, the short story, in which to achieve excellence by recording the intensities of emotion and observation. Ivy's best work is in her short stories and, as in the case of Katherine Mansfield, they cost her infinite pain and even despair in their making.

The other, and totally distinct group, that sustained Ivy during these two years was the Meynells. Ivy was often at Greatham, where she not only saw much of Viola but came to know her younger brother Francis better. At this stage of his life Francis combined being a protégé of Churchill's private secretary, Eddie Marsh, with ardent revolutionary zeal in the retinue of George Lansbury. He had been a heroic conscientious objector, and on the outbreak of the February Revolution in Russia a moving spirit in Lansbury's Anglo-Russian Democratic Alliance, which had naturally brought him into closer contact with Litvinov, whom he had first met through Ivy. Now he was assistant editor of the *Daily Herald*, of which Lansbury was editor.

Lansbury, who is not now usually thought of as a man of the Left, perhaps typifies more clearly than any other figure the profound yearning in Britain that was for a time satisfied by the revolutionary transformation in Russia. The novelty of it, and above all its dramatic call for peace, crowded out of his mind any awareness that the sacrifices called for by the Bolsheviks were and would be no less fearful than those of Passchendaele and Verdun. Later on, for some, this yearning, born of the colossal suffering of the First World War, became a kind of transferred patriotism; and for many it was an escape from immediate and oppressive certainty into a more remote and seemingly more comforting one.

In November 1919 Lansbury visited Copenhagen, where he met Litvinov, and then went on to Russia. The occasion for Litvinov's presence in Denmark was one of the lesser-noticed informal contacts between the British and Soviet governments—the so-called O'Grady mission, which was officially concerned with the exchange of prisoners of war, but was widely rumoured to be the beginning of a negotiation for the end of the 'War of Intervention'.[3] One of

[3] James O'Grady is a curious figure whose memoirs, if he had written any, would be of great interest. He had started life as a working man from Lancashire and a trade union organizer, and in 1906 had become Labour MP for Leeds—a seat he still held at the time of his mission in 1919. He had visited Russia with a deputation just after the Revolution of February 1917, and although he had no sympathy with Litvinov's agitation in England in the first half of 1918 (being a whole-hearted supporter of the

Lansbury's objects in seeing him was to negotiate supplies of paper for the *Daily Herald*, but another was to gain entry into the Soviet Union, which he achieved early in 1920, being one of the first British journalists to do so.

Ivy's friend and Lansbury's deputy, Francis Meynell, was also in Copenhagen at the time of the O'Grady mission, though in his autobiography *My Lives* he mistakenly places the visit in the summer of 1920.[4] And on that visit or another soon afterwards he met Litvinov, taking him, one cannot doubt, news of Ivy, and bringing back subsidies, in the shape of jewellery, for the *Daily Herald*. The subidies ended badly in September 1920 when the whole story came out, and the *Herald*'s headline 'SHALL WE TAKE THE £75,000 OF RUSSIAN MONEY?' was answered with a resounding negative and the resignation of Francis Meynell.

Whether or not Francis was also in Copenhagen in the summer of 1920, Ivy was, though briefly, and met Maxim. She soon returned to England and he to Moscow where he was now one of the council, or Collegium, advising Chicherin on foreign policy. But the occasion for a permanent reunion—all the more necessary since the Copenhagen encounter had resulted in a third pregnancy—came later in that year.

Towards the end of 1920, or early in 1921, Maxim was appointed Soviet ambassador to the newly independent states of Estonia, Latvia, Lithuania and Finland, which allowed him to have his family with him. The posting was a significant one, for the opportunities of regular, recognized Soviet diplomacy abroad were still few, and the Baltic lands—familiar to Litvinov from his *Iskra*-smuggling days— were at that moment the Soviet Union's front door on the West. Almost at the same time Alexandra Kollontai was despatched to Norway, and Krassin succeeded Rothstein as unofficial agent in London.

Ivy's pregnancy was now far advanced, and 1920 had not been a good time in which to eat for two. Photographs of her in that year show her looking haggard and anxious as never before or later. But off she set, with Misha and Tanya, aged respectively three and two.

The first port of call was Oslo, then still called Christiania, where she had to go into hospital, and her third child, a son, was born. She

---

War) he knew and liked him. Later, in 1924, at the time of the first Labour Government, he was transformed into Sir James O'Grady KCMG, Governor of Tasmania, whence he proceeded in the same capacity to the Falkland Islands, where he died.
[4] See Appendix 1.

gave him the name Sigurd, but he died soon after birth, leaving Ivy sick and broken-hearted. Nevertheless the family pushed on through the Narrows to Reval (now Tallin), where they were to meet Maxim. It was the capital of newly independent Estonia, and was as decrepit and turbulent as six years of strife could have made it.

At the moment of their meeting a procession went past and Tanya toddled into it and vanished. The burly Maxim plunged after her and emerged triumphantly carrying his daughter. He enquired sorrow-fully after his lost son, 'asking eagerly what he had been like'. He had also hired a nurse for the children, who was called Nelly Alexeyevna Toop. The journey had been a fearful one, and the next steps were unimaginable, but there was assurance in the reunion; and for the first time she was an ambassadress, a real ambassadress, though in a run-down, dismal little city.

There were letters from Ivy to my mother from Estonia, but they are now lost. Their existence I can confirm only from the stamps torn from them which I later collected and are now, in their turn, lost: they showed a blacksmith with his hammer wildly raised above the anvil, surrounded by the inscription EESTI VAMBARIK, which puzzled me. But a little later I owned a jigsaw of Europe designed to give one piece to each country, however small; and thus I learned about the frayed edges of the old Russian Empire which so preoccupied Maxim Litvinov—Latvia, Lithuania, Estonia, Georgia, Armenia, and Azer-baijan (which was purple). Indeed there must have been many letters, for I had a wonderful collection of improbable stamps, some of them for thousands or even millions of marks, kroner and roubles.

After about a year's embassy in Estonia, Litvinov was recalled to Moscow, this time as deputy to Chicherin. That febrile man, borne down by the humiliation of Brest-Litovsk and unable to break his bohemian habits, was a difficult chief to serve. He summoned meetings in the early hours, at which his colleagues, dragged from their beds, had to listen to him brooding and theorizing over the policy to be adopted by a state which had just emerged from civil and external war as one of the feeblest in Europe. Out of the fog of those meetings it became clear to Litvinov and even to Chicherin that in Soviet foreign policy the cause of international revolution could not bulk large. What mattered was the effacement of that terrible treaty with the Germans which had extruded Russia from Europe and was now built into the treaties made by the final victors; and the re-creation of Russia's external position as a sovereign state.

It was as the wife of Chicherin's new deputy that Ivy arrived for the first time in Moscow. The year was 1922. The Litvinovs were lodged in a flat near the Kremlin which had been carved out of a large mansion once owned by a sugar merchant named Kharitonenko. 'It was all gilt and plush, paintings and panels on the wall and everything,' she wrote later, but there was no heating. She complained to the Commandant, who replied that the house was not cold. 'You heard what the man said,' was Maxim's observation afterwards: 'It isn't cold.' 'He was nervous of him, really,' Ivy wrote, recording the incident. 'It was, I remember, very very cold.' She was never to accept the pig-headed bureaucracy under which she was to live for nearly half a century. But at that moment a small cold finger went on her dependable, self-sufficient husband: 'He was nervous of him, really.'

As she became more confident she could be a swashbuckling, sweeping defender of her adopted country, and her strange position gave her an advantage over English friends whom she loved to shock by affronting their liberal notions and making dismissive comments about the world-famous whom she had met on terms of equality: 'Chiang Kai-shek—an opportunist!' I remember hearing her say: 'Kemal Ataturk—a syphilitic!' But she was incapable of sinking herself in any system, whether it was her boarding-school at Tynemouth or the Union of Soviet Socialist Republics, and perhaps her individualism served her well. Discreet she was not, but since her individualism, and Maxim's profound discretion, prevented her from ever becoming involved in politics, her indiscretions were on the whole harmless. Is it possible, though, that her indiscretion made him, in the end, less discreet than he might otherwise have been, less committed to the cause, lead where it might?

Authority in the Soviet Union was not quite so confident when Ivy arrived there as it ultimately became. It had the benefit, perhaps, of a coinage newly minted. Collectivism had not yet been resolved upon. Instead the New Economic Policy allowed some precarious liberty to private enterprise as the only remedy for a moribund economy. Many old restrictions and conventions had been torn aside and had not yet been replaced by the stony and heartless limits of Stalinism. Much of the old Russia still survived, and there was much experiment. Moscow was uncomfortable and confused, but it was exciting.

Among the many shortages the worst was the shortage of water; but nothing worked, nothing could be had. Nothing, that is, except personal service for those entitled to it. At a time when nannies were growing fewer in Western Europe, Maxim arranged for Nellie Alexeyevna to come from Estonia to look after the children.

Without being aware of it, the rebellious girl from England was becoming part of a new governing class in process of formation, and she found Moscow very puzzling. She had vaguely supposed (so she records) that 'ideas' would be everything in her new country, and that 'things' would hardly count, 'because everyone would have what they wanted without superfluities', but 'when I walked about the streets of Moscow peering into ground-floor windows I saw the *things* huggermuggering in all the corners and realized they had never been so important . . . people dared not throw anything away, for there was nothing to be got.'

At first most of the people she saw were the wives of Maxim's colleagues, who were kind to her, but the only fund of conversation was children or, to her astonishment, the length of London hemlines. Nobody seemed willing to talk about books, and when she tackled Maxim on the subject he said impatiently that she seemed not to want to talk about anything else—and what was more the books had to be novels—and English novels at that. 'When your friends come,' she complained, 'you discuss nothing but other people—at least when I listen attentively.' 'And who', he asked, 'told you to listen attentively?'

As Maxim was well aware, Ivy now knew Russian quite well, both to speak and to write, and eventually she came to speak it as readily as English, though never with the precision she devoted to her native language. So very soon after her arrival in Russia she was assigned (for everyone had to work) to a translation bureau, and translating work was to occupy her intermittently—and profusely—for the rest of her life. One of the not unimportant results was that she usually possessed an independent income.

She found piles of miscellaneous books in the lofty rooms of the ex-sugar merchant's mansion, which looked out towards the Kremlin and was used mainly to house a transient population of delegates from abroad. And gradually, because she was persistent and feared nobody, she began to discover rather more of the cultural life of Moscow. She met Gorky who was agonizing, as so often in his career, between the socialism to whose flattery he was so susceptible, and his dedication to international literary life. He was currently engaged in trying to rescue Russian writers from poverty and oppression by setting up an organization for them, and in so doing coralled them into a Writers' Union in readiness for the oppression which was to come. Soon he was to return to Western Europe for a last period of activity before settling, as an ill and weary man, to fulfil the role of principal Soviet literary hero.

A. V. Lunacharsky, Commissar for Education and Culture, was more of a man after Ivy's heart than Gorky, and a product of that extraordinary, experimental period. He had in his time been very much an advocate of terrorism, but fitted ill with Lenin's notion of a communist, for he was by temperament a *boulevardier* and literary man who had produced a certain amount of verse and drama, and even at the time Ivy came to know him was writing a fairy story called *Vassileca the Wise* for Messrs Kegan Paul in London. He had distanced himself from Lenin in pre-Revolutionary days by espousing (along with Gorky) the heresy of 'God-building', and had suggested that Marx was the last of the Jewish prophets, with Marxism as 'the fifth great religion formulated by Jewry'. His current wife (he later married again a lady whom Ivy was to criticize) was the sister of Bogdanov, the Marxist against whom Lenin had launched one of his most indignant and tortuous pamphlets, *Materialism and Empiriocriticism.*

The Rothsteins Ivy found more congenial still, for they brought a breath of home. He was now back from Persia, and was to spend the rest of his long life as an archivist and historian. But Rothstein's withdrawal from active diplomatic life caused him to see less of Maxim, and so of the Litvinov family. Maxim was a man of action, and although Ivy did not love the business life that went with it, she loved action too. In this she found a friend in 'the Bolshevik Venus', Alexandra Kollontai. 'She was the one Party person who was from the first very kind.' They had never met in London, but found themselves in adjoining flats in the sugar-merchant's mansion, and got on famously:

> She was very beautiful in a kind of way. I met her when she was no longer young, and she was adorable. She always kept a wonderful figure, and was very elegant without giving a damn. In spite of having a rather tight nose she was such an elegant creature, and her eyes were so beautiful. And she was so very friendly.

The trouble was that the Revolution for which Kollontai had worked so hard seemed not to have much use for her. 'She was very depressed because she had such a name and reputation before the Revolution and after that they didn't seem to find her anything much.' She said she would go anywhere—even Mexico—'so in a very horrid, nasty way, thinking it awfully funny, they sent her to Mexico'; and when her heart could not stand the altitude 'she was recalled, and all the Party people laughed at her because she was a woman.'

Alexandra was a great admirer of Maxim's, but the admiration was not reciprocated. He thought she was lacking in realism and tough-mindedness, and deliberately made her flesh creep by emphasizing the darker sides of politics. On such occasions Ivy would try to change the subject. 'I would say: "We can't sleep now, we shall have to play gin rummy or something," terrible, frightening political things he used to say. Things he foresaw, dreadful darkness, and then he'd say, "Why do you take it seriously?"' Gin rummy, in any case, was not Maxim's game.

Maxim had been soaked in the ways of the West, and the notion of perpetual revolution made no appeal to his matter-of-fact outlook. As a public man he was now a Russian rather than a revolutionary, and however much of an internationalist he might appear, his internationalism was based on the idea of nation states, of which the Soviet Union was one. The Comintern, when it came into existence, seemed to him a tiresome irrelevance, even as an arm of Soviet foreign policy, and in the struggle that was to come he would be a supporter of Stalin, not Trotsky.

But he was not then, nor was he ever fully to be, in the inner circle of either Lenin or Stalin. His caution and unpretentiousness forbade it. Even with Lenin, whom he had known for years, he adopted a more respectful and distant form of address after the Revolution, and 'Dear Vladimir Ilyitch' became 'Respected Comrade'. He reminded Ivy that they were Jewish, and that this was a more distinctive status in Russia than in most other countries. One day in the street, coming home from school, their daughter Tanya heard something which made her shout, as soon as she got home, some anti-Semitic remark. Her father gravely rebuked her.

8

The Moscow Mystery

In 1924, when Misha was seven and Tanya six, Maxim was able to arrange for them to spend the summer with Ivy in England. Part of the time was spent with Ivy's sister Letty (now also, in some measure, drawn into Clan Meynell at Greatham) and part with my parents at Hawthorn Cottage near Great Missenden in Buckinghamshire, where they were then living. Things seemed to be going well with the Litvinovs. One of the first acts of the new Labour government was to recognize the Soviet government, and Maxim's old friend Leonid Krassin, from being an unofficial agent in London, was transformed into an ambassador. It was an odd transposition from pre-Revolutionary days for him and Litvinov, with the latter now home-based. Bureaucracy had not yet fastened its talons on cultural life, and Moscow was vibrating with daring, earnest artistic experiment. Isadora Duncan had trodden in the footsteps of Lansbury, Russell and Wells.

Ivy's friends in England regarded her with a mixture of geniality because they knew her so well, and deference because she was now mingling with persons in power. She had met Isadora Duncan[1] and Gorky, and had even seen Lenin.[2] But she was not identified with the adventure of her life. It was literary achievement she hankered after—even down to the placing of short stories and miscellanea in the evanescent columns of the Woman's Page of the *Manchester*

[1] Isadora told Ivy she found a night spent without a man was wasted. Ivy worshipped her.
[2] She never met him face to face. At a public meeting where she was in the audience and Lenin was on the platform, she was convinced that Maxim (also on the platform) had been discussing his English wife with Lenin's wife; and was deeply disappointed to learn afterwards that this had not been the case.

Guardian. Sometimes, to her rage, they were refused. 'Have you noticed', she wrote to my mother a little later, 'that they always seem to have a rather amateurish touch about their last-page stories? I often think this is intentional, and perhaps quite a good policy.'

The history of the correspondence between Ivy and my mother is curious. My mother's contribution is almost entirely lost, but what remains of Ivy's is voluminous, though unhappily the earlier part of it is lost also. A letter from my mother records what happened when Ivy enquired about it in 1944:

> the bundle of your letters and photographs were in 2 small cottage rooms I keep as my life line in Essex and last night was the earliest I could get down to them. Here then are all I have and I'm sad to part with them even temporarily. I've always regretted that in the desperation of one of our great clearances I destroyed an earlier, and I think, bigger, lot, which might have been more valuable to you and was of great interest and value (sentimentally) to me too . . .

The sixty-four letters thus recovered by Ivy, then in Washington, moved back with her to Moscow and finally to England when she returned to spend the last years of her life here. They begin in 1926, and the last is dated, significantly, 1936.

This long correspondence, which must have continued for another ten years until my mother died in 1946, was extremely intimate—at any rate to judge by Ivy's side of it. Running through it, as so often in an intimate correspondence, there are threads of quarrels, criticism and jealousy. Ivy felt Catherine was censorious, and Catherine, apart perhaps from feeling that Ivy sometimes went too far even for a liberated Scotswoman to bear without a word of admonition, was struggling to live by her pen. There may have been twinges of disapproval and irritation towards a friend who continued to nourish literary ambitions (and asked for help in placing her work in England) when she was married to a husband who, if not prosperous, was well on the way to becoming famous. What the letters most obviously lack is any political content whatever, either direct or indirect. Discretion no doubt played its part on Ivy's side, and Catherine knew no politicians except Walter Elliot and John Buchan; but the real reason was that although Ivy had married a politician, the more she saw of the Soviet Union, the less interested in its politics she became. She was a being without reverence (except for literary figures) and she regarded men of power, authority and doctrine with a kind of withering cynicism which dwelt on the shape of their eyebrows, the cut of their suits, and the convincingness or otherwise of their false teeth. Nor do the aspirations or the propaganda of the Soviet system find any place in her letters.

In the summer of 1924 the gates had not yet closed. It must have seemed as if living in Russia, even as the wife of a Deputy Commissar, was not going to separate Ivy seriously from her friends and ambitions in England. There were plans to repeat the summer visit in 1925. But by then relations between Britain and the Soviet Union had been marred by the 'Zinoviev Letter', and a new Conservative government had suppressed the Soviet Trade Mission, Arcos, as being a base for subversion. Among the casualties of that event were Maxim's old colleague Klishko, who was a senior official of Arcos, and his English wife Phyllis, Francis Meynell's favourite dancing partner. Klishko returned to Russia to continue his work in the Commissariat of Foreign Trade until his life was claimed in one of Stalin's execution cellars in the 1930s and his wife was consigned to a period of imprisonment which did not end until the amnesties of Khrushchev.

When Lenin died in 1924 the Litvinovs were still living in the ornate rooms that had been assigned to them when Ivy first arrived. The house—now the British Embassy—was mainly given over to foreign delegations in the style that has now become conventional in communist countries. Ivy was rarely introduced to them. She saw them on the stairs sometimes, 'but we might have been ghosts.'

Among these foreign ghosts she suddenly saw and made a new friend in a German brain specialist named Vogt. He had a curious reason for being in Moscow. Officially he had been summoned there from the institute of neurosurgery he directed in Berlin to advise on the foundation of a similar institute in Moscow. But he also had a private commission from the Central Committee of the Communist Party. The canonization of Lenin had been resolved upon and, as materialists, Lenin's colleagues considered his brain must have been extraordinary in its characteristics and dimensions. Dr Vogt had undertaken the delicate task of verifying this hypothesis by dissecting, measuring and assessing the brain of the deceased leader. He later told Ivy that he had been obliged to report that Lenin's brain presented no unusual physical features.

Maxim thought Ivy would like Dr Vogt, so he introduced them. Perhaps he recollected her veneration for Dr Eder in pre-war days, though Vogt was a surgeon, not an analyst. But he was also by way of being a hypnotist and Maxim thought that might interest Ivy. 'I think you have to be a very special sort of person', was her scornful reply, 'to get anything out of hypnotism.' 'Well,' said her husband, with diplomatic opacity, 'I don't know who is a very special sort of person if you aren't.'

For Ivy being a special sort of person was writing novels, not being the wife of a Deputy Commissar who sat all day at his desk with the radio on playing foxtrots. She had written scarcely anything for ten years, and in that rambling palace she had read voraciously through the piles of Tauchnitz reprints which had once belonged to the sugar-merchant. But she had not been able to get down to writing, and she had no idea what to write. The most obvious inspiration—her own extraordinary adventure—was denied her by the need for discretion she found creeping round her like a hedge. She conceived the idea of getting Vogt to hypnotize her into writing a book.

For a visiting doctor to agree to hypnotize the wife of the Deputy Foreign Minister is unusual, but Vogt did so, though he was careful to arrange that his wife should be present every time he had a session with Ivy. 'I stretched myself obediently on the sofa', she wrote, 'in the Professor's sitting room and tried to keep my eyes fixed on the brass knob of a candelabra. . . . I listened respectfully to his mild injunctions to relax . . . to mild assurances that there was nothing to prevent my writing a book, that I had nothing to fear, nothing to reproach myself with, in effect that everything was simply splendid.'

After a number of such sessions the time came for the Vogts to depart for Berlin. 'You will sit down', Vogt assured her before he left, 'at your husband's writing table as soon as he leaves every morning, and write a book.' 'What makes you so sure?' she asked. His reply was idiomatic: 'Ihr ganzes Wesen' ('Everything about you').

Vogt entered Ivy's Pantheon. She loved and revered him with the same force as she tossed aside the claims of other far more famous men whom she encountered. She was to see Vogt again on visits to Germany and for the rest of her life referred to him in the same breath as Eder, as a chosen hero.

He did certainly help her to write another book, though one must subtract something from her account of how she wrote it under a single glorious wave of influence. It was a detective story, but a very strange one. In style and structure *His Master's Voice* belongs to the family of Agatha Christie and Freeman Wills Croft. What makes it unique is transposition of the scene to the Moscow of the mid-1920s. As Ivy later said, it was the first work of fiction to escape from the Soviet Union that had no missionary content.

The detective, District Procurator Nikulin, bears a certain resemblance to Maxim, but a great deal more to Wills Crofts' Inspector French. The murdered man (stabbed at his desk in his luxurious flat) must certainly have been an exemplar of Lenin's New Economic Policy, since he was the manager of a timber concession in the hands of an American firm. The principal suspect is a ballerina, and the murderer turns out to be the stage manager of the Bolshoi Ballet.

Ivy also put into it the Moscow to which her adventure had brought her: a Moscow that, despite the Revolution which had made it a capital once more, was still very much the Moscow of the old Tsars, where watchmen stamped in the snow, sledge-drivers crossed themselves as they passed under the Ivor Gate, and the streets were infested with street arabs considerably more mischievous than the 'Baker Street Irregulars'. It is a Moscow of dirt, discomfort and shabbiness, in which everyone has an entirely comprehensible and selfish motive. In 1943, when Ivy was in a position of much greater eminence, and the book was reissued, she wrote a preface explaining with some nostalgia how things had changed. The watchman's family would have had a small flat instead of the single room where his whole family slept in a single bed. 'The little wolves of society' had long since been rescued to become 'engineers, truck drivers, scientists, and musicians'. One would search in vain for 'the sprawling markets, cluttering and cramped pavements with the bodies and wares of vendors of hot pies, shoe-laces, butter-brodi and brassières'. The only character who was still the same (she felt bound to admit) was the manicurist. 'I should not be surprised to discover that she still receives clients in her room, for she is one of those women who does not change.'

Ivy was a slow worker, even under hypnotism. The book was begun in 1925 and she was still working on it in 1928, all the time knowing there could be no question, even in those comparatively liberal times, of it being published in Russia—'absence of ideology if you know what that means'. The slow pace was not due to idleness, for she found she now had far more to do than just sit down at her husband's writing table when he went to the office. He was a member of the Central Committee, and his star as an expert on foreign affairs was steadily rising. With the struggle for supreme power between Stalin and Trotsky he had little directly to do, but he was a supporter of Stalin and even during the worst of what followed gave it as his private opinion to his family that Trotsky in power would have been still more terrible. As a negotiator abroad he was in constant demand, and Ivy regularly accompanied him. By 1926 he was in fact, if not in name, the head of the Soviet Foreign Office, a man untouched by the shameful surrender of Brest-Litovsk, and so in contrast to his nominal chief Chicherin. Although Litvinov was very far from being a personal friend of Stalin (Ivy only met him once in her life), Stalin's ascendancy improved Litvinov's position. Stalin, knowing little of the world outside Russia, needed a Foreign Minister who did; and both men saw Soviet diplomacy in terms of national interest, not universal revolution.

The Narkomindel, as the Soviet Foreign Office was called, was an organization largely created by Litvinov. He recruited its staff and designed its system, for Chicherin was not interested in such matters of mere management. Indeed the Narkomindel filled an odd and in some ways inferior position in revolutionary Russian government, for reasons attributable to both theory and practice. It was very far from occupying the central and rather superior social status that the Foreign Offices of older sovereign states held. Its officials ranked lower, not higher, both in social standing and in emoluments, than the diplomats of Western countries, because in principle the Soviet Union was not a sovereign state, and had only adopted the characteristics of one for a transitional period. It was a territory controlled by revolutionary forces which possessed worldwide validity, so that the whole notion of relationships between sovereign states would gradually become obsolete, along with the conventions of diplomacy that governed them. Trotsky, on assuming his brief term of office as Foreign Commissar, had said as much.

The sovereign states, however, continued to exist, and the Soviet Union had to go on behaving like one. Stalin perceived this very clearly, and in Litvinov found a man devoted to the subject of international relations. But the Narkomindel remained an executive department. Its chief was not (until the great changes of 1939) a member of the decision-making body, the Politburo, and did not have access to all the information on which its decisions were taken or deferred. Other agencies for the exertion of Soviet influence abroad, such as the Comintern, lay wholly outside its authority. One of

Maxim's principal preoccupations was the tension and competition that lay between his own office and the Comintern and undermined the confidence of foreign governments which he sought to foster.

Ivy was not told much about the office, and would not have been very interested if she had been. Someone in the West had just sent her a copy of *Ulysses*. 'I still cannot think without emotion (or speak without tears)', she wrote to my mother, 'of the month I have been through. . . . I now feel afraid to pick the book up, as if it were a bomb that might go off.' It could no more be published in Russia, of course, than her own Moscow mystery. The law would be as much against it as in England or America, 'perhaps more so'. Joyce, she felt, in his refusal to write an ordinary novel, had triumphed over temptation like Jesus in the wilderness. Beside him Huxley was insignificant: 'Naive stuff with no mastery of description, little feeling for character'.

She was writing herself of course—and not just the detective story to which Vogt had set her to work. There were stories, one of which, 'Married Love', she hesitated to send to the *Manchester Guardian*, or even through the post. She was, as she put it, 'getting very ribald in my old age' (she was only thirty-six); but she showed it to two men friends 'who are both delighted'. One of them was a Scotsman who worked in the same office as Ivy as a translator. He was 'most uninhibited. The way he fell upon *Ulysses* was most remarkable. It didn't depress him, not a bit, all was sheer joy from the first.' The other may well have been the American Joe Freeman, with whom Ivy was at that time in love; perhaps with the deepest passion she ever felt for any man.

She began to find outlets for her work in Russia, and placed a story, 'Petya the Englishman', drawing on her children's duality of cultural background; and this was followed by two others—'She Did Not Understand' and 'Train Fantasy'— all, of course, in Russian. And she met many Russian intellectuals on friendly terms—Eisenstein, Oransky, Marshak and Tatlin, among others. But her chief literary consolation, perhaps, was in the friendship of Kornei Ivanovich Chukovsky, whom she met through the poet Vera Imber. Chukovsky was a remarkable man. He was entirely self-educated and had none of the dogmatism or love of innovation that characterized the literary world of the 1920s. In earlier life he had spent some years in England as correspondent of a Zionist periodical (though he was not Jewish), and had acquired a considerable knowledge of, and love for, English nursery literature. He earned his living, first in St Petersburg, and later in Moscow, as a critic and a writer for children. In due course he became the intimate of the whole family and in the end was closer to Ivy's daughter Tanya than to Ivy herself.

During Ivy's many years in Russia Chukovsky was one of the Russians of whom she grew really fond, though he was never part of Ivy's 'woodnotes wild', as she was to describe a sexual adventurousness now growing within her. Maxim was over fifty now, and a flighty wife did not match well with the sober-suited statesman he had become. But if he felt some uneasiness, both personal and political, at Ivy's behaviour, he did not show it, though he may have sought some quiet consolation elsewhere, such as a middle-aged man of business might. On the whole, in their new, more modern and slightly larger flat, they were a happy family. The Deputy Commissar, with his wing collar and formal clothes in the cupboard, sat happily in a pullover eating his breakfast egg surrounded by his wayward wife and growing family.

The children were now well into school. Ivy, writing to Catherine, was in raptures over them: 'Their vitality, high spirits, and charm have dissipated quite a lot of the heavy clouds.' Tanya, on being told she would have to take an examination in music 'turned on me with glowing eyes and said "I've always been *longing* to go in for an examination." What a thirst for life.' Ivy was thinking in terms of having at least three more children, in spite of anxiety about a spreading figure and the liberal abortion laws introduced by Kollontai. 'It is quite the fashion here. . . . Amazing people! They always calmly let it come to a baby and then calmly get rid of it!'

The two children were already developing in rather different directions, though both were full of vitality and intelligence. Misha was taciturn: Tanya, to whom English always came as readily as the language of the country in which she was being educated, was voluble. Misha at this age could be rude, wild, wilful, even ungovernable at times, whereas Tanya had a dark, demure intensity, even at eight years old, which went well with the studiousness that delighted her mother. But Ivy was in despair about the conditions in which they were growing up. 'Our poor children are growing up in such chaos, both at home and at school. . . . The rooms are always desperately untidy, garters are perpetually lost, galoshes cannot be found at the last moment, and generally speaking life is all confusion and rush for them. And I can't help it, really and truly I can'..'

She had been reading Freud as well as *Ulysses* and was already more familiar than were her English correspondents with the language of dreams (or so she claimed)—that is, with the fear of losing a train signifying fear of impotency, and 'I don't know about the violin, but I at once got—instrument—organ. To me the whole dream was like a flash of lightning. . . . but then of course I have more than the dream to go on—I have the knowledge of the night on which it was dreamt.'

There are signs, even at this early stage of her stay in Russia, that there was a reverse side to the atmosphere of liberation and excitement with which she was impressing her London friends: an anxiety rather different from what a knowledge of Freud enabled her to read into dreams. 'Do let me have a line of acknowledgement', she scribbled as an afterthought on one letter, '*at once* or I shall feel anxious about this letter.' Elsewhere she makes it clear that the reply was not to be direct. 'What makes you address *Bitner*?' asks one postscript. 'Address Chesham House.' And in another letter it seems the answer was to come through the Soviet embassy in Paris: 'M. says you addressed the Embassy wrong. You must either say Ambassade Russe or Embassie de Russie.'

Maxim, as always, was exact about protocol; but it is interesting, too (though the indication is slight) that he was concerned to maintain the link with England represented by his wife's correspondence with her literary friends. He must have realized it was an outlet for her loneliness. From the evidence, fragmentary though it is, one can suppose that the predominant motive was not political but arose obscurely from a sense of a need to reinsure—if not himself, at any rate his wife and children. That he knew the correspondence went on is certain, and he may well have read the letters Catherine wrote to Ivy. That he read those which Ivy wrote to Catherine seems inconceivable, as we shall see.

9

Disarmament

Towards the end of 1927 Maxim was sent as the principal Soviet
delegate to the preparatory commission for the Disarmament
Conference at Geneva. His influence in Soviet foreign policy had been
that of an *éminence grise* for several years but this was the first time
he had appeared in his own right on the international stage, and Ivy
accompanied him as a member of the official party. Indeed, as an
assistant in preparing English drafts and translations for Maxim, she
was formally a delegate, and attended all the meetings of the
Commission.

Litvinov's success as a European diplomatic figure was immediate
and lasting. It would be safe to say that no Soviet politician, before or
since, has inspired the same confidence and sympathy abroad as
Litvinov during the following twelve years; and that few of his
competitors from other countries made an equal impression. Gone
was the mysterious shabby refugee emerging from obscurity to
address left-wing meetings and negotiate in tea-shops. Plump and
cordial in the contemporary statesman's uniform of wing collar and
dark suit, he was the very picture of the moderation he had persuaded
the Kremlin to espouse. 'Look at him closely,' the French statesman
Barthou was to say in 1932, when Russia formally joined the League
of Nations, 'Does he look like a bandit? No. He does not look like a
bandit. He looks like an honest man.' Something must be subtracted
from such rhetoric, but it remains true that no diplomatist of his time
entered more convincingly than Litvinov into the spirit of Geneva
and all it stood for by way of collective security and disarmament,
and none was more successful in persuading the wider European
world that his country stood for moderation and peace.

This is not the place in which to assess or criticize Litvinov's policies and achievements. The materials for judging his personal contribution are for the most part locked in the archives of the Soviet Foreign Office. But from this distance in time one grave charge cannot be evaded, which lies not in the foreign policy he adopted, which was realistic for the exhausted country he represented as well as reasonable for Europe as a whole, but in serving so respectably a government that was becoming increasingly dependent on terror and repression at home. In 1927 the worst was still to come, but in due course this dilemma was to develop into a personal tragedy in which professionalism and commitment on the one side came into damaging conflict with the inner man.

Ivy's irreverent spirit did not fit at all well with Maxim's diplomatic sociability. She patiently discharged the drudgery of turning his memoranda and speeches into correct English, but the company at the Conference was not to her liking. She particularly resented the pervasive presence of the second Madame Lunacharsky with her excessively large wardrobe: 'a fourth-rate actress who only gets parts through her husband's influence and follows me about like a brother', and had nails so long that her maid had to help her off with her stockings. It was also a trouble that Madame Lunacharsky, for all her faults, was rather slim and 'effective-looking'. Ivy noted sadly that she herself was not getting slimmer.

She gazed round the conference table and decided she rather preferred McNeill, the British delegate, to any of the others. The Frenchman, Paul-Boncour, was too much of a performer: 'a great orator in the pathetic style I can't stand. . . . dramatic lowerings of the voice—smitings of chest—throwing back of white locks'. McNeill on the other hand was 'most impressive and expressive. Dry humour, perfect correctness and brevity'. She was charmed when he sought her out at the end of the Conference to say goodbye, called her by her Christian name, and then turned to congratulate Maxim on his excellent English.

Her liking for McNeill did not prevent her from being very much on her guard against the diplomatic world in which she already felt herself being cocooned and flattered. 'Why on earth should people think that the change and excitement of my life is really interesting?' she reflected.

I am my sole appreciator, my only flatterer myself. . . . At first I

was sensitive about many things but now I realize that the whole
game of politics is one grand game of bluff and that in this game
brother politicians don't so much criticize and condemn each other
as say their lines with their tongue in their cheek. I see that neither
hatred, ridicule, nor anything else can affect the career of a
politician, but merely the popularity or otherwise of his career at
the time.

There is something of a deliberate trading-off in all this because
(especially, perhaps, in writing to Catherine) Ivy was conscious of her
importance as Maxim's wife, and in fact rather enjoyed the deference
and the limelight. But certainly her heart was not in politics or even in
political life: it was in writing, in sex and in her family. So far as the
first was concerned she noted sadly that it was her ill luck never to
have fallen 'among people who would be good for me in the sense of
bringing out my best abilities in the way of writing'. True, she had
had Vogt who, though not himself a writer, had hypnotized a
detective story out of her; and an unkind critic might have said she
was in a better way of meeting literary people than most. And would
she have found the competitive bohemianism of the Western literary world more conducive to her aspirations, if fate had cast her
there?
Against this she correctly perceived that her passionate desire to
write and to be published was frustrated by the great adventure of her
life, and by Maxim's success, in a way the gods might have contrived
for Tantalus. Surely her marriage to a Commissar, the opportunities of
a diplomatic life, the sheer interest of the adventure, should help her
to write and get published? Yet when she realized this would mean a
writer called Ivy Litvinov she began to see it could not be so. The
author had to be Ivy Low, and do without any help from Ivy Litvinov,
who could have helped Ivy Low so much.
The conflict was for the time being resolved in another way, for her
'best abilities' in a different sense had been brought out in Berlin, a
month or so before arriving in Geneva. In Berlin she encountered
another German doctor named Kurt, and as a result felt 'sort of
happy. Had something I never had before. Beginning with an "o".
And now feel serene, domestic, and self-respecting.' Once at Geneva,
'I don't seem to care much about the "o"s. You know how it goes.'
Once back in Moscow she wrote more guardedly. 'I fear there's no
possibility of any chick or child of ours going to England for a bit' was

followed by lengthy discussion of the climate and hairdressing. Apparently hairdressing was remarkably cheap in Russia and the silver which was beginning to appear in her black mane could be kept in check for only 30s a month.

In the midst of all this the two children, were her constant care. They were developing in very different ways. Misha was growing uproarious and ungovernable, and the earnest Soviet schoolteachers were reporting that they really didn't know if they could deal with him any more; while Tanya 'mows people down wholesale and even we who live with her daily can never get used to her sweetness and charm . . . I sometimes wonder if her nose and gums are positively ugly. However nothing short of a squint could spoil her.'

Early in 1928 a plan was being made by Catherine and some of her friends for a holiday in the south of Brittany which would bring together a number of families with children. The place chosen was Quiberon and the scheme was communicated to Ivy: she was tempted, but there were difficulties about 'getting out', especially since 'one lady [it might have been herself, but was more probably Madame Lunacharsky] had so discredited Soviet wives at Geneva as to make things very difficult.' The words are perhaps those of Maxim rather than of Ivy, and it may have been he rather than she who surmounted 'countless insuperable obstacles' in getting permission for her to accompany him once more to Geneva in March 1928. It was to be her longest absence from the Soviet Union for a very long time.

The road to Geneva again lay through Berlin, where she fell on the bookshops and bought another handful of D. H. Lawrence, only to find that all her enthusiasm for his work had evaporated. *Sons and Lovers* she still stood by, but 'I find the other two [*Women in Love* and *The Rainbow*] boring, slightly ridiculous, and even technically weak. I do think Lawrence has always lacked self-criticism and after all shirked the hard thing, which is to get your story told.' She was still working on getting *His Master's Voice* completed.

By the early summer, after translating (as she put it) an excessive amount of words and hot air, she had moved, without Maxim but with the children, to the Villa Flora at Malente-Gremsmühlen, a little village looking out onto the Plönsee in Holstein, just between Kiel and Oldenburg: 'three rooms right under the roof, the garden goes right down to the landing stage and the house is new, pleasant, and scrupulously clean'. Maxim had decided to spend his holidays at

Carlsbad, in Czechoslovakia,[1] after admonishing Ivy that the expense of a journey to France for herself and the children could not be afforded.

For Ivy, the great thing was that the children should have English books. She herself found she was forgetting the right English word and beginning to use 'Europeanisms'. Could Catherine get Misha copies of the *Boy's Own Paper* or *Captain*, with the back numbers if possible so that he could start the serials at the beginning? 'Do treat this as an SOS and send a sub for me to the *Children's Newspaper* or anything cheap and easy you can think of.' She had brought all the old favourites with her and was reading them aloud again and again: the two Alices, Hudson's *A Little Boy Lost* and *The Purple Land, Lob Lie by the Fire* by Mrs Ewing, and Stevenson's *Child's Garden of Verses*, 'which they know backwards'.

Catherine rushed to Bumpus and within a very short time Misha and Tanya were being enthralled by *She* (poor Soviet school-teachers!) with *The Study in Scarlet* to follow. Ivy herself was gloating over *Robinson Crusoe*: 'What a book! What a writer!' On the strength of it all she ordered *King Solomon's Mines* herself from Bumpus and asked Catherine to send some coloured comics and *Pip, Squeak and Wilfred*, which duly arrived, to the delight of the Litvinov children.

But in spite of the Villa Flora's nice clean rooms and the pleasant lake, the weather was beastly, and she was oppressed by the ambiguity of the life on which she had embarked. *His Master's Voice* was nearly finished, but had to be by Ivy Low, whom British publishers had forgotten (it was thirteen years since *The Questing Beast* had been published). What would Maxim say if she signed it Litvinov? She wanted to join in the French holiday plan, but hesitated. Could her friends perhaps all come to Holstein?

Early in July Ivy was forced into a decision of sorts. Maxim's holiday was over and he proposed to travel back to Moscow by way of Kiel, where he would pick up his family. On 4 July she decided to make a bid for at least temporary escape and, with the circuitousness she had now learned was necessary, she asked Catherine to arrange

[1] These visits became a regular habit with Maxim. In this, as in other respects, his style of life was that of a diplomat of the older school. He used to say that he was happier in Carlsbad than anywhere else in the world. The fact that it was in Czechoslovakia was an additional pleasure. He found its comfortable, relaxed atmosphere under the liberal social democracy of the post-Masaryk regime more congenial than that of any other country in Europe, including his own.

for the hotel in Brittany to send her terms for the booking 'so that I may have something to discuss with M. The strain and loneliness and bad weather is simpy breaking me.'

Somehow all went well, and at the latter end of August Ivy, Misha, and Tanya joined in the collective family holiday at Quiberon which (so far as I can remember) mustered eight children, all ten years old or less, governed by four adults, only one of whom (my father) was a man. The proceedings were rowdy and disorderly, but after the departure of the two other families Ivy and Catherine prolonged the holiday by venturing along the coast to the quieter haven of Le Pouldu in its gentle, almost unvisited estuary, once the resort of Gauguin, where Breton dress and Breton speech still unaffectedly held sway.

Ivy left Brittany not only refreshed, but reinforced and in a liberated mood. She still had a week or two before having to return to Russia, and had been thinking of spending the time in Paris where she proposed to meet James Joyce. But on arrival there she found a message from her German friend Kurt who some months earlier had introduced her to sexual fulfilment. He was now in Hamburg for a medical congress. To Hamburg, therefore, she decided to go, but Joyce must come first. After obtaining an introduction through his publisher Sylvia Beach and consigning the children to explore the Eiffel Tower, she called on the author of *Ulysses*. It was a disappointing interview in which Joyce, never a tactful man, brushed aside Ivy's wish to discuss literature and style, and concentrated on ways in which Madame Litvinov might be able to promote his works in the Soviet Union. When she said that *Ulysses*, for all its greatness, was a rather difficult book to read, he demanded whether something that had been toiled over for five years should be treated as light literature to be read in the spare time of a week.

She left for Hamburg that very night, 'the children all the time angels'. Her adventures there can be told in her own words in letters two days apart on 18 and 20 September 1928. Under the year 1928 at the top of the first letter she wrote the date of her birth and a little subtraction sum, leaving the remainder 39.

Kurt arrived at 3. He came straight up to me and we simply fell upon each other with delight. He thought he had never seen me looking so nice and loved my hair.[2] And I thought him ever so much

---

[2] She was wearing it in a new way, very short, accentuating the shape of her head, with a silver forelock left undyed.

more attractive . . . there is something clean and compact about him that is almost irresistible. We went together to Friedel's[3] hotel at 6.30 and found her with her friend Beatus and to my dismay an 'orgy' all fixed up for us 4.

I couldn't say anything as they all seemed to want it, but of course what I really wanted was Kurt all to myself. They all agreed that my hair was an enormous improvement and of course Friedel found it 'a little perverse' so that was all right. We had a nice dinner and coffee together and I liked Beatus very much. A fat man, distinctly Regency, with an eye-glass and soft white hands. Then we went upstairs to Friedel's really huge room and all undressed and I may say tho' it was rather amusing at moments (especially the eyeglass of Beatus, to which he clung) I got no satisfaction out of the whole evening, tho' Kurt had me at least 4 times and at incredible length. He only had Friedel once and that made me frankly unhappy. So today I feel quite cut up in a little way. However they all said I was wonderful and beautiful and I'm glad they're glad. Kurt went home this morning early and I won't see him again. We slept together all night, in fact I went to sleep in the middle of things and woke up in astonishment to find Kurt still at it. He saw I was unhappy to see him with Friedel and came to me and whispered 'Ich liebe dich mehr' and wanted to begin all over again, but I felt limp and wretched. Orgies may be all right where one's feelings are not involved. Oh well, what's the good of grousing—it couldn't be helped, but I feel I've had too little of that kind of happiness, so terribly little that I do grudge what might have been the happiest night of my life being spoilt, for I doubt if I shall ever have a man to suit me like Kurt, and I don't know if I shall ever see him again to make up for it . . .

She did, the very next night, along with Friedel in the best hotel in Hamburg: 'the way we boldly spend the night with anyone who takes our fancy in *The Atlantis* fairly takes my breath away': and she had to embark in the *Herzen* for Moscow in a day or two.

But the wild adventure was not yet over. Before the *Herzen* sailed she found herself more attracted to Beatus, especially when she was told

that he could only dream of me and when he was re-elected

[3] Through whom she had originally met Kurt.

Vice-President of the Deutsches Society for the History of Medicine [whose congress was the occasion of the gathering] he was quite unable to remember his speech and could only wonder if I was coming to the hotel again. . . . Somehow I felt I had to go to him. I felt such an unassuaged thirst for caresses. . . . We dined at the hotel and talked for about an hour and a half and then went boldly up to his room. . . . and we certainly had a wonderful night. Of course Beatus is infinitely more subtle and intelligent than Kurt. . . . He has not Kurt's marvellous potency and it is obvious that this could not be expected. You can't have everything. Besides he was not bad. Only snatching about twenty minutes sleep until about five in the morning, when he rose as fresh as a daisy. We talked for about an hour and really found much to interest each other. In type he is rather like Maxim, but taller, and not Jewish. . . . He has a large plastic face and thin flexible lips and his skin is fresh and pinkish. He is also rather Roman emperorish which I have sometimes thought Maxim, with a slightly bullish neck. Very foppish, with spats and eye-glasses and all that, but much too much corporation. . . . What I specially like about Beatus is that he made me feel I was wonderful for him and said he could never forget me, while dear Kurt always makes me feel that it is *he* who is so wonderful. Of course Kurt would hardly have understood a dozen words of mine, our minds are so different. . . .

But the *Herzen* sailed on 20 September, and Ivy had to leave with her.

Back in Moscow, Maxim's eminence was marked by a new flat for the family, larger than the last, with two bedrooms and a sitting-room. Ivy was free to concentrate on her children and the placing of her now completed detective story. As for Beatus and Kurt and her Hamburg adventures: 'I cannot believe they ever happened. They are far away in the mists of time, and hardly interesting to remember. However I do know they did me good, if only because everybody I meet tells me I am looking nicer than they have ever known me. No substitutes here. Nothing.' There was more in those last few words than appears at first sight. Her return to Moscow that autumn marks the end of the physical side of her married life, and she and Maxim never slept together again. They continued to depend upon each other, and as the years passed he came to depend more on her; and they never parted. But sexually they now began to drift apart.

[Disarmament]

While Ivy was in Germany she had managed to interest someone connected with UFA, the German film company, in the idea of making a film of *His Master's Voice*, with the prospect of 'a good sum down'. But these hopes were disappointed. Curtis Brown, her literary agent, failed at first to place the novel in London, and an American publisher's reader reported sourly that 'readers of mystery stories don't want a lot of atmosphere. . . . We advise Ivy Low to cut out the stuff about spring over the Kremlin and put in another murder or two.' Nor was it published at all for more than two years. No doubt with Dorothy Sayers in mind, as well as the Left Book Club, it was sent to Victor Gollancz, who turned it down. It would hardly have suited his picture of the Soviet Union. Later it was accepted by Ivy's old publisher, Heinemann, who had a modest success with it in 1930, in the depth of the Depression.[4]

Meanwhile all the Western public heard of Ivy was an occasional contribution to the Woman's Page of the *Manchester Guardian* in a vein which could just as well have been written from Hampstead as from the neighbourhood of the Kremlin.

She cheered herself against the tedium of a Moscow winter reading *Tristram Shandy* and, with more enjoyment and greater understanding, Arthur Machen's translation of Casanova's *Memoirs*—'What a joy!'—though by the seventh volume she was finding his dependence on women tedious. 'That's why, I suppose, I always feel I should be bored by hopeless, whole-souled adoration, because one always feels that men with anything in them can't be entirely swallowed up in a woman.' She even found a copy of Conrad's *Under Western Eyes* in a secondhand bookshop but found it 'forced and harsh, and it reads like a translation from the Russian'.

Translation from the Russian, so far as she was concerned, was needed to sustain the family income, perhaps in particular the payments to the music teacher for Misha and Tanya, for a piano had now been wedged into the family sitting-room. She seems to have been an odd kind of translator, and one wonders whether the State Publishing House ever discovered that what she was doing to the crudely propagandist 'cultural bulletin' they sent her was 'not really translating. I am practically rewriting, with excerpts from the original. And the nice thing is that I get heaps of praise as well as

[4] Gollancz made ample amends by republishing it in 1973, after Ivy had returned to this country to live in Hove. It had eventually been published in America in 1943 by Coward McCann Inc., under the title *The Moscow Mystery*.

pence for it . . . as a matter of fact I am going to use the material
shamelessly for the *M.G.*'

The different temperaments of the children were showing more
than ever. Ivy sat over Misha with his homework, admired his
handwriting, scouted Maxim's fears that he would never be able to
write an intelligent letter when he grew up. 'He'll most likely be a
writer—has a tremendous feeling for words and can express himself
extremely neatly, when absolutely forced to express himself at all.'
But she was hardly interested (at that moment) in Tanya's schooling.
'To tell you the truth the student idea doesn't appeal to me a bit! . . . I
see sometimes in Tanya such gleams of spirit and a sort of spiritual
elegance and I long for her to be launched in life.'

It was a dismal winter, and she pined to escape once more to the
West when the Preparatory Commission on Disarmament should
resume its labours in Geneva. In April it did, and Ivy was writing
triumphantly on 8 April 1929 in the train on the Polish-Austrian
frontier en route to Vienna. In her luggage was a quantity of
second-hand books picked up in Moscow which she hoped to sell in
aid of her European holiday. She could even offer 'a whole set of
Transition, if worth anything' (the latest number, containing extracts
from what became *Finnegans Wake* she found wholly unreadable).
Maxim, she hoped, would decide to stop off for three days' rest in
Salzburg before the Conference. She was very much looking forward
to meeting Friedel and her friends again.

10

High Places

In 1929, although he was not yet formally Commissar, Litvinov's ascendancy over Soviet diplomacy was complete. He had already encountered and gained the respect of most of Europe's circle of senior negotiators—Ataturk, Grandi, Titulescu, Briand—the last of whom he much distrusted. He had even talked to Austen Chamberlain after a comedy in which Ivy had been given the task of exploring the ground to establish that a request from Maxim for an interview would not be rebuffed. In the context of Soviet diplomacy at that time any such meeting was a success in itself, even if it led to no substantial discussion; but Maxim could point to some solid achievement as well in pursuit of his policy of moderate internationalism. Against considerable resistance from his colleagues in Moscow, especially those who controlled the Comintern, he arranged for Soviet accession to the Kellogg Pact renouncing war as an instrument of national policy, and in February 1929 built on to it the so-called 'Litvinov Protocol' under which the Soviet Union and all its immediate neighbours in Europe, with the exception of Finland and Bulgaria, specifically accepted the Kellogg principle. Though not expressed as such, this was an acceptance of an international order of sovereign states.

Whether the meeting with Friedel in April took place as planned we do not know, but later that summer Ivy was able to spend some time in Berlin. The projected UFA film of *His Master's Voice* had fallen through owing to the intervention of 'a beastly politician who owns half the shares and is leader of the Nat. Deutsch. Partei': probably Hugenberg. 'They wanted my name as an advertisement, and now my name has spoiled it.' German politics were indeed changing.

However on this occasion Ivy certainly made contact with Friedel again and 'I sleep with anyone who wants me to. Fall violently in love for a night and take up with another next day. . . . Oh, the eyes of the men in Berlin streets—hungry, searching, like lost children.'

She also met 'my darling Vogt', and was reflecting how good *Winnie the Pooh* really was (she had just been sent a copy for the children), when she was induced to write a chatty article about Berlin through foreign eyes for the *Berliner Tageblatt*. Luckily for her she had the prudence to show what she had written to Maxim before sending it off, but its appearance was followed by a ferociously pompous denunciation by the organ of the German Communist Party, *Rote Fahne*. 'How', it demanded, 'could the wife of a Soviet Foreign Minister write such frivolous stuff?' 'The Lord knows if I shall ever get out again,' Ivy wrote pathetically, glancing over her shoulder at the increasingly forbidding Soviet frontier.

But all was well. Ivy and Maxim returned to Moscow that autumn to a new flat, with no fewer than four rooms, for the man who was Foreign Commissar in all but name. Ivy was asked to give lectures on English literature 'from a socio-economic point of view', and communicated her intended theme to Catherine (along with a request for advice and ammunition) thus: 'The early Victorian rank and file were simply calmly convinced of the blessedness of prosperity and the sanctity of the established principles and virtues, and now no one is quite convinced of the necessity for anything.' Whether the lectures were ever delivered or not, the theme would hardly have been acceptable to a Bolshevik audience. In the meantime Ivy recorded that she was immersing herself in the works of Agatha Christie and Edgar Wallace.

Maxim's exertions had opened a window on the West, and important British visitors—most of them far from sympathetic to communism—were coming in droves. 'We have had staying with us', Ivy wrote on 29 August 1929, 'Arnold Bennett, Beaverbrook, Lady Mountbatten, Sir E. Montagu's widow, Mrs Norton who runs the New Gallery Cinema, and also-rans.' Ivy took at once to Arnold Bennett, and found Lady Montagu 'distinguished and sympathetic'; but Beaverbrook reminded her of her stepfather. 'Bad-tempered lines from nose to mouth, maniacal eyes, terrifying changes of mood'. Lady Mountbatten put her in mind of Isadora Duncan, but lacking Isadora's vitality—'Beaverbrook purring around her all the time.'

The talk was of Gerhardie 'and all seem disappointed in him'—a feeling Ivy shared on reading the novels they brought. 'All I can say is that they make me appreciate G's distinction, tho I fear he's not got much more in him somehow.' Nevertheless both the Litvinovs were admirers of Gerhardie's work, Maxim's favourite being *The Polyglots*: and they called their terrier 'Me—Too'.

The only lasting friendship derived from this strangely miscellaneous party was with Amabel Williams-Ellis, wife of the architect and daughter of St Loe Strachey of the *Spectator*. 'People liked her no end here.' Ivy began by being censorious in her heaviest manner, finding that although Amabel was so 'sweet and nice', 'her mental insignificance and uncriticalness simply amazed me from Strachey's daughter. . . . As a soul I think I like her. Her books—children's and all—are flat.'

Maxim was not altogether happy about his wife's devotion to English ways, or about his children being brought up on the *Boy's Own Paper* and the adventures of a teddy bear in Hampshire, and he was troubled over Ivy's continued pining for literary fame. With eight years in a publishing house behind him, he opined that nobody ever made any money from books, and said crushingly that Ivy was mistaken if she thought the fashionable English visitors were genuinely interested in her literary aspiration, since they were already distinguished in their own right. He recommended that she should see more of his colleagues and their families, and that the children should make some Russian friends of their own age.

Much as both Ivy and Maxim loved their children, there was serious tension between the parents over the upbringing of Tanya and Misha. Ivy could not prevent herself from seeing them as English children, whereas the realistic Maxim was clear that they were and must be Russian. It was not a matter of politics (though he thought they should join the Young Pioneers, which they did) or a matter of nationalism. It was how things were. Ivy's Russian by now was fluent, but it remained incorrect, and when she began to write stories in the language they were (somehow) not Russian but English. To Tanya she succeeded in transmitting a love of English literature, a lasting bilingualism, and a whole English dimension, but even Tanya gradually became more Russian than English.

Perhaps she longed even more that Misha should be English in his outlook, but he did not inherit his mother's passion for literature.

Maxim hoped his son would follow a scientific career, but—to look ahead for a moment—Misha showed increasing uncertainty about the course his education should take. He left school early and instead of going to university at once, as his father had planned, he went to a technical college and then took a job in an aircraft factory. Maxim was heartbroken. 'You'll die a common draughtsman,' he told his son severely. As in many middle-class families with similar problems, Misha ultimately solved them by obtaining a scientific qualification and going on to a respectable career after serving with distinction in the War.

However, in one important respect Misha and Tanya were alike, despite their differences of temperament and career. Neither would join the Communist Party, though both they and their father knew that in the Soviet Union this was the only road to success in any profession.

Ivy sadly recorded that she felt her husband was 'indifferent to people', but this was not entirely true. He was cautious, and life had taught him a lot about the less pleasant sides of human nature. On the itineraries he planned there was always an alternative route which could be taken if the weather broke; and although he was in some ways an autocrat to his children he truly loved them, and they in turn loved and respected him, though both, even at an early age, had a turn for rebellion. Their father's importance in the world they simply took for granted, and it never crossed their minds that it could be otherwise, or that they should not be privileged Kremlin children with servants, car and deference shown to them. What they did know was that if they kept a car waiting for two minutes there would be a lecture from papa about consideration for the driver.

In July 1930 Chicherin finally shuffled into retirement and Maxim became the People's Commissar for Foreign Affairs. The Narkomindel, and many of the principal posts abroad, were already filled with his friends and nominees. So began almost a decade in which an outgoing, genial and constructive Soviet foreign policy contrasted grimly with the repression of high and low at home.

Litvinov's achievements during his nine years of office were of a piece with his earlier career. Looked at as a documentary record they are technical. In 1934 he secured the long withheld recognition of the United States; and in 1935 the pact with Laval which suggested a resuscitation of the pre-War entente between France and Russia. He made the League of Nations, to which he was responsible for gaining

Russia's admission, his platform, and coined the epigram 'Peace is indivisible'.

A few months after his promotion, Ivy accompanied the new Commissar to Geneva. She produced mordant verbal sketches of the statesmen assembled there. The British delegate, Lord Hugh Cecil, attracted her especial scorn: 'I defy any impartial observer not to feel the insincerity of Cecil's manner. He is a sawney old crocodile and his "deprecating" toothy smile when he says "if I may say so" and disagrees with anyone fairly makes me puke.'

That winter the Litvinovs came to London—'a flying visit to the home town'—as Ivy put it. She took me to a Christmas show of which even the name now escapes me; but what is still vivid is the tall, dominating, fur-coated figure sweeping me across the wintry promenade outside the Golders Green Hippodrome, to a torrent of commentary.

The summer of 1931 saw her in Britain once again, but this time it was a visit to Wales, where Amabel Williams-Ellis had tempted her to newly built Portmeirion. Ivy's original reservations about Amabel had wholly gone and she longed to live at Portmeirion for ever. But she had to take the boat back to Leningrad in July, and on the voyage made the acquaintance of Julian Huxley and his wife. Nor was it only the Huxleys. 'It is very difficult for me to refuse love,' she wrote regretfully. Who offered it on this occasion she does not say; 'But I very soon discovered he was a most interesting man.'

Once back in Leningrad she found out what it was really like to be a Foreign Minister's wife. It was to be Geneva in a fortnight, and a state visit to Ankara in September. In the meantime she was required to entertain a party consisting of Bernard Shaw, Lord and Lady Astor and Philip Kerr, later Lord Lothian, of whom Maxim remarked that he looked as if he had just buried capitalism and was standing in mourning beside the grave. Ivy thought him 'good-looking and nice' but could make little of Lord Astor. As for Lady Astor she was 'pretty ghastly but a good woman *au fond*' who 'screams and yells when she is kept waiting.'

Shaw, as one would expect, captivated her, even at the age of seventy-five. When they went to the Hermitage he 'ran, ran, ran, up our enormous flight of steps and [Lady Astor] ran after him and caught hold of his coat tails, but he sent her away and said he wanted to see the pictures all to himself.' He was asked what he thought was the most admirable thing in the Revolution, and replied. ' "That it survives in spite of Madame Litvinov," sucking his false teeth and smiling all the time.' Ivy thought him a 'dear old man'.[1]

September, and Geneva again followed hard upon these visitors, and Ivy found herself again oppressed by the tedium and formalities of the Disarmament Conference. Parties with Turks were bad, and those with Lithuanians still worse. She found some relief again with the British representative, Lord Lytton, and with Lord Balfour's daughter Dame Edith Lyttelton, the British representative, whom she found charming;[2] but the person to whom she found herself most drawn was Mussolini's Foreign Minister, Count Dino Grandi:

> He is interesting and might be a fascinating study, but we can never get beyond courtesies with Maxim there all the time, and then his English makes everything he says insipid and somehow goody-goody and academic. His face is fascinating—eyes and brows quite flat, oval renaissance outline and exquisitely white, beautifully shaped teeth. I quite feast on his face. He does not drink at all, which I find disquieting. I wonder much about him.

However, she was already preoccupied by a very different man from Grandi. This was J. D. Bernal, whom she had met during her summer in England and who in the following years was often to be in Russia. He was then about thirty and on the verge of a career which blended science and politics in a manner which hardly has a parallel in this century. Bernal was a man after Ivy's own heart; particularly for his views on love. His political views were of far less consequence for her, though no doubt it was these that first introduced them to one another. The details of her relations with him are obscure—in this she had some vestiges of discretion—but that they were close is certain. It even seems from one of her letters that Ivy contemplated a more open alliance with Bernal but it was clear to both (perhaps more to him than to her) that this could not be. 'He said he and I ought to live together in (temporary, I suppose he meant) permanency, or let each other alone, and I know what he means, but I think the latter the better alternative.'

So she wrote from Geneva in September 1931. This letter to my

[1] Shaw had an interview with Stalin. later published. in which he gave a better account of himself in discussion with the dictator than Wells did.
[2] Dame Edith was a woman of many parts. She had a great hand in organizing the Women's Land Army. sat on innumerable committees. and wrote three plays and a number of other works. She was also. on several occasions. British delegate to the League of Nations.

*13a and b Ivy as a teacher
at Sverdlovsk, 1937.*

14 *(left) Ambassadress at large, Washington DC, 1943.*

15 *(above) Maxim reading the papers; drawing by Ivy.*

16 *The Open Air Art Fair in Washington DC; drawing by Ivy.*

mother contains another quite open communication which could
have got both her and Maxim into serious difficulties, although the
fact it records was to solve problems later in Ivy's life. 'About the
money I asked Maxim how we were.' It seems that Maxim, during his
visit in the summer, had left with the impoverished Carswells a sum
of about £200 which had been paid to a deposit account in his name at
a bank in Hampstead, where in fact it lay undisturbed for thirty
years. It is not to be supposed that Maxim, in his prudence, made
this provision unadvisedly, and as Ivy unwisely wrote, 'the longer
we don't touch this last £100, the better.'

By the time that letter was received in London Ivy was
accompanying Maxim on a state visit to Turkey:

> Turkey was marvellous, but quite 'external', if you know what I
> mean, and not much to do with ME, except for the warm bath of
> flattery side of it, which does one no harm I think, and makes
> tedious engagements more bearable. I mean the flattery of REAL
> cordiality and welcome.

This was written after the return to a grim Moscow winter and
another new flat in the Spiridonovka, this time with five rooms,
whence she wrote a description of home life on 1 February 1932:

> I had so utterly let the flat go and entered one of my phases when I
> let the things on my desk mount skywards for weeks—a vicious
> circle. It is a weak concession to depression and makes you still
> more depressed. The hades-like untidiness of the whole flat (except
> of course M's room, always a model) was enough to drive one
> desperate and of course my quite fairly good little servant got
> demoralized by it too. In that way the move to a new, roomy, light
> and airy flat has done me all the good in the world, by calling forth
> all sorts of energies and imaginations, and making me work like a
> black to get things in order. . . . I had a row with the 'girl', sacked
> her, to her deep astonishment (she was sure I was such a fool I
> would stand anything) and anyhow it is all but impossible to get a
> decent servant nowadays, they all go into factories, naturally. She
> couldn't stand my sudden access of house-pride and resented
> bitterly being given shelves and hooks for everything, having got
> beautifully used in two years with me to having comfy glory-holes
> all over the place—under her bed, on tops of cupboards, under the
> kitchen sink, etc. The kitchen drawers held a lyrical jumble of

pencils, onions, stray lumps of sugar, account-books, ration cards, the stoppers of lost scent bottles, and horrors crown of horrors—a discarded finger-stall—and not even a finger-stall but an old bandage that had taken on the shape of the finger! Surely the abomination of desolation standing in the place where it ought not! I was in despair at the thought of having to find a new servant just before leaving Moscow, but had tremendous luck, an elderly woman who used to be a neighbour's servant, and whom I knew quite well and—crowning luck!—whose secret dream had always been to come to me because our kids are so civilized with servants—she left our neighbour because she couldn't stand their boy—instantly threw up her place and became a really beloved member of our family. She is a little bit the house-proud landlady type, used to have her own furniture and even some little estate, but is reserved rather than garrulous.

Ivy was in this letter at her most inconsiderate because she was worried. 'Spiteful scandals' about her were 'going the round of the various sanatoriums and rest-houses where our elite spend their summer holidays'; and these were 'rejoiced in by the political and other enemies of M'. It was only to be expected, but she was defiant:

> I don't care a pin what anyone says or thinks about me, it seems to me, for I feel heads and shoulders taller than anyone who can gloat over such outworn topics of scandal as who sleeps with whom, but the torture was to feel it might come to M's ears one day. Of course now it is being saved up for a convenient time. I never have the feeling (ought to, of course) that as Caesar's wife I must be above suspicion and think of M's career. I don't care a pin about his career, considering he has already had several men's careers and knowing how utterly without ambition he is, but I do feel awful remorse at the thought of him losing face because of my conduct and being *personally* humiliated, and I worried and worried for weeks of sleepless nights. . . . However you know my happy disposition. . . .

What she did not yet know, writing in 1932, was the formidable nature of the system in which she and Maxim were enmeshed, or the consequences that could result from the personal conduct of those highly placed in Soviet society. 'I would rather write than be happy, wouldn't you?' she demanded of Catherine.

If she did not see the dangers, she saw the realities clearly enough in the context of her children. 'Tanya', she wrote cheerfully, 'is surprisingly and refreshingly showing the cloven hoof': a golden child at home, but at school

> a teacher's terror . . . leading a band of eleven devils who obey her blindly. . . . When I asked her about public meetings and public disapprobation, she said: 'We have other things to talk about that are much more interesting. I'm sick of school.' She nurses some resentment against the authorities—considers them petty and bureaucratic (as they sure are!) and that all her zeal and idealism for the pioneer movement were exploited to bore her to death with what she considers unnecessary meetings and office work when she wanted to be alive. The thing is she is too mature for school and too full of life and integrity not to get a shock when she comes up against our careerist-bureaucratic brand of idealism.

Maxim shook his head and said that Ivy was ruining their daughter's career. But Ivy was faithful to her star, and in those last few words—jargon though they deliberately were—she saw and clearly described what she found deeply inimical in the world which surrounded her. It made her almost unbelievably reckless and the recklessness cut deeper and deeper grooves in her determination that her destiny was not to be the wife of a politician but a writer. 'NOW WRITING' is the proud headline of a letter written only a month after all these reflections. 'I cannot complain [she writes on 1 February 1932, now again in Geneva] but neither can I consider my life really stimulating or what I need (who does I wonder).'

Indeed, at the end of that month, left behind in Geneva for ten days by Maxim who had unexpectedly to return to Moscow, she demonstrated her indifference to all scandalous rumours: 'I am left here alone with about 22 gents and three typists (latter quite uninteresting—two hopelessly plain and the other not at all good-looking . . . of course there is no such thing as twenty-two uninteresting men.' She pondered among them, and began imagining 'a semi-political variation of The Admirable Crichton' as a possible novel: 'a delegation stranded on a desert island'. Then comes a strange, unexpected note, asking for Cynthia Mosley's address. She must have met this tragic figure, Lord Curzon's daughter, 'one of God's gentlest and loveliest creatures' according to Chips Channon, on a recent visit to England. 'I constantly find myself thinking with affection of her. She wrote me two touching and unconsciously pathetic letters.' Cynthia, Oswald Mosley's first wife, died barely a year later, in the year in which Mosley lurched from his New Party into Fascism, and Hitler rose to power in Germany: the year also in which the first of the great show trials was held in Russia, the trial of the British engineers.

II

Independence

Geneva and its unexplored men were soon left behind, and by April Ivy was in Berlin, once more sponsored by her hero Vogt: 'he has set me down in a charming little flat here all by myself, with a car to go into town whenever I will, and practically locks me into my terrace room with my typewriter.' But although she tried hard ('I am making a brave attack') she was not in a mood to write, and 'the old crowd', though she went to see them, was, not surprisingly, breaking up. Friedel, who had inspired it, was dead. The storm troopers were on the march. Instead there was Walter, a man who bore her father's name.

Walter was a communist, engaged in producing and distributing a secret newspaper, but that was not the source of what Ivy felt about him. Her feelings for him were among the tenderest she records:

It has been getting better and better between us, but this was the climax. I reminded him of the times when I used to come for a few hours and how furtive and inhibited he used to be, and how our goodbyes had seemed almost like trying to forgive each other for partial failure—how different from our frank and eager contests now. I enjoyed tremendously lying on the divan in his room in the morning and watching (without helping) Walter—terribly handsome and Spanish in a black hairnet! tidying away the break-fast things . . . then, neatly dressed, exquisitively shaved, rather like a dapper little cock robin, only dear, pale, and rather saturnine . . . his life is so complicated, materially, so precarious, and, poor devil, so comblé with work and anxiety, and I know it, but I just lay there, enjoying his silhouette against the open window and a tracery of leafless trees.

After this she returned to Moscow for a month or two, but in the autumn managed a whirlwind visit to England to see her relatives—mainly her mother. From her letters it seems as if she spent her time dashing about in an embassy car driven by an impassive chauffeur called Braithwaite, and leaving her possessions behind at various ports of call, including a ladies' lavatory where she was changing for dinner. 'Admittedly I'm beastly to mother,' she scribbled in her long report of her adventures, 'but I honestly don't know how to be anything else.' That letter was written approaching the Polish frontier, and she was careful to get out of the train and post it before crossing, in October 1932.

She imported into the Soviet Union something more than reminiscences of amorous and social adventures: something that was going to give a backbone to her life for some years to come. This was Basic English.

She had always been fascinated by words—their structure, their sound, the possibility of making them out of one another. In the end the fascination furrowed her whole existence and became more important to her than any hope or search for literary fame. Her work as a translator had sharpened her skill with words, and had made her alert to the Soviet problem of gaining access to the literature and science of the West. Her own translations had been from Russian into English. Why should not the Russians be taught English on a grand scale? The inheritance of Walter Low, the popularizer, and of the line of Indian army officers on her mother's side, was brought to bear on this problem.

Basic English came from the fertile mind of C. K. Ogden, a man who mingled intellectuality, business acumen and sheer crankiness with elements of mystification. His importance in the intellectual world of the 1920s and 1930s has perhaps been underestimated, since he was responsible, among much else, for recruiting the authors of the 109 little brown volumes of the *Today and Tomorrow* series, and the weightier 98 of the *International Library of Psychology, Philosophy and Scientific Method* ('Method' was one of his favourite words) which offered a new and eager public the whole gamut of modernism from Piaget to Wittgenstein. He was an aggressive rationalist and a zealous pacifist, with considerable insight into not only themes that deserved to be presented but ways of presenting them that ensured they would be noticed and taken seriously.

How Ivy came into contact with Ogden and his ideas I do not know.

She can hardly have found him interesting from the sexual viewpoint, for his activity in that side of life was minimal. He was unmarried and formed no sexual attachments of any kind, permanent or temporary. In appearance he was Pickwickian and rather insignificant, and his favourite haunt was the Athenaeum, where he occupied a table to himself. But his tentacles were everywhere, and in addition to the Athenaeum he belonged to the more avant-garde Nineteen Seventeen Club, which included J. D. Bernal, Bertrand Russell and Francis Meynell. No doubt it was through one of these connections that he met Ivy and introduced her to Basic English, which he had first proposed in 1931.

'Basic', as its devotees and promoters like to call it, is a system by which 850 well-chosen English words can be made to do duty for the whole range of language, and so provide a universal medium of communication, both written and spoken. The implications of such an idea, as Ogden and his disciples tirelessly pointed out, are vast, and he counted many converts, including, at one time, Winston Churchill. The scheme (or rather the dramatic claims Ogden made for it) had its critics and detractors as well as its supporters, but it cannot be denied that the way Ogden had worked out and promoted the idea was original, ingenious and potentially far-reaching.

Among other things it was an answer to a problem which had beset thoughtful Bolsheviks ever since the Revolution, and even before it. The Revolution, after all, was supposed to be a universal phenomenon arising from ineluctable historical and economic laws affecting the whole human race; but the fact that it had occurred in Russia, with traditions and culture so distinctive as to cut it off from the more developed parts of Europe, was embarrassing. In the early years, accordingly, a great deal of attention had been paid by the Bolsheviks to the synthetic universal language Esperanto, and in the 1920s stamps in honour of its inventor Zamenhof had even been issued by the Soviet Union. But the trouble with Esperanto was that being native to nobody, it would have to be learned by all; and the task of translating the literature and science of the world into it would be beyond the resources of even the largest institute.

The solution offered by Basic to this problem—and the more practical benefits which a knowledge of her native language, even in attenuated form, would confer on the Russians—made Ivy a crusader for Ogden's plan in the Soviet Union. In this mission she was seconded by an American music teacher named Jock Rantz, who makes his first appearance in her correspondence soon after her return to Moscow in the autumn of 1932.

Wandering American intellectuals were not uncommon in the Soviet Union in those more relaxed times, and Jock Rantz's presence in Moscow requires no particular explanation. He had become involved in Basic through taking up with one of Ogden's other brainwaves—the association of musical harmony with colour. As I remember him, Jock was large and amiable, and spoke with a buzz or drone of extreme slowness and deliberation. He was an affectionate and good-hearted man, but he got on the nerves of the practical, level-headed Maxim.

Maxim was now on the threshold of the greatest triumph of his career—the successful negotiation of recognition of the Soviet Union by the United States, a triumph even greater than membership of the League of Nations which was to follow shortly afterwards. Both were as much triumphs over the doctrinaires in his own country as over the opposition of conservative Western statesmen. They could not have been achieved at all if they had not suited Stalin, and if the time should ever come when they did not so suit, the position of the minister associated with the policy would indeed be perilous.

But Ivy was less and less interested in Maxim's career, and it cannot be that he did not feel this. They were drifting apart, though they were never to sever. 'I may be a sinner,' Ivy wrote to Catherine, 'but I have become infinitely more tolerant, understand my husband through other men, and am generally a sunshine round the house.' When Maxim went to the United States in the autumn of 1933 to conclude the recognition arrangements and impose his friendly, practical image on future relationships with the Americans, Ivy did not go with him. 'I didn't go to America because I couldn't be bothered,' she wrote, and whether this was true or not, the elaborate radio conversation which was arranged between Maxim (speaking from the Oval Office in the White House) and herself in Moscow rather bears out her lack of interest, though admittedly she was just seeing a manual of Basic English through the press:

Litvinov: I am now in the White House.
Ivy: Yes, I know.
Litvinov: I have just been talking to the President, and his last words were to give you his regards.
Ivy: Thank you very much. I have them.

Litvinov: Everybody here is very sorry you did not come with me.
Ivy: Oh!

Still, he 'came back full of buck from America[1] and we have a
luxurious house in the country'. It had, in fact, at one time belonged
to Stalin, and was one of the best dachas at the disposal of the
government.

Only a week before Ivy wrote this, Maxim had delivered his report
to the Central Committee. It contained two interesting remarks: a
courteous reference to Comrade Molotov (of whom in fact he had no
high opinion) and the sentence 'Germany has lost the Second World
War.'

Ivy's 'great interest' was still Basic, she reported, and she had lost
her voice teaching it to a class of forty-five students. She went into
hospital for a fortnight, and then to a professional elocutionist, as a
result of which she acquired 'a pleasing (they say) singing voice'. A
more serious thing was that the professional teachers of English and
their friends at the Commissariat of Education were up in arms
against an unqualified teacher who taught English in an unapproved
way. Representations were made, but Ivy was not abashed or
deterred, and her classes continued to flourish.

She was, however, no longer to have the support of Jock Rantz. The
day of the amiable foreign wanderer in the Soviet Union (there had
been so many of them in the 1920s) was fast drawing to a close. One
morning in the spring of 1934 two sober men called on Jock and asked
him to pack his bags, since they were about to conduct him to the
frontier. His fare had been paid, and all formalities had been
complied with. He later appeared at our house in London where his
prolonged stay induced my father to tell my mother that he found in
himself a hankering to be a Commissar which he had never felt
before.

Poor Jock. Even Ivy's letter of commendation, though it praised his
profound musical knowledge and his friendly disposition, was not
unqualified. '. . . I'm sure you ought to see him. And the quality of his
disposition— extremely friendly, but aloof however intimate you get,
gay and amusing over a deep pool of melancholy, and devastatingly
acute, you ought to find something to like in him . . .'

[1] Not only America. He had also been to Paris and Rome where he had a meeting with
Mussolini (3 December 1933) with whom he had concluded a non-aggression pact three
months earlier.

Jock's removal, though in no sense an emotional break in Ivy's life, symbolizes the end of one phase in it, and the beginning of a much grimmer period in which her chief, and almost her only, consolations were to be the children whom she had tried to cocoon in the Englishness of her own childhood:

> I think you would find them both good-looking now [Misha was seventeen and Tanya a year younger]—but Tanya unreservedly beautiful—there is what the Victorian novelist used to describe as a 'mild radiance' about her. Misha is always handsome . . . occasionally ravishing (as what mother's son is not?) but Tanya's sweet balance of gaiety and thoughtfulness never seems to desert her.

Ivy set about forming an oasis for herself and the children, and very soon found a new recruit for it—a recruit who in due course would first complicate, then disrupt it. S—— was a girl of about Tanya's age; the daughter of a Russian whom Maxim had known of long ago in England and who had worked, like Klishko, in Arcos. Her childhood had been spent in England, and she found her way to Ivy's oasis initially, about 1930, simply through living in the flat above: 'She was a rather low type of animal life [Ivy wrote afterwards]—very pretty, decidedly vulgar, and very sexy indeed. She fascinated me because she was simple and blunt. In those days I felt she would be a wonderful catalyst.' S—— was unhappy in her own home and it is reasonable to guess that as she entered adolescence the prospect of attaching herself to a family very much above her own in the Soviet hierarchy was attractive and exciting for her. She gradually became part of the Litvinov household. Ultimately she was formally adopted. Her father perished in the purges.

Meanwhile, as a kind of extension of Ivy's English oasis in the Soviet world, there was Basic. Whatever Maxim had felt about Jock Rantz, he could see there was something in Ogden's idea, and a class of junior Foreign Office officials was organized for Ivy to teach. 'Not at all exciting, not very bright youths. At least they are above the average by education and perhaps even intellectually, but they are so dim in themselves, such poor specimens.' How this reflection on the staff of the Narkomindel got through the censor is a mystery. Nor was this class the only one. There were at least two others, and Ivy now had two assistants. Basic was catching on, despite the resistance of the Soviet educational establishment.

[Independence]

In 1934, with the assassination of Kirov, the worst horrors of Stalinism began. Trial followed trial, slaughter was piled upon slaughter, death and destruction fell year after year on hundreds of the prominent and tens of thousands of the obscure. One by one Maxim's most trusted colleagues whom he had placed to further his policy, Krestinsky and Sokolnikov (his two Assistant Commissars), Bogomolov (China), Yurenev (Japan), Davtyan (Poland), Karsky (Lithuania), Asmus (Finland), Brodovsky (Latvia), Svirsky (Afghanistan), Tikhmenev (Denmark), Bekzadian (Hungary), Raskolnikov (Bulgaria), Yakobuvich (Norway), Barmine (Greece), and even his own private secretary Gershelman, were shot, imprisoned or deposed; or, in terror, they defected and took refuge abroad. Of the service Maxim had created very few significant figures survived to the end of the decade—Maisky in London, Umansky in the United States, and the ailing Kollontai in Sweden were the most prominent. The tide was clearly lapping round his own feet. Though the policy of the Narkomindel was not changed, the control of foreign affairs was slipping from his grasp after 1935.

Nor were things well between Maxim and Ivy. The introduction of S—— to the family had resulted in a growing association between the Commissar and his adopted daughter. If Ivy found official parties boring, S—— did not, and to the scandal of many she began to make her appearance at them in company with Maxim. She even, to excited commentary, came to collect him from the office wearing riding breeches.

Ivy found the humiliation unbearable. There was in her a streak of conventional pride that lay deep, however inconsistent it may have been with her other beliefs. And at the same time her own oasis was failing. She had originally brought S—— into it; and its first inhabitant, Tanya, was moving into a phase of independence and defiance. Along with all this went the creeping shadows of terror,[2] from which foreign origin carried no exemption. Long afterwards Ivy herself was to write of the tragedy that overtook one idealist from Western Europe, Rose Cohen.[3]

In a situation partly self-inflicted, partly imposed, Ivy made and

[2] On returning from a reception one evening with Maxim, Ivy commented that Yezhov, who had recently succeeded Yagoda as chief of the secret police, had looked more genial and sociable than was his wont. 'I expect he's had a blood transfusion,' was Maxim's grim reply.

[3] Appendix 2.

carried out a remarkable and independent decision. She would leave Moscow and the protective shadow of Maxim, and set up the standard of Basic English in some provincial centre, thereby embarking once more on a career of her own. She approached an official of the Ministry of Higher Education, and in due course received an appointment to teach English at a teacher training college in Sverdlovsk, in the Urals, several hundred miles east of Moscow.

The reasons for her 'exile' have been the subject of speculation—refuge, caution on the part of Maxim, offence given in high quarters, have all been thought of. Certainly her departure, even though independently decided, did not put her beyond the range of risk. It took her away from knowing the worst that was happening, but means were found of conveying much of that by covert phrases in apparently harmless letters. It did not produce a total breach with Maxim, furious though she was with him. Both of them were conventional at heart, but he was more conventional that she was, and she was so much part of his life that he could never contemplate an end to their marriage. He must have been beginning to foresee that his policy, with which his personality and emotions were deeply involved, might diverge from Stalin's interests; and in spite of the complexities of his life, it was impossible for him ever to abandon the ideas of of internationalism on which he had built his reputation and his concept of the survival of the Soviet Union. With these ideas his marriage was in some way irretrievably involved.

Ivy's step of moving to Sverdlovsk placed her in a new kind of exile, and separated her from the world of contingent privilege in which she had lived for so long, and in which her children still, uncertainly, existed. For the first time since her rebellion against Alice and Sandy, she found herself truly on her own; and in a totalitarian state, as the dubious, foreign, semi-separated wife of a prominent but threatened man. Yet by thus demonstrating her total indifference to politics she may have saved her life, and possibly Maxim's.

She wrote brightly enough from Sverdlovsk to London in October 1936 that she was in 'an old town spreading into a new town by eating into larch forests':

> I am working and living all by myself for the first time and finding it suits me. . . . I have at least a hundred students and one or two contacts in the town so I don't get solitude. But I do get a sort of isolation and freedom from domestic cares (not that they ever

weighed very heavy on me) and above all those damned diplomatic
parties. . . .

The worst was being separated from her children, particularly from
Tanya. But the letters she wrote to Tanya during her long stay in the
Urals, which lasted until the war broke out, are among the most
impressive and interesting of her career.

Naturally enough, these letters say little in direct terms about the
terrible period through which she, her family and all Russia, were
then living. Though a little they do say. As a whole they mark a
growing and decisive movement in Ivy away from the reckless
discontent that marked her earlier life. Self-centred and opinionated
she would always be, but there is a new warmth, a new solicitude and
a new satisfaction in the work she was doing—difficult though that
was.

Well—25 people—(6 of them men) in a half dark school-
room . . . Class very raw as regards discipline, but very essentially
attentive. I had prepared every detail of the lesson the day before.
This gave me a sense of Olympian calm, and of foreseeing all
possible events. The alphabet [this was a piece of apparatus] went
splendidly. First I put only the Russian side, then both, then the
English only. . . . Then I went round with three blades I had
brought, lending them to the bladeless, and we all cut our
books. . . . Then I went round with a Marmite jar of water, which,
bless its little heart, didn't spill a drop on the way and some dry
powdery red stuff which responded to the wet paint brush with
heavenly, rich, poisonous blood-like red. And everyone was so
awed that they didn't even ask 'what for?'

So they began their English letters:

The awful man sits in front 'spikinglishes' to a marvel and is
desperately cultural. He came to me afterwards and said 'Nextime
you give me make reports. I like very. I help students no can' etc.
etc. Of course I will CRUSH him, but he is very wearing. I consider it
a shame to have given him to me, it was distinctly stipulated I
should have beginners only On the other hand he is so bustly and
kind . . . that I find it hard to be absolutely firm and one hates to
worry the poor director who . . . can't sleep at nights for thinking
that Moscow will suddenly go back on her.

[Independence]

For the time being the PEDKURS (as the Russian passion for acronyms labelled Ivy's course) went ahead with Ivy cheerfully writing 'I shall be a Stakhanovite yet', and congratulating herself on the absence of 'sovmeststitelsvo [double life], no tearing oneself from one absorption to another. Not grinning through a diplomatic reception and wondering anxiously if one will be able to be up by 7 tomorrow.' But the resistance of the educational establishment was not so lightly brushed aside, and the director of the college to which Ivy was attached was justified in her anxieties. A correspondence was stirred up in *Pravda*. 'The Philistines are upon us,' Ivy wrote to Tanya on 17 February 1937. She had written a letter herself to *Pravda*: 'of course it's so much money thrown in the letter-box; but I had to try. . . . There is a rather now-or-never feel in the air now I think.'

The classes lasted well into 1938, but under increasing difficulties, and Ivy was driven more and more into music and to deep re-reading of English literature: Trollope, Fielding, Jane Austen. She was almost completely cut off from England, and there is reason to think foreign correspondence was forbidden to her—at any rate her long correspondence with my mother ceased. She saw the *New Yorker*, however (Thurber she adored), the *New Statesman*, and *The Times Literary Supplement*. Maxim sent them, reminding her that they should be returned, since they belonged to the Narkomindel library. It was not exile in any technical sense, and sometimes there were visits to Moscow; but there were restrictions.

Tanya, then at a college of art, was a life-line and her heart-line., 'All my happiness seems to depend on being in touch with you,' Ivy wrote to her daughter in December 1936. It was through Tanya that she maintained contact with Russian friends, such as Oransky, the musician, and even Maxim, whose carefully drafted letters left little even between the lines from which to guess at his situation and feelings. She had occasional visitors from Moscow—the children, of course, but also two artists, Goncharov and Tatlin. Tanya was helping to paint scenery for Favorsky, attending the rehearsals for Meyerhold's last season and was in touch with Eisenstein. She had been late, however, in arriving for a speech by Stalin himself, in which the great man, after ordaining that there were still two classes in Russia (workers and peasants) observed severely that the intelligentsia were not, never had been, and never would be, a class.

Although Ivy had a regular correspondence with Maxim, she felt they could no longer meet. 'I simply can't go down to the dacha with

Papa and S——. I can't and I won't and Papa must not expect it.'
Nevertheless, though she blamed him for his extreme carefulness
about money and his 'petty-bourgeois Hebraic paternalism', there is
increasing affection for him, and increasing concern as he struggled,
amid growing personal dangers, for the survival of his policy.

In February 1937 Maxim was complaining to the American
ambassador about the blindness of the British government to the
threat Hitler presented, and expressing his fears that they would try
to reach an accommodation with him. At the end of the year he went
even further, saying to an American journalist (J. T. Whitaker) that
in his opinion Britain and France would be Hitler's first objectives;
and dangerously further still by adding that, despite the Anticomin-
tern Pact, 'when the Germans are prepared at last to embark on their
new adventures, these bandits will come to Moscow and ask us for a
pact.' In January 1938, Zhdanov, Stalin's henchman, delivered a
public attack on the administration of the Narkomindel, and
although he did not mention Maxim by name, shoulders were
deliberately turned on the Foreign Commissar at the reception
afterwards. 'Forgive me,' said the heavily bemedalled and bewhisk-
ered Marshal Budyenny, who found himself next to Maxim, 'but
I'm an awful coward'; and moved away, glancing at the draught from
the open window. In the Munich crisis that summer it was clear there
was no real prospect of Soviet intervention, and the German
ambassador in Moscow commented to his government that 'the
attempt to arrive at an objective policy towards the Third Reich is
striking.' In August Molotov referred to 'those short-sighted people
who, carried away by over-simplified anti-fascist propaganda, forget
about the provocative work of our enemies'; and in October the
German Embassy reported to Berlin that 'the policy of Litvinov has
suffered a complete fiasco'.

In what she called her 'Sverdlovian remoteness', Ivy had to depend
on hints and inferences, such as the weary letter from Maxim in June
1938 saying 'this year nobody is even speaking of holidays. Anyhow I
shall certainly no more go abroad for a holiday.' It was a typically
restrained epitaph on the annual relaxation in liberal Carlsbad that
had meant so much to him over many years past, and a realization
that for him the gates his visas had once opened had closed. Ivy was
wise enough in the ways of the Soviet Union to be able to infer much
from little, and in November 1938, in one of her longest letters to
Tanya, which deals among other things with her views on art and the

stylistic detail of *The Newcomes*, she speaks of being kept from depression by 'a perpetual melancholy sense of proportion' which

> makes everything seem more or less unimportant except the immediate suffering of the moment. And that is a sense of utter doom, universal and personal. And this sense keeps me strangely cheerful, because you can't keep thinking of it all the time, and it dwarfs everything else.

'Last night', she wrote two months later, in February 1939

> I felt especially ominous and wondered so about all and sundry. I am making a careful revision of all my underclothes and keeping two of everything in a box, mended and clean. Like that I would at least have what I wanted at hand in case of need.

So might one of her ancestresses have written at the time of the Indian Mutiny, and the picture is completed by her triumphant report, in the same letter to Tanya, of a woman with whom she had completed some transaction saying, 'Ivy Walterovna, you behaved as you always do, like a lady.'

She had some unladylike thoughts on the theme of possible captivity:

> Tortured self [so a fragment of diary reads] with thinking of being in the power of coarse women. Humiliation. I think no one knows what a RULING PASSION pride is with me. Of course even in camp sure to meet with some decent people. Wonder if I would continue the sessions of sweet silent thought that runs parallel to my life in conditions of confinement and cruel regulations. B. V. told me how she slept between two huge women and their bottoms touched one another all night. And I wouldn't be able to READ. . . .

She enquired for poison from the father of one of her pupils; and 'didn't I see a woman, her pale face uplifted to the neighbours over my floor, her two hands lifted to give a quick sign of crossed bars, and then all fingers on each hand spread out to signify ten years.'

She was growing towards Maxim again in their common danger. In the spring of 1939 she wrote to Tanya: 'I wonder about Papa. If by any chance it should be like last summer I'd want to be with him, I see him so little. . . . My love to Papa, longing for a letter from him.' And he did indeed write only a few days later, on 3 April, in one of the few letters from him that have survived. He begins by describing a visit from the British Department of Overseas Trade, headed by R. S. Hudson, and the exhausting round of talks and social engagements it imposed. The letter is infused with weariness and ends 'how I would like a few days' rest if only at our dacha, especially as the spring is coming on so quickly!'

Ivy was still at Sverdlovsk when the blow fell, exactly a month later. She arrived at the Institute to a sudden hush. 'I heard myself addressed: "You know Vyacheslav Mikhailovich don't you, Ivy Walterovna? He'll make a splendid Foreign Minister, won't he?"' A copy of *Pravda* was placed in her hands and her attention drawn to a small paragraph announcing that Molotov, retaining his post as chairman of the Council of Commissars, had assumed control of the Narkomindel. M. M. Litvinov 'had been relieved of his duties at his own request'.[4]

It was not only a change of Foreign Ministers, or even a presage of a momentous change of foreign policy—namely the pact with 'those bandits' of which Maxim had spoken to the American Whitaker more than a year earlier: it marked the direct assumption of control over foreign policy by the governing group of state and Party.

Ivy went at once to Moscow. No restraint was placed on her, nor, for the time being, were any of Maxim's obvious privileges withdrawn. The dacha, the chauffeur-driven car, the servants, the visits to opera house and theatre—all these continued. Maxim had an interview with his successor to discuss the office, in the course of which Molotov asked which of the senior staff rated highest in his opinion. Those named favourably were removed within a few days. He complained to the new chief of the GPU, Beria (for he was a courageous man), that the security patrols round his dacha had been unnecessarily increased. 'You don't know your own worth, Maxim Maximovich,' was the soothing reply, which elicited the parry: 'I do, but some others seem not to.' He was, after all, still a member of the Central Committee. But the private telephone was thereafter cut off.

He no longer went to the office, of course; he was a man under surveillance. Moreover, as Khrushchev relates in his memoirs, a plan was laid to murder him in a contrived 'accident' on a bend in the road leading to his dacha. And he had been led into further difficulty by Ivy. In her desperation that spring, she had entrusted a letter pouring

---

[4] The formula, though graceless, was not entirely without meaning, or indeed, an element of truth. It represented the nearest to resignation that was—or is—permitted to a Soviet dignitary.

out her fears to the hands of an American couple, apparently friendly, who were leaving Sverdlovsk and promised to post it abroad. Instead it found its way to Stalin's desk, and Maxim was confronted with it. 'You have', Stalin had said, 'an extremely courageous and outspoken wife. You should tell her to calm herself. She is not threatened.' The letter, however, remained on the file.

Many explanations—all equally speculative and unconvincing—have been advanced for Litvinov's survival at this, the most perilous moment of his adventurous career. The suggestion that Stalin had some kind of particular affection for his loyal supporter can be dismissed at once. More elaborately, it can be asserted that Litvinov's whole tenure of the Foreign Ministry was a conscious fraud cloaking other designs, and that his services were recognized by his master accordingly. All the evidence available, including the testimony of those who knew him best, is against this suggestion: but even if it were correct, the reward from Litvinov's master for faithful service was not invariably pleasant, nor was the interpretation of faithful service always consistent. Then, with undoubted force, there is the argument that even if Maxim, the Jewish internationalist with his Western connections and success with the liberal public, had to be discarded now for reasons of state, he might be useful later on. This has a ring of truth, and is borne out by later events, but is hardly sufficient.

One other explanation may be put forward. For at least a year before Maxim's dismissal, and probably longer, the major decision of foreign policy had been deliberately held in the balance at a level inaccessible to him, by Stalin. To Stalin, it would have appeared that if Maxim's policy of a combination to contain Hitler succeeded, well and good; and if it did not, its effect would be to drive 'the bandits' to seek an agreement with Moscow. The decision was deferred for so long that (as against those members of the Politburo who favoured an earlier understanding with Hitler) Stalin, in the eyes of his colleagues, became in some measure associated with Litvinov's policy. In that case, proceeding to extremities against Litvinov would, from Stalin's point of view, be unwise. It would be better to let him and his reckless English wife drop into convenient obscurity if circumstances required it. In terms of Party politics it was not important enough an issue on which to destroy a Bolshevik of the first generation who had a unique understanding of the West.

12

Switchback

Ivy was once more united with Maxim, but in misfortune—Jewish,
and in disgrace in a totalitarian country allied with Hitlerite
Germany. It is not surprising that the outside world heard little about
her between the summer of 1939 and the summer two years later
when the Nazi armies—as Maxim had foreseen—were hurled against
the Soviet Union and crushed the forces of the antiquated and
time-serving Budyenny.

Though danger brought them together, their new domesticity
could not exclude the creeping shadows. The spacious flat in the
Spiridonovka was soon, and abruptly, withdrawn, and they were
moved to a flat in which most of their neighbours were security
officials. But strangely enough they kept the dacha (which had once
been Stalin's and would in due course be Khrushchev's) until the
advance of the Germans put it in the war zone. There Ivy began
cultivating Maxim's one artistic interest by giving him music lessons,
and Maxim, in enforced leisure, achieved some proficiency.

But much of his time was spent writing—or rather typing
laboriously with two pudgy fingers—a long manuscript which he
would trust to no secretary or even member of his family. When he
travelled, it travelled with him. What it was we do not know, but it
was not a diary of current events or an account of his political and
diplomatic career. More probably, from hints he gave Ivy, it was a
commentary on international affairs as he saw them and as his
successors at the Narkomindel, Molotov, Dekanozov, and Vishinsky,
did not. If so, it was the basis of the long document addressed to Stalin
which Maxim left behind on his death and is no doubt still in the
archives of the Soviet Foreign Office.

[Switchback]

The problems of the children also had to be faced. Neither Misha nor Tanya showed any disposition to join the Party, and both were involved in love affairs which Ivy looked on with a sympathetic eye. To the deposed Commissar, deprived of all information except what he could extract from *Pravda* and *Izvestia*, the unsuitability of his children's choices increased his depression. Misha's girlfriend Flara he found uninteresting; Tanya's sculptor seemed to him a man unlikely to succeed in life. And he brooded from behind his newspaper about his successors. 'All that man knows about foreign policy,' he declared of one of them, 'is what he picked up sitting next to Ribbentrop at dinner.'[1]

But there was worse—far worse—to face than the discontents of being out of office. There is every reason to suppose that at this time a show trial was being prepared for Maxim—witnesses selected from his former subordinates were being groomed for one. He slept with a pistol under his pillow, and had arranged with Ivy that she would answer the midnight knock when it came and, if the visitors were those expected, give a coded tap on the bedroom door to ensure that he was not taken alive to face humiliation.

In the winter of 1940–1 the preliminary step was taken of depriving Maxim of the one public position he retained—membership of the Central Committee of the Communist Party. Such membership was by then more honorific than significant. The Central Committee was a large body and rarely met, even for formal business. Like all other supposedly representative or considerative bodies it had been drained of authority by the Stalinist machine acting in the name of socialism and the people. Nevertheless, it still symbolized the Revolutionary regime more than any other of its institutions. Maxim had for many years been a member of it, he valued his membership as a mark of his life's work; and, even more than that, expulsion from it could hardly fail to be a stage towards something far worse than private life.

One evening in February 1941, as Ivy relates, he was summoned to a meeting of the Central Committee,

and by his jerky movements as he flung down his newspaper and started to his feet I could see that he had forgotten nothing. Tanya

---

[1] Maxim attached supreme importance to knowledge of foreign countries as a qualification for statesmanship, and considered that even Stalin could not be considered a great statesman because 'he had never been further than Finland.'

and I looked palely into each other's eyes when we heard the front door slam behind Maxim, and I asked 'Can you believe that papa will never come back again?'

He did return, that same night, but stripped of his membership of the Central Committee. Nor had he been the only one. Madame Molotov, also Jewish, was expelled at the same time, and her husband, holding one of the highest offices in the country, had been powerless, or unwilling, to defend her.

Later events suggest that this humiliation—nay, destruction of the purpose to which he had devoted his life—was an important stage in Maxim's disillusionment with the 'reality' which the Revolution claimed to have created. Indeed, it may have confirmed doubts which had begun long before, but had been silenced by his immersion in foreign affairs and his hopes that by establishing the Soviet Union in an international system the sources of repression at home would diminish. Nevertheless his resolution and his presence of mind had not—as he later told Ivy—deserted him. Stalin, as became his pre-eminence, had been the first to leave the meeting, the others respectfully standing as he retired, and as the dictator reached the door Litvinov exclaimed, taking courage in both hands, 'Does this mean you consider me an enemy of the people?' The question, he and Ivy thought, saved his life. The dictator turned and said, with his heavy Georgian accent, 'No. We do not consider you an enemy of the people.'

This was only a few months before Molotov's vaunted pact was torn up and Hitler's armies invaded Russia. Yet in those few months there had been talk of the Soviet Union actually joining Hitler's war against the West, and despite Stalin's surprising forbearance, the whole Litvinov family, with its Western background, naturally went through a difficult period. The dramatic reversal of June 1941 justified Litvinov's views, but opened up the prospect of catastrophe for the Soviet state. By October the Germans were within striking distance of Moscow, where confusion gave place to panic.

Domestic was piled on public confusion for the Litvinovs. Misha, who had of course been called up, had married Flara and provided Ivy and Maxim with their first grandchild—Pavel. Tanya, expelled from her art school for excessive interest in 'decadent Western art' after Maxim's demotion, found herself working as a camouflage artist on factory roofs. Her sculptor friend Slonim, known to the family as

'Elephant', had also joined up. S——, perhaps uneasy about Maxim's sinking star, had married a security man—a move of which her former lover strongly disapproved, holding as he did that security men of all descriptions were to be avoided as members of a discreditable profession.

And yet, by the autumn the whole family apart from Misha and the security man, had reassembled at Kuibyshev in Eastern Russia, where most of the government had retired; Maxim, Ivy, Flara, Pavel, S——, Tanya, and 'Elephant', who had now been discharged from the army and was working on a bust of Shostakovich (also at Kuibyshev, and thus able to give him sittings). In addition there was Maxim's faithful personal secretary from Narkomindel days—a middle-aged woman named P——. Over this diverse group S—— tried briefly to reassert her old authority until Maxim arranged for her to be dispatched to Novosibirsk, to which distant place her policeman husband had been posted.

But Maxim was at Kuibyshev for only a few weeks. In November 1941 he received an urgent summons to the Kremlin, and the man who only six months earlier had been in peril of his life was declared the new Soviet ambassador in Washington. Ivy was to go with him, and he asked Tanya to go too, but she refused, so he told her she had better get on and marry 'Elephant'. Misha he tried to see, but the fog of war prevented it. Naturally they both felt it might be for the last time.

Within the month Maxim and Ivy set off eastwards across central Asia, the far East and the Pacific, as yet outwardly unaffected by the war, though Pearl Harbor was only a few days off and Japan's intention to enter the war was probably known already to the Kremlin. At Singapore, where he made a brief stop, Maxim commented on the atmosphere of complacency and unpreparedness. Their arrival in Washington could not have been more dramatic if it had been contrived, for it was on the day of Pearl Harbor itself—a day which turned the USA and the USSR into allies without the slightest exertion of high diplomacy. If Maxim's mission was to secure American support for the war against Germany, it was accomplished as he set foot on American soil.

It was nearly eight years since he had been in America, but Roosevelt was still President. That earlier visit had been so carefully prepared in advance that Maxim had thought of it as almost a formality. 'The question of recognition', he had said, 'will hardly need half an hour of conversation to settle satisfactorily.' Now, with a *de facto* alliance already in existence, his task was very different. He was sixty-four. His support of the War was as great as it had ever been. But he had lost faith in the regime he represented.

Ivy was a most successful partner in this remarkable mission and found a new bloom. She was only fifty-two and extremely handsome, although she was increasingly worried about her weight. She had never been in America before, and had never been a real ambassadress, and she found that both, especially in combination, suited her. Her strange history, her autocratic yet informal ways, her robustness and her vitality, appealed to the American public. She got a marvellous press; and despite her repeated denial that official functions could be pleasant, she enjoyed some of the American ones.

America, with its quick-burning enthusiasms and starry-eyed hustle in many ways suited Ivy's temperament better than any other country she had lived in. The restraint and inhibitions of the English, which galled her as humbug and perpetually put her in mind of Sandy; the cowed, furtive, atmosphere of the Soviet Union, with its deadly perils: both were absent. She adored the humour—and the letterpress—of the *New Yorker*. And Americans liked *her*. She quickly made many new friends, and rediscovered some old ones, among them her old friend Walter, of Berlin days. She even saw Jock Rantz again, and his sister Berta, who had also been in Moscow some eight years earlier. With Berta she carried on a voluminous correspondence, which has survived.

There was only a single shadow in Ivy's tremendous love affair with America. During the bad days just ended, which had brought her and Maxim together, they had been on an equal footing, almost for the first time since 1918, and with all the danger that surrounded them, something of the old interdependence had returned. The new, unexpected prosperity carried them apart again. Ivy had fresh grounds for jealousy in Maxim's secretary P——, who had accompanied them to America,[2] and in any case she much preferred her own friends to the diplomatic circle of the embassy. She became something of an ambassadress at large, writing, travelling, broadcasting, going to parties without her husband and, so far as one can

[2] There had been much family debate on the subject, for the relationship between Ivy and P—— was extremely stormy. Maxim felt he could discuss business with P——, and she was very good at bridge.

judge, without clearance from anyone. She even boldly got note-paper of her own printed which read:

Ivy Litvinoff
1125 Sixteenth Street
Washington

It must have caused great anxiety to Mr Gromyko, who was then Counsellor of Embassy and Maxim's deputy.

For the first time in her life Ivy found herself being cultivated for her own sake. *Vogue*, the *Woman's Home Journal*, the *Atlantic Monthly*, agents and editors from all sides, sought stories, reminiscences, sketches, interviews. She even wrote a lively interview with herself, taking the interviewer's part as well as her own. Of course she said that Stalingrad would hold out, above all because Russian soldiers were all breast-fed in their babyhood, but that was what Americans wanted to hear at that moment. Everyone was on the same side.

She wrote a vivid account of her expedition to D. H. Lawrence in Italy during these halcyon days. She wrote reviews, and lunched with Mrs Roosevelt.[3] She went to Hollywood, and encountered a princess (of what origin she does not state) who proposed to give up her chair to Ivy, as an ambassadress. Ivy, contrary to her true nature, protested, whereon the princess insisted she had not been born one, and Ivy, saying she had not been born an ambassadress, took her seat.

Her old detective story of 1930 was republished as *The Moscow Mystery* with a preface about how Vogt had helped her with hypnosis to write it. It was, as she said to Berta Rantz, 'a year or two of moral oxygen', above all when she could get to New York. 'NY, NY' became her favourite spot on earth. While Maxim laboured on the details of lend-lease, and persuaded American contractors that a bay leaf had to be put into every tin of meat if the Russian soldier was to eat it (which was perfectly true), Ivy rejoiced as lioness. The dollars came rolling in, and after her expenses had been paid, the balance went on comforts for the troops. The letters leave no shadow of doubt that she was handling her own finances, and any embassy accountant who

[3] But provided no account of the conversation. Maxim, who had many conversations with Roosevelt, had the greatest respect for him, but considered the President was stronger in domestic than in foreign policy, being prone to oversimplify the issues in the latter field. Roosevelt moreover irritated Maxim by addressing him as 'Max'.

tried to make out what Ivy was earning would soon have found himself in a morass.

Despite her comparative alienation from Maxim, there was an understanding and confidence between them. One example of this she called their 'code'—certain words in letters and telegrams which had a special meaning: 'expect', for instance, meant 'must'. And she carried out a service for him which could not be entrusted to any of his staff, or even revealed to them. He was now a deeply disappointed and disillusioned man, subordinated to a successor in Moscow whom he regarded as unprofessional, heavy-handed, and wrong-headed. He foresaw that the victory which he was striving for would be misused by his masters for dangerous aggrandisement. He began, using Ivy as his amanuensis, to dictate secret memoirs of his diplomatic career.[4]

Writing, social life and dealing with Maxim did not exhaust Ivy's exuberance. She discovered a new talent in herself, namely drawing, and for a time applied herself to it with enthusiasm and success, taking lessons from Grosz, and producing, among other things, a vivid sketch of Maxim at work on the daily press—something he always took with the utmost seriousness. She had a genuine gift for line, as that and other surviving drawings testify.

> She was standing dead center in the middle of the path [wrote a friendly journalist] looking critically at a small blond girl painting. . . . She wore a pair of blue canvas shoes, a blue and white linen frock, a black knitted cape, and her curly white hair was tied in a knitted black band. She was very intent on her own sketch of the rear of the small blond girl and started slightly when I spoke.
>
> 'I didn't know you could draw,' I said. Mme Litvinoff turned quickly and laughed. Oh yes, it was the ubiquitous and unpredictable Ivy Litvinoff, caught in the act of giving the open-air fair the once-over . . .

It is a pity Ivy did not develop this talent earlier, and did not pursue it later. Much as she loved words they were a kind of prison to her, and needed to be purged, chiselled, and endlessly altered before they

---

[4] A considerable part of this memoir was completed. Litvinov (according to his daughter) arranged to deposit it in a bank in the United States before he was recalled. In some way or other, however, it was recovered by Soviet agents and ended up in the archives of the Narkomindel.

could be presentable; whereas her drawing flows with effortless confidence of line.

So did her letters—perhaps too effortlessly:

I have had a rotten time here [she wrote from Washington to her confidante Berta Rantz] and am completely defeated. At the same time so is she, and our little Napoleon neatly keeps bits of himself for each of us. Well, oh, hell, anyhow. We* went to The Great Dictator yesterday and I am still amazed and entranced (*He and me).

That autumn they stayed together with the Davies's (Roosevelt's ambassador in Moscow) at Camp Topridge, in upstate New York—'not so much in the lap as the very womb of luxury,' as Ivy put it. 'Maxim very creased and crumpled, and Ivy quite neat and sporting—all would have the necessary pinch of salt if there was someone here to retire with and crab it all a bit.' Ivy never entirely merged herself in her surroundings, whether pleasant or unpleasant. Then it was off to Hollywood as the guest of Warner Brothers in 'a bungalow which costs a dollar for every breath you draw'. Once more united with Jock Rantz, she signed a contract for a film about Basic English (it was never made, but she got a substantial advance) and was introduced to the great columnist Walter Winchell.

By the spring of 1943 it was clear that the war against Germany was going to be won and the prospectively victorious powers were each privately beginning to consider their policy when the threat of Hitler was removed. In this context the Kremlin was becoming increasingly dissatisfied with its ambassador in Washington, and possibly with his wife as well. There were signs that Maxim was beginning to talk to the Americans about his old schemes of collective security, and was unreceptive to thoughts of territorial security for the Soviets in terms of a belt of dependent states, which charmed the imagination of Stalin and Molotov. 'The old man seems to have gone absolutely mad,' a Foreign Office friend confided to Tanya in Moscow: 'He seems to be ignoring his instructions.'

He was. In April 1943 he was instructed to return to Moscow 'for consultations'. On 7 May he called on Sumner Welles, then Assistant Secretary of State and (according to the official record of the conversation)

complained that he was unable to communicate with Stalin, whose isolation then bred a distorted view of the West and in particular an underestimate of Western public opinion. He assured Welles that once back home he would do his best to improve matters but was not at all hopeful that he could. He gave vent to his frustration about the rigidity of the whole Soviet system and especially about Molotov's tight grip on the Foreign Commissariat. He still abstained, however, from any criticisms of Moscow's policies.[5]

In his own mind, however, there were many such criticisms, and he was in fact contemplating disobedience to his orders to return, and passing the rest of his life in America, where he could complete his political memoirs and his critique of Stalin's foreign policy.

Various reasons must have led him to reject the idea: the discipline of long service; the hatefulness of exile and dependence; his family in pawn; hopes that he might even yet, if he were on the spot, recapture the dictator's ear for the policy he felt to be in the Soviet Union's best interests. And Ivy was against it when they discussed the idea:

> When Maxim thought he was going to stay he felt terribly dependent on me. He said to me, 'You're much more to me than P——'—you have no idea how much that meant from a man like him. He had to force every intimate word out of himself, he resented it—such a neurotic! He began calling me darling, and I thought, 'I've got a man's fate, a man's life in my hands!'; but I began to feel more and more that I could not do this to the children. I lost pounds. I was sick with worry. At last I told him, 'I can't do it'. I wonder if *he* could have. I felt terribly sorry for him. And the world has lost something. It would have been a real book. But of course they would have done their best to get rid of him. . . .

At first it seems they were planning to return together—on 28 April Ivy was telling her friend Berta that inoculations had begun and tickets had been ordered; but then it was decided he should go first, and so we find Ivy writing in August to Berta from a comfortable hotel

---

[5] Quoted by Vojtech Mastny in 'The Cassandra in the Foreign Commissariat', *Foreign Affairs*, January 1976. Mr Mastny visited Ivy before writing the article, and she loyally denied her husband could ever have said such a thing. But the record is clear, and her own papers confirm it. Indeed they suggest his disillusionment went back many years: 'He said he knew the moment when the Revolution went wrong. He had been unhappy for a long time. There was the time when he came to Copenhagen. It was just at the beginning of the New Economic Policy. He was terribly depressed. Afterwards I suppose he knew that things had to be like this, but how depressed he was! He felt everything had been sold.'

in upstate New York about the excellent swimming. She was putting the finishing touches to her memoir of her encounter with D. H. Lawrence. 'How I love not doing my own room in the mornings: I have breakfast in bed at 8.30 and am still in a nightgown typing at 11 am. That is the way to work!'

She had confided a good deal in Berta, especially on the subject of her jealousy of P——, and the possibility that Ivy might not follow Maxim back to Russia seems to have been raised between them. But there could be no question of that:

> Now I feel like this. I suppose I'll have to go, and I hate the idea of either harming the family or going round hat in hand here. But just as certainly I'm determined not to go back to family life. I will try to get a job organizing Basic English groups in any town they like, so long as a room goes with it. I will not go back to dependence. After all I could take a lot of stuff back with me. . . .

But there was some stuff it was her duty not to take back with her. These were the papers Maxim had left behind in her care. She deposited them in a numbered safe-deposit box in a New York bank, and entrusted the key to an American friend.

During these last months in America, before returning to the dangerous tunnel of life in the Soviet Union, she could not escape her lifelong task of writing about her youth:

> I am still slugging away at writing. . . . I'm working on the destiny thru books bit: meeting Viola Meynell thru her book, meeting Cath thru her [sc. my] book and LEAVING home, and H. James and the Lawrences, and also the bit about my mother coming to Moscow.[6] Unfortunately I feel I still need weeks of work. . . . So far I don't feel lonely.

Ivy did not leave for Moscow until December 1943. 'It seems incredible that I should have had to give up NY life prematurely, with all that it meant, but on the other hand, once you're going, you feel you've got to go.' There speaks the ancestral memsahib side of her character. The notion of parting from Maxim in any formal sense was

---

[6] Alice Herbert had visited her daughter in Moscow in 1933. There is a remarkable photograph of her standing in the garden of the dacha formerly owned by Stalin, making it look like Harrow in summer. She died in 1942, and the news reached Ivy just as she arrived in Washington.

inconceivable, even if it meant a return to the shadow of a prison camp. And there were the children.

The fact that all her thoughts had had to be bottled up over a period of more than twenty-five years worked on Ivy's natural egotism to form a carapace of truly remarkable toughness. Her experience of a totalitarian society made her strive never to merge, always to be herself; but as a result something of the indifference of that society communicated itself to her personality, and was adopted as a protective shield behind which the 'real Ivy' could continue her perpetual study of her childhood and youth, 'slugging away' at 'the book I've got to write' but which was never written. Her natural warmth, her vitality, even her courage, were driven inwards and emerged only in spurts and gusts.

> I sometimes think you may find something disconcerting [she had written to Berta in April 1943] in the way I cut people out the moment they show the cloven hoof of poor frail humanity. I would not have done so before. I would cling thru all stress to anybody I had been intimate with. It is just that I feel I can't afford extravagant complications.

So, at Christmas 1943, the Litvinov family was once more united in Moscow. The War had been won, but it was not over. The Germans were still firmly occupying Western Europe and much of Russia. Maxim, now sixty-seven, was assigned to one of the least influential departments of the Narkomindel with the rank of Assistant Commissar—a step below the one to which he had been appointed on his return to Russia twenty-five years earlier. His membership of the Central Committee was not restored, and he was not very well. Ivy was a still vigorous and excitable fifty-four.

13

Widow of a Diplomat

When Ivy joined Maxim in Moscow once more there was a scent of victory in the air, despite the devastation and fearful losses; and the patriotism that had been evoked to bring it about carried with it also some whiffs of an older Russia. Civil servants, including Maxim, had been put into uniforms. He hated it. He had not worn one since serving in the Tsar's army in Baku nearly half a century earlier, and it did not suit either his style or his dumpy figure. An American journalist who met him in April 1945 commented that 'he looked rather less like a general than anybody I have ever seen. His grey uniform was rumpled and unpressed and there were food stains on the lapels.'

As an Assistant Commissar (the others were Dekanozov and Lozovsky), he was assigned to post-war planning, but his influence was minimal. De Gaulle in his memoirs mentions his presence at a banquet in the Kremlin in November 1944, but such appearances were infrequent. Instead he applied himself to the course he had hinted at in his interview with Sumner Welles, and seems in doing so to have enjoyed a kind of contemptuous licence from Stalin and Molotov, for he repeatedly gave interviews to journalists and others in which he criticized his superiors, lamented their neglect of his advice, and even accused the West of culpable weakness in failing to resist Stalin's inordinate demands. Another American journalist, Richard Hottelot of the *Washington Post*, could hardly believe his ears when 'his host, chafing in the ornate Soviet foreign service uniform, gravely pronounced the words: "If the West acceded to the current Soviet demands it would be faced, after a more or less short time, with the next series of demands."' Maxim made no secret of his view that the

Yalta agreement, Stalin's greatest diplomatic victory, was a disaster for the future of international relations.[1]

That interview, on 5 April 1945, was Maxim's last as an official. It had been preceded by at least half a dozen others of much the same kind with allied public figures and journalists, including Harriman and Edgar Snow, and by two articles under the pseudonym 'N. Malinin' in which he advocated views very different from those of Molotov and Vishinsky. His time was over. 'A bitter, cynical old revolutionary,' Hottelot commented after that last interview, 'isolated and alone: he knows he's had it.' He was dismissed at the end of April, and Hottelot met him once more at the May Day parade standing in the crowd below the diplomatic benches. Hottelot asked him why he had not been allotted a seat.

'I was,' he said dourly, 'but I preferred it down here with the masses.' The way he said 'masses' it was in quotes. His pale, ugly face looked thoughtful and sad; none of the exuberance of a magnificent triumph. He never once looked at Stalin and his lieutenants standing atop of Lenin's tomb. He just stared at the long rows of cannon and marching troops.

Maxim was a man of peace both by character and because he had always been a negotiator from a position of weakness. The politics of strength were repugnant to him personally, and he foresaw that in the longer term their adoption by his country could be damaging to its interests. The stronger sinews still lay with the West.

He was consigned to an extremely comfortable flat and a modest pension, and set out regularly each morning for the public library as he had once gone to the office. He conceived the idea—one can see his diplomatic career may have suggested it—of a dictionary of synonyms, and laboured on a lexicon of saying the same thing in different ways. But his real consolation in the last seven years of his life was his growing family of grandchildren, of whom there were now four. Tanya and 'Elephant' had produced Masha and Vera, and Misha and Flara had a son and a daughter, Pavel and Nina. The flat was large enough for all three families—ten people in all. Maxim

[1] *Washington Post*, 24 January 1952. Litvinov's last diplomatic phase is very fully dealt with in Vojtech Mastny, 'The Cassandra in the Foreign Commissariat', *Foreign Affairs*, January 1976. See also the survey of Litvinov's diplomatic career as a whole by Harry L. Roberts in *The Diplomats 1919–1939*, ed. Craig and Gilbert, 1953; and Cyrus L. Sulzberger, *A Long Row of Candles. Memoirs and Diaries*, 1969.

adored the very small children, tossing them in the air and making much of them: it was as children grew older that his tendency to discipline and austerity began to appear.

Ivy did not carry out her plan of resuming a separate existence teaching Basic English where 'they' sent her, on condition she had a room of her own. Maxim was now dependent on her, not she on him. No longer did he come home from the Kremlin after a hard day and madden her with his formal cry of 'I love you' as he crossed the threshold. She supplemented the pension with translating work and devoted herself to his comfort and defence with an almost dragon-like determination. Men no longer attracted her. On that side of her nature the fondness for her own sex, which had been noticeable even in her schooldays, now predominated. Nearly all her friends were women expatriates of about her own age.

About a year after his final retirement Maxim received an unlooked-for invitation to a reception at the Kremlin. He detected that a mistake had been made in his old office's hospitality department and commented caustically that it was most important to keep lists up to date; but he was unable to resist the chance of a last public appearance, especially as he was no longer required to wear uniform. At the party he found himself talking to Alexandre Werth, then correspondent of the *New Statesman*, who inquired politely how it felt to be in retirement. The reply was that it was pleasant enough, especially as one no longer had to work for superiors who 'refused to believe that goodwill could be the basis of any policy'. At that moment, so Werth records, Vishinsky passed by scowling at the guest who had been invited by mistake.

It is a remark which might easily have fallen from many retired senior officials, dissatisfied with what they could see of the work of their successors; yet in the case of Litvinov, and given the circumstances in which it was uttered, it can be taken almost as an epitaph on his career. There was no necessity for him to say it, and it was a dangerous thing to say. It marks him as a man of independent opinions, and refutes the most damaging criticism that can be made of him—that he was a foil, a man acting a role he did not believe when it pleased his masters to put him on the stage, a cog, or perhaps a gear, in a carefully managed, horrendous machine pursuing consistent, carefully calculated aims of subversion and aggression.

For various reasons, one of them being his marriage, we have a more intimate, clear picture of Litvinov than of any other prominent

*17 The diplomat—
Maxim, 1943.*

18 Ivy as music teacher in the 1960s.

19 *(top) The exile returns—Ivy in London, 1972.*

20 *(centre) Ivy and Masha.*

21 *(left) Ivy at home in Hove.*

Bolshevik. That he put a fair face on the atrocious reality of Stalin's regime is a heavy charge against him. But the impartial reviews of his outlook and achievements show a consistent theme which he pursued regardless of the political conditions within Russia. It was based on carefully accumulated information and patient analysis. As Roberts writes:

> His ability to detect the major trends in the 1930s and to anticipate the course of events indicates an extraordinary understanding of that decade and his speeches describe in mood and in content the tasks facing the world today in its efforts to check the new danger of Soviet expansion.

The theme of the policy itself is expressed thus by Mastny:

> His was the mature notion that Soviet power and influence could best be promoted by cultivating areas of common interest by positive, albeit carefully circumscribed, collaboration with the West.

Even his years of retirement were overshadowed by the possibility of denunciation and trial, which came nearest, perhaps, in 1951 when one of his successors, Lozovsky, was shot. Maxim nevertheless followed the development of Soviet foreign policy with increasing disapproval. Much of his time was taken up in elaborating a long memorandum to Stalin which analysed and commented on what he called 'Molotov's errors'. After his death it was delivered to the dictator, and later came to the desk of Khruschchev, who is said to have been impressed by it.

A single letter survives out of the many Ivy wrote to Maxim during the thirty-six years of married life, and it belongs to this last phase. It is written in August 1950 from Sudak, a seaside place where she had taken their grand-daughter Masha on holiday. She had been reading Pepys's diaries—'You would enjoy them'—but preferred to devote herself to *Clarissa Harlowe* 'which you will never read I'm sure, though no book was more popular in Russia in XIX Century'. It is a long, rather contented letter full of balconies and bathing and happy descriptions of the little girl—'plucky in the sea, I think she will soon be swimming. Eats marvellously, sleeps splendidly, and would be a model child, but whenever strangers appear she becomes a little beast.' It ends, 'Love and Love! Be sure to write about yourself, your doings, your feelings (no, that you have never done, and never will, I'm sure).'

Soon after this Maxim became ill, and after several heart attacks died triumphantly in his bed on 31 December 1951. In the final crisis he gasped out some words to Ivy, which were devoid of endearment, but heartfelt: 'Englishwoman, go home!'

If he had lived a little longer there can be little doubt that, old and ill though he was, he would have been a victim of the anti-Jewish, anti-medical persecution known as the 'Doctors' Plot', which Stalin was preparing during the last year of his life. One of Ivy's first words to Tanya on Maxim's death was an almost exultant: 'They didn't get him.'

Nevertheless they came that very evening of his death to examine, and at their discretion remove, the late Comrade Litvinov's papers. The searchers—Narkomindel officials—may have had orders not to press matters too hard, for after a superficial inspection they indicated that the hour was late.They would return first thing next morning. If in the meantime there was anything of a purely personal nature that Ivy Walterovna wished to lay aside. . . . The search next day was much more thorough, and all Maxim's papers were removed, including two envelopes addressed to Stalin personally. One of these contained Maxim's memorandum on foreign policy. In the other he recalled his long and numerous services, and commended Ivy and his children to Stalin's favourable consideration.

The funeral was obscure and perfunctory. Few people were present to hear a Narkomindel official read a brief account of the deceased man's services in terms of the posts he had occupied. An old lady came up to Ivy afterwards and whispered her indignation that more had not been said; but he had only just evaded a much worse fate.

'Nothing ever made more impression on me', Ivy said later, 'than the arrest of the doctors.' 'It is now firmly established', *Pravda* declared a month after Maxim's death, 'that these murderous healers, these desecrators of the banner of science and the honour of their sacred calling, have long been the hired agents of foreign intelligence.' An atmosphere of rumour and hysteria began to spread among the population in general. Attendance at clinics and surgeries began to fall away. Ivy tried to persuade the father of a sick child who lived in a neighbouring flat to take his son to see the doctor: 'A look of fear crept into his pale eyes. "We can't do that. You never know what these doctors might do to your children. They give them germs so that they die." ' Though doctors were the immediate targets, there could be no doubt, as the propaganda developed, that the aims went far wider. Scientists, Jews, every taint of 'Western' influence, were within the scope of the proposed purge.

The year 1952 was a nightmare of misery made worse by the deaths of several old friends—Rothstein, Surits and Kollontai all followed Maxim to the grave. Kollontai was an especial loss to Ivy, and during her last illness they had seen a great deal of each other:

> Once on my way to the country I called in at Kollontai's flat for some reason. The spring . . . cold and bright . . . and for some reason the door open and everything very quiet. I just opened the door and I saw the little foyer they used as a dining room—there were four women sitting at an exquisitely appointed table—very daintily eating, very quiet. Kollontai in her wheel chair. Lovely flowers and a cat they were fond of.

Ivy and Kollontai had sworn to each other that whichever of them died first the other would not go to the funeral. But Ivy broke that vow.

The 'plot' died with Stalin, almost exactly a year after Maxim's death. Ivy and her friends expected things to grow worse, not better, and the dictator's funeral was an extension of the nightmares over which he had presided.

> The funeral [Ivy wrote] brought catastrophe to hundreds of men and women in the streets. People surged into the capital from all over Russia, and the streets could not contain them. The mourning marchers crushed one another to death in the Red Square on the way to the little temple where, it was believed, Stalin's undecaying corpse would lie for ever side by side with Lenin.

The Kremlin guides, showing the Tsar's state carriage, used to describe how the hysterical crowd had been crushed beneath its jewel-encrusted wheels. After Stalin's funeral the body of the son of one of Ivy's friends who had been lost in the crowd (but later turned up) was sought among the dead piled in a police wagon. But then the worst was over. The Doctors were released.

Under the new dispensation Ivy was allowed to stay on in her flat and was granted a small pension which moved her to recall the fable of the lion's reply to the crane who had removed a bone from the lion's throat and then asked for a fee: 'You're lucky I didn't bite your head off.' Khrushchev later awarded a modest increase, for she still fell within the category of person about whom even the smallest matter went to the highest level of authority.

After the brief interregnum of Malenkov came a rather more tolerant era. The worst enormities of Stalin were revealed and repudiated, the survivors of his persecutions began to trickle back from the camps where they had spent almost two decades, and Ivy found herself meeting once more several ghosts from the past. Among them was Phyllis Klishko, with whom she again became quite friendly for a time. Another was a former Sverdlovsk pupil who had been consigned to a camp for no better reason than that she had been born in Shanghai:

Darling Ivy Walterovna! [ran the letter] You want to know more about me, but there's so much to tell, that all the paper in Karaganda won't be enough to write and tell you everything.

Yes, my darling, twenty years have passed by and even more.

There is a lot to tell, but I'm afraid a part has to be told, and not on paper.

. . . I have been ill for seventeen years. In 1954 28 August I returned to the living land again.

. . . People are surprised that we can still want to have a nice life after all the health is left behind. But we fight for life because so much was lost just because of somebody's mistake. Yes, after 17 years they called me out and let me free and said that *it was a mistake*, well how do you like a mistake like that?? Oh darling! There is so much to tell you. I feel like flying straight away to Moscow to see you, but I suppose I'll have to wait till summer time. . . .

Such letters, of which Ivy must have had several, raise the question of her attitude to the cruelty and injustice of the government under which she had lived. She felt sorry for, and helped, its individual victims. Later she came to admire the stand that her grandson Pavel took against the communist autocracy of his day. She held the compromisers and placemen (such as Voroshilov), who saved their posts and their lives by compliance, in particular contempt. But she was not the person ever to make a general condemnation of what she had never generally supported. Years of exposure to peril had hardened a kind of shell which she may have inherited from her Anglo-Indian ancestors. She was not an unfeeling person, but she had spent her life in a dangerous country, and was not the one to feel guilt or remorse.

This trait was tested not long after Maxim's death when for the first time in her life she had a personal encounter with the security authorities. Summoned to the Lubyanka, she was led through a number of menacing wire-meshed corridors, whose purpose in preventing sudden suicide was casually mentioned to her; and was then confronted with the papers she had last seen many years earlier, when she deposited them on Maxim's behalf in a New York bank. Were they genuine? she was asked. What was their history? What did she know of them? At first she boldly denied all knowledge, but her opponents clearly knew too much. After a family conference she resolved to tell the simple truth in the hope that nothing more would be heard of it. And nothing was. It was not in the interest of the security service that it should be.

She devoted herself to reading and writing, to her grandchildren, and to cats, and accepted the approach of old age. Her letters begin to be signed 'Gammer' or 'Old Ivy', and perhaps she took pleasure in growing eccentricity. When she travelled she had a set of boards with her, which could be set up as a makeshift desk wherever she could find a chair with arms. By now (usually in association with Tanya) she was producing translations from the Russian at the rate of almost one a year,[2] and she read omnivorously. Looking back in 1955 she found she had in the last few years read the whole of Lockhart's life of Scott; the autobiographies of Havelock Ellis and Edward Carpenter; the letters of Keats, Wordsworth, Dostoyevsky, Henry James and Charles Lamb; Alpers's life of Katherine Mansfield; a good deal of MacNeice and Auden; and 'lots of Mark Twain I wouldn't have dreamt of reading but for the book famine'.

Trollope and Jane Austen were her constant companions, and she had now come to prefer the first. 'Trollope', she scribbled, 'was always disarmed by the spectacle of suffering. Jane is never caught without her stiletto.' The novelists of her own early days were another matter. Very few authors could be admitted except D. H. Lawrence, Henry James and Gissing. 'Perhaps that's what youth is for,' she once said about the severity of her choice in this area—'for readng books

[2] Makarenko's *The Road to Life* (1951); Pushkin's *Tales of Ivan Belkin* (1954) and *Dubrovsky* (1955); Turgenev's *Three Short Novels* (1955); Dostoyevsky's *My Uncle's Dream* (1958); Gorky's *Literary Portraits* (1959) and *On Literature* (1960); Posensky's *The Simpleton* (1959); and an anthology of Chekhov's short stories.

one will never read again. And age is for reading books one couldn't read in youth.' Galsworthy she regarded with particular contempt.

Among more modern authors she was prepared to have idols: Graham Greene she admired, but far above him she placed Henry Green and Adrian Bell. She even got hold of a copy of Henry Miller's *Tropic of Cancer*, and conceded he showed talent; but of his claim 'Today I am proud to say I am *inhuman*! That I have nothing to do with creeds and machines . . . I am *inhuman*! I say it with a mad hallucinated grin and I will keep on saying it though it rains crocodiles!' she commented:

> Well it may rain crocodiles any day now, but if the rain ever stops and if the world survives, we may be sure people will spend their time groping back to human society, human values, human culture, despite mad hallucinated grins, till the next time it rains crocodiles.

This shows Ivy at her best. She could seem cruel and be inconsiderate, but she was far more interested in individuals (including herself) than in general statements, postures, and abstractions.

She became something of a wanderer in Russia. Though she kept her flat in Moscow, she spent months at a time in country and seaside towns and in her wanderings became an intent, almost too minute observer of the scenes and people she encountered. As an elderly widow she was acquiring a background of ordinary Soviet existence which she had never known in her married life of cocooned and perilous privilege. The extortions and peculiarities of seaside landladies, the shabby topography of provincial towns and resorts, conversations, incidents, notes on the relationships between fellow lodgers in boarding houses where she spent time: all these are abundant in her letters and memoranda. And she is always one of the characters herself. She made two little girls recite in unison a poem by Nekrassov; describes the scene minutely, and reflects that 'Natasha and Anya will remember all their lives how the old Englishwoman loved this poem.' She sits on the beach talking to her grand-daughter in English, to which the child replies in Russian. 'Why does she speak to you in Russian?' asks a woman sitting near, 'and you answer her in Jewish?' Jewish, Ivy reflects, is in Russian almost equivalent to foreign.

Though now poor and unprivileged she was still something of a celebrity. People deferred to her as the widow of the former minister, and some of Maxim's memoirs, including his own description of his escape from Kiev prison and his early association with Lenin, were published in magazines. Old pupils of the Basic days continued to appear:

A little dumpling of a woman, bright-eyed, frizzy-haired, zebra-clad, came diffidently up to me today. 'Ivy Walterovna, is it really you? And how is Tanya?' Turns out to be someone from the days I used to give Basic English lessons in the foreign library. She looks as if she ought to be wearing a mob cap, a bustle, and a fichu, and bring in a decanter of the Vicar of Wakefield's gooseberry wine on a tray, or be some little woman at a ball in the Assembly Rooms, somebody Emma thought would do very nicely for Mr Elton. But she turns out to be a very swell translator. . . .

Even here turns up the almost inevitable recourse to the models she admired in literature. In an English-speaking country she might have developed wider interests, but as it was she became a kind of natural critic, entirely uninfluenced by either Western chic or Soviet ukase. She had to depend on a few shelves of books of her own, the chance findings of second-hand bookshops, and a public library system where the offerings in English literature were sketchy and unpredictable. She never read reviews, but with a kind of autocratic authority laid down for herself and for anyone who would listen the correct merits of English prose writers.

Thus were laid the foundations of the stories she would write in her eighth decade. Since Maxim's death, indeed since her return from America, she had written almost nothing original, and published nothing except translations. It was a new, widow's apprenticeship, extending from her sixty-third year, when Maxim died, until 1960, when she was seventy. '"Compatible"', she austerely informed Tanya with all the authority of Fowler, 'is so spelt, and not with an "a". The variation from a similar word such as "capable" must simply be learned, or better still looked up if one is not sure.' 'Many familiar words', she noted one night in a seaside villa, 'were invented by great men such as Bentham, who coined "international", and Carlyle, who was responsible for "environment".'

From being untidy and rather indifferent to her surroundings, Ivy was becoming houseproud, and surveyed her Moscow flat with complacency:

I think there could not be a more beautiful room than my room, though I need a couple of decent chairs and better book-shelves. . . . Into this room has gone the experience of a lifetime which has among other things taught me to eschew *all* ornaments. I never was one for much in that way, but now it has whittled down to—nothing. This is perhaps negative. . . . I have learned staying here and there that nothing suits me and soothes me like beautiful curtains and I have beautiful pebbly surface blue-grey curtains at window and concealing bed-niche. I have learned that curtains must fall from inumerable rings with no pulley-nonsense and no lambrequins. . . .

Even as seventy approached she was not beyond the reach of passion, but now it was unhesitatingly homosexual. She made a note on 'Thursday 5th or 6th or I know not what of Feb 1959', from which it is clear that she was having an affair with a woman younger than herself. 'Fantastic day ended. Wild, sweet love. My only desire—that any moment of it should go on for ever. Any—doesn't matter which. With her, not so simple.'

Yet only a few months earlier she had had a serious heart attack. Ivy embroidered and romanced even in scribbles meant only for herself. Almost certainly, at the time she scribbled that, the passion was beginning to fade. Her mind was on something very different. Maxim's last words had made a deep impression on her, and surely in her native England she would still find a welcome, arouse interest in her strange adventures, perhaps even find the literary recognition she could never hope for in Russia. She had indeed sought permission to visit England already, but it had been refused, and at least one old English friend (Desmond Bernal) visiting Russia had been told she was not available, for the invisible curtain which extends to all who have held, or have connections with those who have held, high office in the Soviet Union had quietly extended itself to her also.

In 1959 her application to go to England was renewed, supported this time by a letter from her sister Letty urging Ivy's presence on compassionate grounds, for Letty was not at all well. Such a matter had to be submitted to the highest authority—Khrushchev himself, whose judgement at that stage may well have been swayed by Desmond Bernal, whom she saw for the first time in many years just about this time. However that may be, Khrushchev decided to remove the invisible curtain in relation to Ivy. 'Litvinova', he wrote (according to Ivy), 'is not political. Approved.' So early in 1960 she was permitted to set off for her native land for a stay of six months. She had not been there, even for the briefest of visits, for more than a quarter of a century.

14

Englishwoman Goes Home

Ivy gave no advance warning of her intention to visit England in the occasional postcards which I and others received, her heavily looped handwriting squeezed round gaudy examples of Soviet philately to ask for verification of a literary reference, or to criticize the style of articles in *The Times Literary Supplement*. She simply drove straight from the airport (where, as she afterwards admitted, she was a little disappointed not to find a single reporter) to a small hotel and began ringing up old acquaintances with the aid of a telephone directory which she was delighted to find in the hall 'hanging from hooks and swinging forward obligingly to the touch'. It was a treat for anyone who had long lived in a country where telephone directories were regarded as restricted, if not actually secret documents.

To an amazed Martin Secker, now old and growing blind, she announced herself as 'the Questing Beast'—the title of her second novel which he had published nearly half a century earlier. Her call to our house simply began 'It's Ivy' without any introduction or surname, in an extraordinary contralto which combined the upper-class intonation of the generation before last with a distinctly foreign tang. We then lived in a small house in Hampstead from which, with a growing family, we were very soon to move. For several weeks after her first arrival she stayed with us.

I had not seen her since I was at school, and had maintained only a frail link out of consciousness of Ivy's strange, obviously perilous situation, my own vague memories, and my certainty that my mother would have maintained it. I had never visited the Soviet Union, and was never likely to. I had ceased to have any sympathy with its system during the trials of the 1930s when I was still at school. Ivy was primarily a figure from my childhood, but also a kind of family connection who lived in a distant and dangerous country. I knew, however, through family tradition, about the modest bank account which Maxim had opened when he visited London for the last time, in 1936, to attend the funeral of King George V. What I could not have imagined was that for all those years, to her and her family, we had been thought of as old, familiar friends.

Her hair was as abundant as I remembered it, but as white as snow from the steppes; her figure, though under control, distinctly bulky; the chief impression one of extraordinary vitality. She filled our little Hampstead house. There was a torrent of words, and a longing to communicate, together with a kind of canniness which was the more difficult to penetrate because it was not natural, but had been acquired subconsciously as a kind of camouflage.

Years of diplomatic life superimposed on an upper middle-class education before the First World War, made her appear inconsiderate in the increasingly egalitarian England of 1960. Her eyes were dark and flashing and her whole style imperious. Suggestions she did not care for were dismissed with a sweep of the hand and a toss of the head, and for the first time in my life I felt that servants were a necessity of life which our house unfortunately lacked. It made no difference that such dismissive gestures were often reinforced by some word from communist vocabulary such as 'opportunist' or 'speculator', since these were frequently applied to persons venerated in the Soviet Union. They might just as well have been 'not out of the top drawer', or 'not quite the clean potato'.

She seemed in excellent health for a woman of seventy, whose life had not been an easy one; and in fact she was to live vigorously for another fourteen years. But only a few months before her journey to England she had experienced renewed spasms of heart trouble. Some scraps of a journal she kept about it survives. 'Em here. Lay flat and let her talk and my fears pass over me. Night O.K. but silent decision about packing for going to England. 2 suitcases filled . . .' Her heart worried her, but it made her all the more eager to go.

She walked round her old haunts in the little lanes at the top of Hampstead and was delighted to find them so reassuringly the same, except that there were too many cars, the trees had grown taller, and Golden Square had been asphalted. London seemed full of 'universal benevolence, marvellous accents, homely streets', and when she asked a man the way, 'I thought he was putting on a music-hall turn for me, I couldn't *believe* it was just being natural. Lean, clean, thin-nosed, thin-lipped, what a *thick* confiding London accent, what a cock to his cap, what kindly leering eyes and elegant thumb!' But he was one of the few that had a cap to cock. The general hatlessness of the population shocked her.

She would put up with very little in the way of comfort: her privileged life and remote standards declared themselves in other ways. Toast, for instance. However unpropitious the circumstances there must be toast for breakfast; and also for tea. The simplest gadget (such as a toaster) she regarded with hostile and invincible incomprehension. Her style was a kind of queenly impracticability justified by the modesty of her demands which—modest though they certainly were—could not always and easily be satisfied.

I have said she was cautious, and in the early months of her stay she was particularly wary about meeting journalists or Russians: 'A Russ-ian woman,' she exclaimed scornfully, when I suggested introducing her to a Russian friend of mine (actually the daughter of a prince), 'I don't want to meet any Russ-ian women.' Nevertheless she had much to say about the circumstances of Maxim's death, and the perilous nights after his fall when headlamps from the road outside swept their bedroom window on a passing bend, and mercifully never stopped outside the house.

Her access to Maxim's ancient nest-egg was arranged with comparatively little difficulty, and she thereby became mistress of slightly less than £300, which she managed with great care, and even in due course added to by her own efforts. It enabled her to move, first to a small hotel in Bloomsbury, and then to a room of her own in Handel Street, nearby, where she spent the next nine months in delighted independence.[1]

Several of her contemporaries were still alive and vigorous: Peter Kapp, the artist, her first boyfriend; and Desmond Bernal, one of her last; Ivor Brown, Francis Meynell. But these interested her less than the literary figures she had come to worship, Henry Green and Adrian Bell.

Ivy had learned enough from Maxim about diplomacy never to tell anyone everything that she was up to, so large segments of her life in

---

[1] Before doing so she had called on Eleanor Farjeon, in her Hampstead mews, whom she found 'quite alone, dying every now and then, but never quite bringing it off, corrects proofs by day and dresses for dinner . . . Thought she might love to have me in downstairs room, but she showed no sign (rightly, I consider).'

London were almost unknown to me at the time. One such was her acquaintance with Manya Harari, who was then working for the Harvill Press, an affiliate of Collins, and was among several literary people who saw in Ivy the opportunity for a major book of memoirs about Soviet life.

Manya had been born in Russia and had already been known to Ivy before her visit to England, for Ivy's friend Chukovsky had a drawing of the three Berenson sisters (Berenson was Manya's maiden name) by the poet Mayakovsky. Though she had left Russia as a child she was, perhaps just the kind of 'Russ-ian woman' Ivy's caution told her to avoid. But Manya fascinated her:

> She disturbs my diaphragm too much for me really to enjoy serious conversation with her. Keep thinking how beautiful she is. And then when we talk we cannot be really sympathetic. She is a Catholic. She doesn't understand how much that matters. . . . Cannot forget what a dark reactionary power this is, charm they never so sweetly. . . . Of course I know that I am mystically inclined myself, but I only enjoy it. I never expect to lean on it. I never expect anything but a trance of joy at small beauties, more than itself. Just happy to know I still have the strength of such joy. . . .
>
> Oh dear, the more we have serious literary talks, the cooler my blood. I keep seeing her beauty every now and then with a thrill, but less and less. Begin to understand men who don't want intellectual mistresses. She *stirred* me so and now hardly at all. Liked her in her shrine . . . and then after all her whole attitude is that of a publisher. She made suggestions for dictating various anecdotes about the celebrated that have about as much to do with me as a gossip column would. Certainly if I can give anything in a book it must be only the feeling that pours out of me. And how often none does. The moment we discuss a publishable book everything evaporates.

History was in an ironical mood when it provided Ivy with an itching pen and a keen eye and sent her to observe from a vantage point some of the most extraordinary phases through which the human race has passed, and then muffled her with a passion for English literature and the primacy of her own feelings. But Manya was more successful than anyone else in persuading Ivy to come out of her shell and record something of what she had seen.

She got her to make tapes, first about her early life, and then about the Soviet Union. How many were made, and where the originals are if they still exist, I do not know; but there are considerable transcripts from them among Ivy's papers, in many cases corrected and improved in Ivy's own unmistakable hand. They deal, among other things, with her early married life, Maxim's infidelities, Ivy's friendship with Kollontai, and the dark period of the Doctors' Plot.

Ivy lived in a modest bed-sitter, but very soon her sagging clothes and untidy hair had been reformed in favour of a smart, even soignée figure and a neat permanent wave. She compared herself favourably with her younger sister Letty, and began enjoying herself very much. 'He was marvellous,' she wrote home about a lunch with Henry Green and his wife: 'she was marvellous. I was marvellous.' She discussed Dostoyevsky with William Sansom, and began placing little pieces in the magazines, which pleased her very much and helped to keep her little ship financially afloat as well.

A fragmentary diary she kept at this time shows how completely she had abandoned Maxim's political faith. Writing of her woman friend in Moscow she reflected:

> She is, or was, a Red, and she can't understand that political disagreements should come between us. Then she doesn't take her convictions seriously, that's all. I do, and cannot have a deep relationship with a person who disagrees with me on the most important thing of all. But one can fall in love unfortunately.

But what *was* 'the most important thing of all'? Ivy, as Khrushchev himself had said, was 'not political', and he was right. Ivy not only held no political opinions, she was against politics. That was the source of her political disagreement with her Moscow friend, and that was 'the most important thing of all'. She hated politics with all the hatred of one who has seen their worst consequences.[2]

So she devoted herself to the observation of the people and things that came immediately under her eye—the man upstairs she thought was beating his wife; the kitten; the sink:

> Watched drop forming under rim of tap for about five minutes. Forming gradually, purposefully, so clear, so strong, in the certain

---

[2] 'She couldn't—couldn't, you see, take it [the falsity of the Doctors' Plot]. That it was sheer evil, you see. It was hard for her to. She longed to be very Soviet and the rest of it. She really does want to be. And you know, you can't be. No, no, you can't be' (*Tape*).

knowledge that when it is fully formed it must drop . . . didn't think I had looked away but suddenly, with no apparent movement, with no sound, the drop disappeared.

Then there was her music pupil—a small source of income:

She's having treatment all the time to get down her weight— beautiful, slightly too mature arms and legs, nice, rather broad waist, but neck running up into cheeks . . .

Her ticket of leave had originally been for six months only, but after a number of disagreeable interviews with Soviet consular officials, which they must have feared almost as much as she disliked them, her right to return was prolonged until January 1961. The suspicion must have crossed their minds that she never intended to return at all, since as a native of Britain she was entitled to stay there.

The second six months were happier and more productive than the first, and she was beginning to settle down to what she had always longed for, a literary life. With her pen, slowly though it moved, she managed to bring more than £500 to augment Maxim's old bank account, and placed a story called 'That Uncertain Feeling' with the *New Statesman*. A kind of liberation was going on which, though never completed, would permit her to be more creative in her eighth decade than she had been since her third.

She made the acquaintance of Dennis Cohen, then senior partner in the Cresset Press. Dennis was a massive man, about the same age as Ivy, or perhaps a little younger, tall, with a face like an ancient Assyrian. Being possessed of ample means he had no need to run a publishing business, but did so out of love for civilized life and desire for a congenial occupation. He lived in an impressive house which he had built in Old Church Street, Chelsea, and filled with objects in exquisite taste, including a collection of Tang horses. He was a widower. His much younger wife, whom he had discovered on a chorus line in New York and put through medical school to create her as a psychiatrist, had died tragically of cancer. He was a proud, lonely, noble man, and enough of a publisher to see he might get a book out of Ivy, and perhaps a partner.

I escorted her to dinner in Chelsea, the other guests being John and Ernestine Carter, and the friendship between the widow and the widower developed. I have no doubt that Ivy seriously considered that Dennis Cohen could offer—was offering—a great deal: comfort; a place in the literary world; a distinguished, prosperous husband; security, even devotion. It is a credit to her that she declined all this on a *mélange* of practical and emotional objections. She would be cut off from her children in the Soviet Union. Then there were other reasons—Dennis, however devoted, would still be interested in her memoirs which were to her like a child that could not be delivered, an endless labour, something whose birth was surrounded with an impenetrable mixture of longing and resistance, conscious and subconscious.

So she stayed on in Handel Street, with its worn carpet and antiquated gas stove with the hood and fire-clay bars she loved, and a faded curtain that hid the saucepans under the sink. Ilya Ehrenburg, who was in England at the time, considered she was living the garret life of a student, and there was something of the dash of recovered youth in her, even though she was seventy.

More than once she called on Tanya to join her, and if that had happened she would almost certainly have defied the Soviet authorities and stayed in England. Maxim's dying advice had registered. She neither cared about nor understood hierarchies and bureaucracies, and although she knew well enough what Soviet authority could do, the habit of simply treating Russian officials as foreigners in uniform, of sending for the manager, of disregarding their treasured procedures, was too deep-seated for eradication, and had a disturbing effect which more emotional resistance could hardly have achieved.

She even went so far as to write a personal letter to Khrushchev seeking permission for Tanya to come to England. Tanya's telegram on hearing the news was opaque—'I got your letter don't know about him here's hoping love.' The profession of ignorance was justified. Permission was withheld.

Return to the Soviet Union had to be accepted. It was 'back to barracks', as she said to a shocked English communist. In December, as her prolonged stay was drawing to a close, she gave a long interview to Jack Lambert for the *Sunday Times*. It clearly had those at home in mind—that is to say, it left much unsaid. Its purpose in the longer term was to leave behind an impression of her determination not to lose contact with her native land and her resolve not to stop writing. In January 1961, when she left, her bank balance shows a credit of £290. 16s. 3d. despite a heavy cheque for £109 14s. in favour of Gamages and two others to cash for £100 each. Maxim's nest-egg had not been much diminished.

Her year's stay had not achieved all she intended, perhaps, but it had done a great deal. She not only met some old friends but made many new ones, and she had reminded the Western world of her unique existence. Let them think she would one day tell her story. That was not the point. A writer, unknown as yet, even at seventy-one, but a writer still, who for decades had been imbued with English literature in a way the busy English hardly could be—that was the memory she wanted to imprint in England.

Dennis Cohen sent flowers to the airport. They would never meet again. What Ivy took back with her by way of memory, reinforced by her year in England, was a sense that the landmarks had hardly altered, for the changes of the 1960s, which were to transform the landscape of British society, had hardly begun to penetrate the population as a whole, and she returned to a Soviet Union which was on the point of encountering problems which the founders of Soviet communism had not foreseen. The one anxiety of the communist sage Plekhanov, whose authority even Lenin had revered, had been that when all conflicts had been removed by the establishment of a classless society, life would become tedious. He need not have worried. New conflicts were on their way in Soviet society, and in these Ivy and her family, with their odd nucleus of Englishness, were to play a not inconspicuous part.

15

The Eighth Decade

Foreign travel is a privilege in the Soviet Union and Ivy's year in England added considerably to her status. The higher reaches of Soviet society were not, of course, for her—nor were the official literary circles of the Writers' Union. Her friends were mostly women, and mostly English-speaking expatriates like herself, who at one time or another, through idealism or marriage, had found themselves inhabiting the Soviet Union, and now, in their later age, were caught there. Journalists, especially American journalists, on visits to Moscow, sometimes stumbled into this little circle of which Ivy was the centre. But above all she moved easily into the role of a matriarch.

Her family now had a flourishing third generation of three girls and a boy moving to maturity. Of these Pavel Litvinov, the son of Misha and Flara, bore a striking physical resemblance to Maxim, his grandfather; and his sister Nina, and the two daughters of Tanya and 'Elephant'—Masha and Vera—were extremely pretty. None of the family was a member of the Party, and although none of the grandchildren had ever been to England, they regarded it as a promised land, of which their grandmother could give an authentic account: an account which was based on the authority of Richardson, Fielding, Jane Austen, Trollope, and Henry James. It was an England of tea and toast, bacon and eggs, red omnibuses, squires, archdeacons, and literature; of freedom and literature; of diversity and literature. 'Sholokhov!' exclaimed one of the family to an English visitor who thought it might be a congenial subject, 'No, no, we don't read *Sholokhov!*'

For Ivy herself, the year in England seems not only to have stimulated but cleared her mind. She had thought so much about being a writer that finished work had become almost an impossibility for her. Unlike Michelangelo, with his claim to see the statue he proposed inside the block of raw marble waiting to be carved, Ivy created huge blocks of raw material from which she found it infinitely difficult to quarry a detached work of art. Again and again she had launched herself into the same episode, rearranging the words, drafting yet again, retyping and altering, cutting out paragraphs with scissors to paste them in elsewhere, until the whole thing was cast aside for a game of scrabble or lexicon. There are many sheets of her manuscripts on which a passage is struck through in favour of another which hardly differs from it, which is again struck out, only to be followed by another which is almost the same; and there on the back is a list of words extracted with weary ingenuity from 'unavailable' or 'passionate'.

She spent the summer of 1961, the summer after her return from England, at Lielupe, a seaside place on the gulf of Riga, and there she came as close as she ever did to confronting her problems as a writer. She recorded her experience in a diary where egotism, courage, and self-doubt are mingled:

> Everyone (especially in England) wanted me to write a straight autobiography. But I can't see how that can be done. I am only interested in intimate things. . . . I turned to the writing of various short stories that have been in my mind for about forty years. Some I have tried in the course of years to write again and again, without ever being satisfied.

She dreamed she was in a garden of fountains, one of which, the fountain of truth, was denied to her. 'There are one or two things like this, very important, very significant in my own life, and the hardest of all to write about. They turn out banal. Make no impact. What are these things? The Holy Ghost—begging it to come; the Fountain of Truth.'

> What then am I trying to write? I seem to have the amiable intention of proving that all my sorrows, misfortunes, and character defects come from my mother. I imagine that if she had not forced me and sabotaged my true interests I would have been a brisk (perhaps distinguished) professional woman . . . my sex-life, though no doubt complicated and unsatisfactory, would at least have been dignified.

A word from the world of diplomacy floated into her mind. She saw the opposition to her desire to write, to produce finished work, as a 'bloc' (and at the same time a 'block'), 'and only now and then can I get round it, undermine it'.

> I turn again and again to the hard task, with never the reward that I feel I have accomplished anything yet, just believing that this is what I HAVE to do. Nobody asks me to write a book, nobody specially wants me to, and yet there is this feeling of compulsion.

Instead of writing an autobiography, the one book everyone thought she was so well qualified to write, she devoted herself to what she called 'Sorterbiography' in long episodes extracted painfully from accumulated recollection, observation and what might have been, mostly harking back to her childhood and youth. 'Now what am I going to write? Still waiting for Mother to Ring the Bell?'

Freud, whom she so much admired, would have said she was punishing herself for the sins of her childhood; and she did betray some symptoms of conscious remorse, though it tended to stop short even in her private musings.

> There are things I do and don't do that nice people don't and do, and there are holes in my self-respect. I read other people's letters, freely; I don't wash and change my clothes more than I can help. I sort of cheated to help my pupils in exams ('sort of' is good—I corrected their papers after they were sent in). I tell other people's secrets. But it is not these things that torment me now. . . . What torments me is the memory of cruelties. How *could* I have done this, said that? What suffering I have caused.

Naturally she at once absolved herself of all these venial sins. 'Still, I think the HG won't let me down after a life-time of begging.' The Holy Ghost had not done badly for Ivy, all things considered, and he was to do a little more yet. That first year after Ivy's return to the USSR was marked by the twentieth Congress of the party and the dismantling of Stalin. A milder political climate began to prevail, though only for a time.

Ivy was beginning to feel old. From Lielupe she wrote:

> I think I must have come to the last row, a kind of border, not yet the tattered fringe. What seems to make old age different from the rest of life is that expectancy of change is gone from it. It need not

necessarily be hopeless, though it hopes for nothing except to make the best of this last phase. In my case I want to have time to finish my book, if possible, but this isn't exactly a state of hope. It is more active. Then I know, too, that if I don't have time, it won't matter, I shan't know. The great thing is—time is precious because I want to get something done, not something to be spent as peacefully and painlessly as possible, which is another way of waiting for death. I am not *waiting* for death. I am trying to race death. It is death that calmly waits. Which is very confusing because it sounds as if I'm trying to get there as quickly as possible. I suppose what I'm trying to do is I'm trying to cheat death, leave it to catch me up.

Trying, trying, trying, the sense of effort, the rejection of passivity, ring through the passage. Her virtues, like her faults, came from the intenseness of her vitality.

This was the period in which Ivy at last began to find her feet as a writer. There had been 'That Uncertain Feeling' published in the *New Statesman*; and there was another unpublished story of about the same vintage called 'Wet Spring', about two young artists sharing a cottage on the Downs, who quarrelled and made it up. Those who had seen it in England had liked it. She began to turn from the 'Sorterbiography' and its endless excursions to recapture childhood and youth, and add to her portfolio of stories, some with an English setting, but others, more boldly, drawn from Soviet life. It was still a terrible labour, 'cutting out, shuffling, sticking sentences into a different order. Real work.'

The number of stories grew, but they were to remain unknown until friends of the American writer John Cheever, whose stories Tanya had translated, came to Moscow in 1965 and were shown some of them. By then the Litvinov family was involved in matters of a very different kind. During the early 1960s, Pavel, following his father into a scientific career, had passed through university and become a lecturer in physics at the Lomonosov Institute of Chemical Technology; and Vera had married a scientist, Valery Chalidze. As the bracing atmosphere of Khrushchev began to give way to the greyer times of Brezhnev, dissidence began to make its appearance. It was an obscure, amateurish movement, but it affected particularly the new intellectual generation springing from privileged revolutionary families: people who should, according to prediction, have taken their places in the leadership of the communist society whose foundations had now been securely laid. In 1965 small gatherings began, first in Mayakovsky Square, then in Pushkin Square, to pay silent but ironical tribute to the Soviet Constitution whose liberal language that seemed to guarantee every human right had been promulgated in the midst of political trials, purges and the despatch of thousands to gaol, camps and death. The underground paper *The Chronicle of Contemporary Events* began to circulate, and many of those concerned in its circulation were well-born young intellectuals such as Pavel Litvinov and Yakir, the son of a Soviet Marshal shot in Stalin's purges. The age-old pattern of Russian history—intellectual-ized rebellion against a conservative bureaucracy—was reasserting itself.

Ivy was not a Russian intellectual, inheriting the Russian intellectual tradition, but an English intellectual in exile. Her effect on the events which followed was indirect and even unintentional. But her indifference to the claims of authority and her unassimilated character had a certain influence on her family, and in 1968, when Pavel was arrested for demonstrating against the invasion of Czechoslovakia I had a postcard from her referring enthusiastically but anonymously to 'the hero in the house'. She was proud of her grandson and sympathetic to his protest—not on any doctrinal ground but because it was her nature, and she felt the whole Soviet hierarchy ineffably oppressive and dreary. Old and cautious, she was committed to her literary career, and was busy quarrying stories from mountains of over-corrected manuscript. Through the meeting with John Cheever's friends her stories had made landfall with Rachel Mackenzie of the *New Yorker*. 'Sowing Asphodel', the first of Ivy's stories to appear in that magazine, was published in 1966, the year after the first demonstrations in Mayakovsky Square.

'Sowing Asphodel' is a homesick story whose scene is an upper middle-class English interior with a central grandmotherly character clearly based on Ivy herself, but wickedly christened 'Amabel'. It is a piece of self-expression, but it has the economy and internal strength for which she strove. Its riddle of an adolescent son (modelled on Pavel) who disappears and as mysteriously returns, is left unsolved, but every detail contributes to an atmosphere and an interplay within a family which is recaptured in a kind of winning conviction.

The thought of escape must by this time have been beginning to cross her mind. Long ago Stalin, in conversation with Maxim, had said in reply to some question about foreign policy, 'It is not for me to judge, Maxim Maximovitch—you are sitting by the window and you can see.' What could be seen from her window was becoming more and more attractive, and the stories were crowding into the *New Yorker*. She had now been in Russia for more than forty years, with one spell of home leave. She wanted to lay her bones in England.

'Farewell to the Dacha' appeared in 1967, a gentle and vivid picture of suburban life in Russia and a scene she already did not expect to see again. It was followed in 1968, the year of Pavel's arrest and trial, by another short piece in a Russian setting, 'Babushka', and what was in effect a first instalment of her 'Sorterbiography' under the title of 'She Knew She Was Right'.

'Babushka', the story of the death of a grandmother, is one of Ivy's best. It is economical, vivid, even dramatic, and unlike most of her work it does not draw obtrusively on personal experience. 'She Knew She Was Right', however, introduces us to the childhood of Ivy (Eileen in the story) at the time of her mother's widowhood and choice of a second husband, who proves to be the detested Sandy—he is even allowed to retain his real name. There is a twist into fiction at the close, when Wyn, the mother, and her two children visit the rejected suitor some time afterwards and discover what a mistake it would have been for Wyn to choose him: but on the whole this story, distilled from many accounts Ivy made of that part of her life, could have been entitled 'What Happened When Mother Rang the Bell'.

Another long episode from her 'Sorterbiography' already existed, and had been in existence since 1966 when she had contemplated publishing it abroad under the title 'Litvinov's Wife'. I was indeed involved in placing it in a London periodical, but for reasons she never wholly disclosed, Ivy suddenly decided to withdraw it. The text is not quite the same as the long piece describing her strange courtship and marriage with Maxim ('Mr Belkin') which was published in the *New Yorker* in November 1969. The earlier version is much more openly autobiographical and contains a great deal more about the details of their meeting and the ripening of their love affair: the Eders appear in this earlier version; so do the Klishkos; and so does my mother Catherine as Ivy's closest friend at the time.

'Call It Love', as she decided to entitle the *New Yorker* version, is a somewhat fictionalized account; but even if the words of the dialogue it reports were never actually spoken, they convey very closely what must have happened:

She says you're a political émigré.

And what do you know about political émigrés?

I've read Prince Kropotkin's *Memoirs of a Revolutionist* and I've got a Socialist uncle and aunt.

And are you a Socialist?

Sort of. That's why I left home, really. I couldn't stand the atmosphere.

Too reactionary? he suggested.

That's it! Reactionary! she echoed radiantly. My mother's quite broad-minded—she believes all politicians mean well, and it doesn't matter much whether they're liberals or conservatives. But my step-father's awfully reactionary. . . .

All the caution, all the twinkle that so attracted even Litvinov's opponents are in the portrait of Mr Belkin: his insistence on proper form, his preference for business English, his insight into the characters of those with whom he was dealing. And yet he fell for this naive, enthusiastic girl-clerk in the Prudential at the most important crisis of his career. That is the point of 'Call It Love', which is probably the best, and certainly the most memorable, of Ivy's stories.

Four more stories followed in 1970. All had a Russian background—'Bright Shores', 'Apartheid', 'The Boy Who laughed', and 'Holiday Home'. These, along with 'Babushka', 'Farewell to the Dacha' and one other not then written, make up Ivy's small but unique contribution to English literature—scenes from Soviet life by an informed but wholly detached resident English author.

'Bright Shores', which is the longest of Ivy's Russian stories, is also her most complex—almost too allusive and intense. Its setting is a Soviet seaside resort, municipalized, dreary, yet inspiring transient love affairs between the unhappy men and women who find themselves among its concrete and rubbish, its sunsets and cliffs. It is a kind of Soviet Skegness into which the deprived visitors of Frinton have been compelled. The steep street, the untidy spinneys, the paths which do not quite get you where you mean to go, interplay with personal relationships which are described rather in the way of maps where part of the detailed survey has been completed and the rest left to be explored.

But 'Bright Shores' marks more than an advance in the author's technique or an emancipation from the 'Sorterbiography'. One of its scenes—treated with great sensitiveness—concerns a quite commonplace adulterous lunchtime arrangement which is interrupted, while the woman is still waiting for her lover and preparing the festive meal, by the unexpected arrival of a woman colleague of long ago who has just been released after many years in a prison camp. Tragedy is mixed with comedy in the opening words of the unwelcome visitor: 'There wasn't a single day out there when I didn't ask myself, "Is Malishka all right? I wonder where Malishka is?" And you haven't changed a bit. I'd have known you anywhere.'

The love affair is frustrated, and the former prisoner hovers in the watering place, pathetic and continuously unwelcome, continuously upsetting the trivial sins of those who have suffered less, until a crisis comes:

'Happiness! Nobody thinks *I* have a right to happiness! Vera wouldn't have that clear baby complexion if she'd spent ten years in a camp! Look at you—for all I know you may be older than me, but nobody would think it. *Your* mouth hasn't fallen in through losing all your teeth from scurvy! *You* weren't bald as an egg before you were forty!' Almost frenetically Vera Ivanovna put her hand to her head and pushed back a coarsely made wig exposing an expanse of waxy skull.

Ivy knew those watering places, and had spent many summers of the 1960s sampling their landladies. Much of the society she found there, regrettably, she despised, and a few individuals, rather as an English visitor might have found in an earlier age, were admired for their bearing and their interest. All had to cope with this formidable old lady, propped up in a chair or in bed with a board across her knees, writing and writing and then collapsing with despair into the relaxation of word-games.

The three other stories in this collection—all in a Russian setting—are increasingly critical of her surroundings and sombre in their content. 'The Boy Who Laughed' is a tragedy achieved with unusual skill: the story of a mentally defective boy, his mother and his grandmother, against a background of miserable overcrowding and a strange persistence of the old Russia in the idiot who wanders away from his devoted relatives and finds temporary shelter with an old woman who lives in a shed she has been allowed to retain among a new development of high-rise blocks. The spectre of the concentration camp crosses both the other stories—'Holiday Home' and 'Apartheid'. In the latter, it is the key to the barrier between the respectable Soviet family and their landlady whose child eventually blurts out the word 'Magadan'. 'Magadan's a big town', the paterfamilias says, not lowering his newspaper, 'there must be a permanent population you know.' 'You know very well I'm not talking about the town,' his wife replies.

In 'Holiday Home' the spectre is more transient and concerns only the peripheral character of a distinguished but unproductive woman poet who is inflicted on the miscellany of guests in the ghastly holiday home at Drozdovo where Nina Petrovna finds herself. Nina has some of the defiant characteristics of Ivy (though she is made a Russian) and from the first, when she finds that the rules require the top floor to be occupied before the others, she is in a running dispute with the authorities. Their unconscious hard-heartedness and lack of imagination is the main theme. The girl who receives Nina is not unsympathetically drawn as she comes into the picture but:

> At the first landing she turned and cried out as if Nina Petrovna were half a mile away. 'Don't hurry, Babulya! It's two more flights to your room. I'll wait for you at the top—I simply can't learn to go slowly upstairs. Hold onto the railing, Babulya. Here, let me take your bag!' When Nina Petrovna did not give up her handbag the girl vanished around the turn of the staircase. She was waiting for Nina Petrovna on the top landing, and the moment her head appeared the shrill young voice rang out: 'There she is. Here I am Babulya! Don't hurry, I'm waiting for you!' 'And you don't shout,' said Nina Petrovna; 'I thought it was supposed to be the rest hour.' 'Oh, I pay no attention to that,' said the girl merrily. 'That's for the guests, not for the staff.'

Nina Petrovna finds companionship in the holiday home with a vulgar, bulky, good-hearted woman with whom it is impossible to discuss Galsworthy or Iris Murdoch, let alone Paustovsky or Solzhenitzyn, 'for Olga Vassilievna never read anything but illustrated magazines'. Nina has to admit a mean resentment that she had been so long cooped up with a person so far from her real interests, and feels that she might have cultivated the poet: yet all in all it has been a happy friendship, perhaps above all in its rejection of authority.

Ivy's Russian stories, like almost all Russian stories, are shot through with the presence of authority, but in her case it is authority studied in ordinary society—not clothed in the uniform of the government, the police or the Party. It is the ingrained habit of authority at the periphery, the instinct of anyone entrusted with even an atom of authority, to set themselves at a distance from those they administer.

By 1970, when these stories had been written and many had been published, Ivy was entering her ninth decade, and had made up her mind once more to return to England. It is difficult to say she had made up her mind to stay and leave her bones there. Such pension as she had could not follow her. Misha, and above all Tanya, were still embedded in Russian life. Pavel was still serving his five-year sentence, imposed in 1968, in a place not far from where the Decembrists had been sent by Nicholas I. Her life was not altogether uncomfortable. She had a little flat in Moscow and rented a room for the summer in the country. And she had many visitors. But the helplessness and dependence of the mournful group of broken exiles—English and American—who were her most frequent companions, and above all the image of herself she saw in them, now began to repel her. She had served her time. She had stayed by Maxim, through all his perils, to the end, and in the 1960s had seen his vindication as a loyal servant, with respectful commemorative articles in the Soviet press on his achievements. She began to think of herself as Jonah, swallowed in the whale's belly, but with a mission to preach against Nineveh. She began to make plans to give up Soviet life, and return permanently to her native country.

16

Hove

For so long now Ivy had been at the centre of a kind of do-it-yourself Bloomsbury in Moscow. The audience had not been large—her own family and two devoted American women expatriates who 'went to bed with Virginia Woolf' and hoped some day to escape from the grey world to which youthful enthusiasm had brought them. But as the 1960s went by Ivy's obstinate devotion to literature began to bring its reward. Her *New Yorker* stories enlarged and revived the circle of her friends and admirers abroad, and her own vitality was nowhere near ebbing.

Almost all her new friends were women. By 1968 she had developed a close link with Rachel Mackenzie of the *New Yorker* who had been her contact for the stories, and now began to plan a collection of them in America. Anita Loos wrote enthusiastically that 'your style has a perfume quite unlike any other'. Leona Schechter, the journalist, became another friend—but only for a time. The strongest and most lasting of these new friendships was with Beryl Graves, wife of the poet, who visited Moscow with her husband Robert in 1968.

All these were in one way or another literary contacts, windows on to the world in which Ivy still longed for recognition. There was one other contact of a very different kind. During her last stay in London she had taken refuge, after a difference of opinion with another landlady, in lodgings kept by a widow named Mrs Nellie Seddon. The stay had lasted only a month or two, but the time was enough to allow Mrs Seddon to become deeply attached to Ivy. The series of Mrs Seddon's letters, all of which Ivy kept, stretches down to her death, and ends with a touching note of condolence to her daughter. Mrs Seddon was devoted to Ivy, and Mrs Seddon kept lodgings in London.

Increasingly Ivy thought about Maxim's last words to her—that the Englishwoman should go home. When he had gasped them out she had been puzzled that he should call her by a name he had never used before, but now she saw clearly that even at that moment his mind had been as precise as ever. Not that such departure would be easy. She was not a political figure herself, but Pavel, her grandson, was still in Siberia, a marked man. Neither Misha, his father, nor Tanya as his warm sympathizer, could leave, and in any case both had family commitments of their own; but without family support, especially the support of Tanya, Ivy found it hard to contemplate life at all. Tanya had been her pupil, her confidante, brought up in the worship and experience of English literature.

Her Soviet pension would not be payable in England. Nevertheless Ivy calculated that she would not be destitute. The *New Yorker* royalties had been prudently paid into a London bank, and they were bound to come to something, though she had always been careful not to enquire how much.[1] And there was the possibility that it would not have to last very long—after all, she was not far short of eighty. But Ivy's calculations were not consciously of this sort. She had been an adventurer from the first, and remained one. If she took the decision, fate would look after her, and she might have the chance, a last chance, to live by her pen and enter the 'world unrealized' of English literary life.

The forces of history are not perceptible to those who move under their influence, however much they may think they understand them. In reaching her decision to move westwards Ivy was responding to much the same wind as had carried her grandfather in the same direction from Hungary, and herself eastwards to Russia, and would soon blow most of her family westwards again. But she was aware of her own influence. 'At least one thing I have given you all,' she wrote about this time, '—a feeling for the English language, roots and all.' Indeed, she had done more, and to most of her descendants had handed on a personal outlook very different from Soviet conformity.

In 1971, her eighty-first year, the Viking Press published a collection of her short stories under a title feminized from her favourite Trollope, *She Knew She Was Right*. Although it would not

---

[1] They amounted to about £4,000 (some £17,500 in today's money). But even at that time Ivy's evaluation of the pound was entirely obsolete, and she regarded £4,000 as a considerable endowment.

have occurred to Ivy in that light, the very title was a defiance of the orthodoxy the Soviet Union had inherited from Russian tradition along with the weapons for defending it: among these being not only civil punishment and social ostracism, but literal ejection from the country of the offender's birth. The procedure is quite logical but to the modern Western mind deeply objectionable; and under the Tsars it led to the accumulation of dissidents in exile that organized from without the overthrow of their autocracy.

But Ivy had always been an exile, never quite at home anywhere—not in Westbourne Park or Harrow or Hampstead or in the sugar-merchant's expropriated mansion with a view of the Kremlin. Life in the Soviet Union had reinforced her sense of not belonging; and as a widow she had wandered from one watering-place to another, returning to Moscow for a time, then setting out once more for Lielupe or Sochi, so that she became an inveterate camper and wanderer. She accumulated books, it is true, but even these she did not treasure as objects. They were scribbled in, lost, left behind, given away. Her only true possessions were her papers.

She left the Soviet Union for the last time in July 1972 with leave of absence for six months, but the amount of paper she took with her suggested that the idea of returning was not very strongly held. Though she added to her archive later, the papers she left on her death that had clearly originated from her days in the Soviet Union were alone enough to fill a sizeable trunk. Even if there had been an official patient enough to scrutinize the bulging folders of drafts, stories, letters, scribbled thoughts, chance recollections, fragmentary diaries, all filed in such impenetrable disorder that hardly two successive pages of a single script could be found together, he would have found little to ban. Far more probably, the owner simply swept all officials defiantly aside with one hand, firmly grasping in the other the ancient portable typewriter on which she had taken dictation from Maxim all those years ago.

She made landfall at King's Cross, where Mrs Seddon now lived, and was received with open arms.[2] One of her first acts, the symbolism of which escaped Mrs Seddon, was to release a pet

---

[2] Ivy had endeared herself to Mrs Seddon in a curious way, by convicting her, and then curing her, of racial prejudice. During Ivy's earlier visit she discovered Mrs Seddon had refused a coloured lodger; and proceeded, in Mrs Seddon's absence, to let a room that happened to be vacant to the next coloured applicant that presented himself. In a short time Mrs Seddon became quite converted to the new lodger.

budgerigar from its cage. The bird was never seen again. Having established her headquarters, Ivy—who as usual had given no advance notice of her arrival—proceeded to ring round her friends.

Her appearance had altered since I had last seen her, though she was as vigorous and masterful as ever. She had grown shorter with age, and all attempt to discipline hair or figure had been given up. Her snow-white hair cascaded on to her shoulders to give her the appearance of a sorceress, which was enhanced by her shining dark eyes and a face from which all plumpness had retreated to reveal stern, unforgettable features. The throaty contralto, sometimes endearing, sometimes menacing, was still the same.

For a time she was something of a celebrity, and her reputation was enhanced by the publication, almost simultaneously in Britain and America, of her collected short stories. The American edition was dedicated to Rachel Mackenzie, and so, to Ivy's fury, was the British edition which she had meant to dedicate to Adrian Bell—something on which she had built a great deal, for her admiration of Adrian Bell, with whom she had maintained an active correspondence since her visit in 1960, was infinite. Explanations that the same book could not be dedicated differently on either side of the Atlantic were brushed aside; and it is very probable that her indignation over this led her into declining a very advantageous broadcasting contract which her English publisher had thoughtfully arranged. She was courted and invited, but already the other mood, the hatred of being lionized, was beginning to take possession of her.

Just five months after her arrival in England, the husband of her grand-daughter Vera, Valery Chalidze, travelled with his wife to the United States and began a series of lectures on human rights in the Soviet Union. On 13 December he was called down to the lobby of his New York hotel to see two Soviet consular officials who requested his passport, pocketed it, and offered in return a decree depriving him of his Soviet citizenship. His wife, of course, could return to the Soviet Union if she wished, but he should, they advised, get on as best he could where he was.

This must have strengthened Ivy's resolution against ever returning to Russia herself, and her future hopes began to be built on the idea that the rest of her family would one day follow her westwards. But she sadly began to find that the survivors of her own generation who had been in England to sustain her on her visit ten years earlier, were now few. Her two sisters were now dead, and their families, though she saw something of them, were scattered.[3] England itself was visibly seedier and more egalitarian, and she could no longer find so many of the signs about London that had reassured her a decade earlier. She had to look to younger people for company, and they in the main wanted to hear the truth about the Soviet Union and not about English literature.

She was befriended by Mrs Kaiser, whose son she had met in Moscow when he was correspondent there for an American paper: Mr Kaiser senior was in the American Embassy in London. For a time she was the retired ambassadress once more, inhabiting the Kaisers' impressive flat in Knightsbridge, but it was no more her proper scene than it had been when she was a real diplomat's wife. Somewhere in her autobiographical writings she describes how she and Maxim, suitably dressed, would make their way from their modest flat to the gorgeous rooms in the same building to preside over a diplomatic reception and afterwards 'like actors on whom the curtain has fallen hurry back through the connecting passages to reality'. She felt now that she could not go on being helped by the Kaisers, and had 'an almost straight talk' in which she explained that 'I couldn't bear her for ever shopping for me and kept worrying that I didn't perhaps pay her back. She murmured and said I enriched her life and I said I valued that very deeply but it was not enough in itself.'

So Ivy left London, and I think never returned to it save once on an important visit just before her death. For a short time she found haven and hospitality with her half-sister Rose and her family, but the Holy Ghost was still to provide her with independence. There was a flat in Hove which belonged to an academic she had met in Moscow some years earlier when he was on a visit. It was unoccupied and he offered it to her at a token rent.

Ten, Salisbury Road, Hove was the most suitable place that could have been found for Ivy to spend her last years, and she often said it reminded her of the houses where she had spent her childhood. Salisbury Road, broad and Victorian, slopes in brownish brick gently down towards the sea front and contains both a church and an institute for the English language—a feature Ivy noted with approval. Number 10, unlike many of the houses in the road, was and always had been a private dwelling, and the ground floor flat must

---

[3] Rose, her half-sister (the daughter of Alice and Sandy) was still alive. She and her children were loyal friends of Ivy's, and she stayed with them for a while.

once have been quite smart; but when Ivy took it it had not been redecorated or refurnished for a long time.

The tall, cavernous rooms were approached through a door glazed with stained glass and a murky passage. On the further side of the vast sitting-room lay a dilapidated, glassed-over balcony which served as a dining-room and looked over a modest, disorderly garden. The massive darkness of the sitting-room furniture was partly relieved by Tanya's cheerful impressionistic landscapes of Russia, several of which Ivy hung on the walls. Firmly planted in the middle of the room was the loved and hated sixty-year-old typewriter and most of the surfaces were quickly covered with puddles of papers.

Her needs were modest in the material sense. She did not smoke, and hardly tolerated others doing so; rarely touched alcohol, and ate simply and sparingly, if not always frugally. Her clothes were usually simple to the point of shabbiness—a pair of baggy trousers, a jersey and heavy clumping shoes. Her snow-white hair was pulled back with a black velvet snood. Apart from the heart condition which had troubled her for many years, and from which she eventually died, she was not subject to any of the ailments and decays of old age. Her eyes and hearing were good, her movements vigorous, her mind as sharp and masterful as ever. And when she chose she could still behave like an ambassadress, and dress like one.

She was not unheralded in Hove, and from the first attracted much attention. Chaim Raphael, the novelist, who had been in the British Information Services in Washington during Maxim's embassy, lived not far away. She was invited to neighbouring Palmeira Square by the celebrated connoisseur of the bohemian twenties, Miron Grindea, who saw in her a possible contributor to his magazine *Adam*, and her appearance there brought her a number of other friends.[4] And there was Marjorie Eliot, whom Ivy had met some years before in Moscow and was now not far away with her husband Ian, a lecturer at the Brighton Polytechnic.

Nor did she lack visitors from further afield. Beryl Graves came from Mallorca to spend a week and so did Ivy's old Moscow friend Peg Wetlin on her way back to Russia after spending a holiday in America. Her grand-daughter Masha Slonim was now in England. It was not a lonely exile.

But it was an exile just the same, and she was growing less sociable.

[4] I have referred to several of these valued friends, from whom I have had much help, in the Preface.

She expected deference in a way people were no longer used to, but dreaded exploitation, and so gave the impression of accepting rather ungraciously such deference as was offered. Letters meant more to her by now than actual company, and she pined for them. The correspondence she maintained with Beryl Graves, of which I have been privileged to see both sides, bears witness to true affection and amity; and of course there were many letters from old friends in Russia.

Her resolution was focused not on social life but on registering herself as a writer. After all she had an extraordinary story to tell, if she could manage to tell it. The trouble was that the Kremlin revelations which literary agents and publishers longed for her to provide she regarded as beneath her, and the imaginative writing to which she aspired was now beyond her. Soon after her arrival at Hove she haughtily turned down a very large sum from an American publisher for memoirs of her life in Russia, and set to work on the chronicle of her childhood and youth.

Her attacks on this great work, which she saw as continuing into her later life, resemble the offensives of the Great War through which she had lived, with slaughtered drafts lying pell-mell in swathes, all telling the same story. Here a few yards are gained, a small salient begins to appear, ordered formations are still to be seen advancing; but in the end the stricken words are thrown back in disorder, the scrawls of correction scuffle across the pages like barbed wire, and one more attack has collapsed in confusion and defeat. Marjorie Barnett, a friend of Beryl Graves, came regularly to spend hours a day imparting and restoring discipline to Ivy's shattered output, but it was no use.[5]

She was more successful in mounting single raids. Unhappily her connection with the *New Yorker* had decayed. Rachel Mackenzie was ill and had not long to live; and for financial reasons the paper was taking less copy. One more story, 'Old Woman', was published there (Ivy described the theme as 'what happens when you do things you're not accustomed to'), but successors were turned down with hints that material about the First Circle would be more acceptable.

She found an alternative outlet in *Blackwood's Magazine* where, in March 1973, she published a summary account of her life down to her

[5] Mrs Barnett has told me how, after much effort, she managed to assemble some fifty pages of Ivy's memoirs in continuous typescript, and returned next day to find it reduced to unusable fragments—literally cut to strips—by Ivy's ruthless revision.

marriage with Maxim under the title 'Early Days'. Its 6,000 words are a far more reliable source than the longer, more elaborate, 'Call It Love' which had appeared four years earlier in the *New Yorker*. It is terse and informative, and contains an admirable portrait of Litvinov as she first knew him, together with much detail about their early life together in London.

To ask why there were never 'Later Days' is not quite fair. In the last year of her life Ivy did manage to publish even on this ground, and among her papers there are a number of passages about her life in Russia. But compared to what she tried to achieve in describing her early life—compared to the mountain of attempts from which 'Early Days' is extracted—the contrast is allowable. No doubt many reasons played their part: the discipline of discretion imparted by Maxim; anxiety for those still in Russia; a strong conviction that Jane Austen counted for more than Stalin in the general scale of things; a feeling that her Soviet experience was a valuable asset and not to be squandered; a mixture of irritation and mischief towards those who were so anxious she should tell; and perhaps a feeling that there was less to tell than an eager audience might expect. Less to remember, anyway. Ivy's memory was not very good, and it was very selective.

However, I do not think the real reason was any of these. The block against which the words hurled themselves and were thrown back in disorder was her own character, compounded as it was of intense vitality and lack of sociability. For her the Russian Revolution was not a worldshaking event but something that had occurred in *her* life. Maxim was not an eminent Bolshevik and diplomat, but *her* husband. The time she had spent in the Soviet Union had not been an opportunity for personal observation (still less one for the exercise of political idealism) but *her* life. To describe all these things from the point of view most people seemed to want them described would be a contemptible betrayal of herself. So she took refuge in the idea that she was a born writer of fiction, and found her text in George Sand's alleged reply to the question why she had not written her memoirs, 'Mais, monsieur, je suis romaniste.'[6]

Several of Ivy's friends in Hove, both men and women, noticed an

---

[6] It is not clear where Ivy got this favourite quotation from, and I suspect it is a misquotation. In modern French 'romaniste' means a person learned in Roman studies. Littré notes a use for a proponent of Roman (i.e. papal) power, and an obsolete use for a coiner of fiction.

intense sexuality about her, undiminished in her ninth decade. She still seemed to be holding herself out for adventure—with women far more than with men. She could offer in its honour great warmth and affection, and thirsted for a return which pride and age could no longer accept. Vast though her experience had been she had never been completely confident on the subject. The prefect at the Newcastle school, Broughy the maths mistress at Kilburn, Maxim, her German lovers, her women friends in Russia—they had excited her and elicited her admiration, but she was never completely sure, and it made her story difficult to tell.

In July 1973 she made a second appearance in *Blackwood's Magazine*, but this time she had taken cover, even though the contribution contained a whiff from her later days. 'Pussy Cat Pussy Cat, Where Have You Been' had not made the *New Yorker*, no doubt because its potentially terrible theme had been too much muffled in an animal fable. The story concerns the concentration camps of Stalin's time.

It begins in almost Beatrix Potter style with the meeting of two cats in a Russian forest. One is a born denizen of the woods, the other a stray from the town. Near them there happens to be a concentration camp for women, whom we first see through the explorations of the two animals and their puzzlement that these particular human beings seem unwilling to part with even the smallest scrap of food, beg though they may.Then the story makes a leap to the period after the amnesties of Krushchev. One of the ex-prisoners has resumed her former occupation as a dentist, but on the black market because release has not restored the right to practise, and she has adopted one of the cats. Among her patients is one of the former 'trusties' who long ago had reported her as not needing rations because she had given the cat some scraps.

The contrast between the brazen 'trusty' seeking private treatment from an ex-victim who is still living on the fringe of society is effectively registered, and the injustice of it all comes out sharply because it is hardly ever mentioned. It is the cats—creatures to which Ivy was devoted and dedicated many pages—that intrude, and fail to convince.

She had now given her 'Sorterbiography' the title 'Worlds Unrealized', and much of it survives. But if it had a plan it is not apparent. Here and there are indications of parts and chapters but she never got beyond her all too realized early years, and there is no sign of how she would have continuued it. At first she had written to Beryl Graves that 'Hove is Heaven' but very soon she was in the depths of depression:

> . . . of course I am a very civilized abbaissée, never rude or hysterical, but the reverse of stimulating I should say. Of course if you thought you could bear it and stimulate *me* to use my abundant material I would be willing to sacrifice you on friendship's altar. But you have been warned. All that is the matter with me is an utter loathing of writing.

That cry for help had been answered by Beryl's visit, and there can be no doubt of Ivy's gratitude:

> Oh what you did for me! Because you were there I could not wallow in depression and tell myself it was no good trying to force myself in such a state. And you made me pick up the old t-writer again and I think there hasn't been a day when I haven't tried to write a line or two. I shall never forget how just before going to bed you suggested we should have another little look at the last page.

Beryl had left a guardian angel called Marjorie Barnett, who came daily from Lewes to encourage and organize, 'so I daren't not have ANYTHING to show her.' She became quite jaunty, in spite of her troubles: 'I am sinking very low in the cash department. Ivy Low. But in between mild fits of panic I plan to spend the enormous advances publishers in two continents are about to offer me.' So continued 'Worlds Unrealized'.

Her life was beginning to assume an iron routine. Her breakfast, at which she often received visitors, was the favourite meal of the day and allowed her to parade her inveterate Englishness. It was usually taken on the balcony where a small book-case stood conveniently near the breakfast table. The tea took about half an hour to prepare, since it involved not only boiling the kettle and warming the tea-pot, but warming the individual cups, and the milk, all in sequence and accompanied by grave warnings that no other method was in any way acceptable. Toast was then made with equal ceremony, using a toasting fork—no grill could in her opinion produce satisfactory toast. Marmalade was of course indispensable. Then the typewriter was set up and the daily battle would begin.

The Chalidzes were already in the West and other members of the family were soon to follow. Pavel had been released on completion of his five-year sentence at the end of 1972 but very soon found himself once more in conflict with the authorities. 'Great things happening here', wrote one of Ivy's correspondents in Russia, 'which I am out of except hearing repercussions and wishing the best to all.' The new crisis was gathering round the names of Sakharov and Solzhenitsyn from whose window another of Ivy's correspondents described 'the brave light shining. They don't mix with the aborigines, but glimpses of them are sought by the latter as eagerly as the snowman of the Himalayas.'

In March 1974 Pavel Litvinov was warned that if he remained in Russia he would face an even harsher sentence than five years, and he decided to leave the country with his wife Maya and his children Dimitri and Larissa. He made his way first to Vienna, then to Hove (where his grandmother received him joyfully but required him to leave the room to smoke) and finally to the United States. Soon afterwards another of Ivy's grandchildren, Tanya's daughter Masha, came to England. Of Maxim's family only three remained in Russia—Misha and his daughter, and Tanya.

It seemed so obvious to Ivy that Tanya should come. She had the right to settle in the country of her birth; she had been brought up to a love of its literature; her mother was old and needed her support; the running battle with the Soviet authorities could never end in victory, and was far more likely to lead to suffering for those fighting it.

> Every day for a few minutes I think to myself; 'can it be that I shall never see Tanya again?' and the answer is 'it certainly can.' Do be energetic while it is yet day. It isn't only a question of me, but things don't seem to get any easier do they?

With 1975 the appeals grew more urgent. 'Hopes. Hopes!' is scribbled at the bottom of a short note in August of that year; and in November: 'I'm so sorry to have so few family photos, and apparently none of my mother even! Perhaps one day you can find some and BRING (not send). Ah, bring, bring. Yourself. to ME.'

In spite of the powerful arguments and even more powerful pressure from Salisbury Road, Tanya hesitated. She was now a widow, but her ties with her brother were strong, and her social world lay in the country where she had been brought up since she was four years old. Strong as were her British sympathies, she felt herself at heart a Russian. Her career had been highly skilled translation of English classics for the Russian reader, not, like Ivy's, the rendering

of Russian into English. Though not herself one of the organizers of
dissidence she felt a loyalty to some of them, and a responsibility to
give comfort and support to those who landed in trouble. She did not
want to become an exile, and she well knew her mother's demanding
character which the end of one of Ivy's letters from Hove showed only
too clearly. She was commenting on one of her friends:

> She thinks I'm exacting. She doesn't understand that I have no
> time left for anything but everything (in reason), and allows herself
> to be distracted by such little things as having the roof mended and
> furniture stored and step-nieces to stay and all sorts of things she
> will always have with her, whereas ME she won't. Damn Real
> Life.

Ivy was too honest to confine such an attitude to private comment,
and the attitude was therefore bound to make itself felt in her circle in
Hove. Though she kept many loyal friends, they were not so many as
at first. She could be alarmingly rude and critical on little
provocation. 'There are no such people as economists,' she roundly
declared on being introduced to one: 'There are only statisticians and
mathematicians. I always told my class in Moscow so.' This particular
economist bided his time and got the better of her at their next
encounter, when she again greeted him with 'There's no such thing as
an . . .' and he completed the sentence for her, adding, 'You are
beginning to suffer from senile repetition.' It was characteristic of Ivy
that he thereby earned her undying admiration.

Tanya, she felt, would be her deliverance, and yet subconsciously
she had hesitations. She saw her daughter in dreams coming towards
her and stretched out her hand, only to see the vision retreat. It was
not just a doubt whether Tanya would come, or be allowed to come.
She was not sure if Tanya could deliver her.

Towards the end of 1975 Tanya made up her mind to pay Ivy at
least a visit if she could. She remembers laying down the telephone
that autumn after one of her mother's frequent calls from Hove and
realizing from the urgency of the words 'I need you' (words her
mother had never, in her pride, used before) that she had to go. This
must have been just before the 'Bring, bring . . .' letter which had
risen to its final call after a sweeping review of George Eliot and the
conclusion that *The Mill on the Floss* 'may be the great English novel'.
It might, Ivy thought, be fashionable to praise *Middlemarch* 'but it is
madly uneven and overpopulated', while *Adam Bede* was 'loathsome

in its priggishness' and *Scenes from Clerical Life* was 'not quite professional'.

So in March 1976 there was a family reunion of four generations at Salisbury Road—Ivy, Tanya, Masha, Vera, and great-grandchildren. Ivy was nearly eighty-seven and experienced even in the life of extreme old age. Inevitably Tanya was prevailed upon to stay, and was congratulated by the British official who handed her the necessary papers on the happy accident which had prevented her father's recognition long ago, in 1918. If Maxim had been granted the diplomatic status he had so persistently sought, his children could have had no claim to British nationality.

Tanya's presence brought a great degree of contentment to Ivy, and the pressure for self-assertion began to diminish. The long struggle for personal independence now was over, and a calmer mood took its place, a quiescence, even an unwillingness to exert herself. Her patent chair, of which she was very proud, became a yet more important feature of her life. Yet one more effort was made to unblock her memories of her Moscow days, under the leadership of Tanya and with the aid of several friends. The result, after weeks of turmoil, was the front page of the *Observer Review* for 25 July 1976.

This article is Ivy's one contribution to the political history of her time. It describes how not only Ivy, the bourgeois foreigner, but Maxim, the bourgeois Jew, were excluded from the hierarchy that governed the Soviet Union. They were, in Bolshevik terms, unclubbable:

> It was Maxim who was the foreign body. . . . He did not drink or hunt or take part in any of the virile sports of the rulers. He wore elastic-sided ankle-high boots, read the *New Statesman*, took long walks like an Englishman, and carried a mahogany walking-stick.

And as early as 1936 'he had begun to see the writing on the wall.'[7]

The article provides many vivid details of Maxim's decline and fall, starting with Zhdanov's attack on the administration of the Narkomindel and continuing with the gradual withdrawal of even formal cordiality by colleagues interested in their skins; his supersession by Molotov in 1939; his expulsion from the Central

---

[7] At the end of her life Ivy used to indicate that he had developed scepticism even earlier, during the 1920s, and that in retrospect he could discern the moment, even in the days of Lenin, when the Revolution had taken the wrong direction.

Committee; and his defiant interchange with Stalin which Ivy considered had saved his life.

As her own life drew to an end Ivy reflected a great deal about the reasons for Maxim's and her own survival. The last task she set herself was a compilation, of which only fragments remain, entitled 'Lucky Old Woman'. 'I am sure they had enough dossiers on me', she told a journalist from the *Washington Post* in 1977, 'to fill this room.' There had been times when friends had been startled to see her in the street, and when she had not been surprised to discover that a friend had vanished. Three times, it was said, orders had been issued for Maxim's arrest, each time to be cancelled. Yet Stalin was not a man ever to err on the side of generosity, or to remember past services.

Maxim's unclubbability and Ivy's oddness were not quite enough to explain their exemption. Tens of thousands who were far less exposed than Maxim had perished, and what he had said towards the end of his stay in Washington, let alone after it, could alone have cost him his life. It almost did. It was a question of time. In the Bolshevik system, even in the bloody mind of Stalin, there lay a calculation that the possibility of Western approval must never wholly be discarded. Total isolation, absolute defiance, were positions to be avoided, and the destruction of Litvinov would have violated this instinct. It can hardly have been that he possessed dangerous secrets—the best way with such possessors is to eliminate them—but that almost alone among the Soviet leadership he had a constituency in the West which had come to associate him personally with disarmament, resistance to fascism, and collective security; and it was a constituency which extended to the highest levels among senior statesmen who felt he would keep his word. His opinion may not have counted for much in the high policy of the Kremlin, but his standing abroad was a factor in its calculations.

Maxim's survival and Ivy's frustration as a writer can both be traced to accidents in their lives which set each of them apart from similar contemporaries. In Maxim's case it was his reputation in the West originating in his long residence there; in Ivy's a marriage through which she had a unique position and a distinction she would never otherwise have achieved. This distinction she found impossible to incorporate in what she felt was her destiny as a writer, and she resented the fact. Her great adventure, which had singled her out, and which she felt obscurely should have helped her in her literary ambition, actually stood in her way like a gigantic landslide into which she could do no more than burrow and tunnel on the surface without being able to bring her gifts of observation or her experience to bear as a whole.

Her last year at Hove, with Tanya, was one of the calmest of her life. She was declining in strength, and troubled by the effects of a slight stroke she had suffered a year or two earlier, but her mood, though melancholy, was more tranquil and she was supported by many friends. The Christmas of 1976 brought a letter from Jock Rantz, who earlier that year had come to visit her:

> I am sad that you are sad. Must it be so? Is there no consolation in books and music and the knowledge that many people love you and wish for your happiness? Here I stopped and played the tape you made in Moscow in 1965—and you are here in this room with me. You are reading a story of Chekhov—only a fragment, unluckily— and the room is filled with the music of your voice—YOUR VOICE. Remember I fell in love with your voice before I ever saw you. I had come to the *Moscow Daily News*, and from the next room came your voice dictating a story, and I was enchanted.

A little later, in February 1977, came a letter from one of her friends in Moscow who was translating *Anna Karenina*:

> Your last letter gave her [i.e. Anna Karenina] a shot in the arm, or rather the leg, because I set out for a walk . . . and kept on going for two hours, all 120 minutes of them filled with thoughts of you, having that talk with you you said you wished for. It was a saddish letter, Ivy, but we have nothing to be sad about, we who have lived so many lives in one; it is the height of ingratitude to expect anything. Surely we never thought it would last for ever and in a sort of crescendo. That would be very odd.

On the back of this letter Ivy scrawled an exhausting game of words out of a word, scoring 15 from 'employment', 33 from 'recondite', 36 from 'endeavour', 45 from 'manifesto', 52 from 'malevolent', and no less than 71 from 'pertinacious'.

Calmer she might be, but her flag was still flying. In February 1977 she gave an interview to the *Washington Post* in which she indicated that even now the gigantic challenge of her book might be conquered and roundly declared that Tanya 'was the best thing that ever happened to me'. She introduced herself to Anna Freud, and made her way to London for a meeting with the daughter of the man whose mind she had venerated more than any other. 'Why', she asked Anna Freud, 'do I feel so strongly about my father, whom I can only just remember?' 'He taught you to read,' was the reply.

Sometimes an evening would be spent, with Tanya's aid, bringing the piles of paper to some kind of order; but after Tanya had gone to bed, or rising before her early in the morning, the aged author would churn all into confusion once more. She began to see things in reverse, and even her beloved scrabble letters sometimes seemed to be upside down. Her speech began to slur.

If you could see me grunting and wortling on getting up from a chair [she wrote to one of her Moscow friends] or trying to turn to the other side in bed, all would be forgiven. I don't know quite what it is—sharp pain in the ribs on one side, sometimes rising towards the chest and climbing to the neck. Fit for nothing but grumbling and mumbling. Well we'll *see* won't we? Love. Ivy.

A few weeks later, in April 1977, Marjorie Barnett had a long, reminiscent conversation with Ivy which she never seemed to want to break off; and on the morning of 16 April, not quite two months before her eighty-eighth birthday, she was found dying in bed from the effects of a massive heart attack—a 'lucky old woman', as she would have said, to the last. There was no funeral. She had donated her body for anatomical purposes to University College Hospital— the hospital where David Eder had qualified.

'Too cerebral', she wrote towards the end of her life, 'but at the same time not really furnished for hard thinking'. The grounds on which she built her claim to recognition actually drew attention away from her best qualities—her courage, her warmth, her powers of survival. No doubt she would always have been a contradictory character, even if she had not accidentally married a future Commissar, but the effect of the adventure of her life was to magnify the contradiction. She was dealt a high card in life, but it was in the wrong suit. So she became one of the most serious of exiles, one who has exiled herself, and was hardly at home between the day she left the barely remembered house in Fairholme Road, West Kensington, until she found a haven at Salisbury Road, Hove, 'an old hag, poring over words like arrows'.

APPENDIX I

Copenhagen 1919–1920

The meetings in Copenhagen between Litvinov and James O'Grady, his contacts with Francis Meynell and Lansbury's visit to the Soviet Union constitute an episode which deserves elucidation and has been stressed since.[1]

James O'Grady visited Copenhagen in November 1919 to negotiate, ostensibly, for the return of British prisoners of war from Russia, but, in addition, to explore an ending of the War of Intervention. Meynell's dating of his own meeting with Litvinov as 'the summer of 1920', 'at the time of the O'Grady mission', cannot therefore be correct on grounds of internal consistency.There are other reasons for supposing that the meeting took place earlier than the summer of 1920. One is that Rothstein, from whom Meynell says he carried a message to Litvinov, receiving pearl necklaces in exchange, left London in 1920, never to return. The other is that in September 1920 the story of Soviet subsidies to the *Daily Herald* was all over the papers, and Meynell had to resign. Yet Meynell's account refers to several bullion-carrying trips between the Baltic and London after the first encounter 'in the summer of 1920', for which there is hardly time.

The inference is that Meynell's encounter with Litvinov took place earlier than the summer of 1920, and if so, at the time of the O'Grady mission in November 1919. The conclusion is significant, because in that case it coincided with Lansbury's (i.e. Meynell's editor's) own visit to Copenhagen, from which he went on to be the first British journalist to visit the Soviet Union, and had an interview with Lenin in February 1920. That Litvinov knew of this is certain: he probably arranged it. It seems inconceivable that Meynell and Lansbury did not know that each was simultaneously in Copenhagen and in touch with Litvinov.

[1] E.g. Walter Kendall, *The British Revolutionary Movement in Britain 1900–1921*, Weidenfeld and Nicolson, 1969; and Andrew Boyle, *Climate of Treason*, Hutchinson, 1980.

Mr Boyle, though he attributes 'a master plan of subversion' to Litvinov, has clearly not studied Litvinov's connection with England even superficially. Mr Kendall throws doubt on Meynell's account, the fullest version of which is given in *My Lives*, Bodley Head, 1971, pp. 116–23.

[Appendix I: Copenhagen 1919–1920]

Yet Meynell does not mention this at all in his account, or even refer to Lansbury's Soviet visit. Lansbury appears only in the sequel as an editor he had embarrassed and who expressed sorrowful agreement to his resignation.

Two explanations are possible, both of them consistent with Meynell's omission of any reference to Lansbury's presence in Copenhagen. One is that Meynell's exchange of messages for jewellery was a matter wholly secret to himself, which should not be allowed to compromise Lansbury. The other is that he was acting with Lansbury. If the latter was the case, Lansbury's subsequent conduct does not appear in a very agreeable light, though Meynell's does. In either case the episode provides no evidence of a master plan for subversion on the part of the Soviets.

APPENDIX II

Rose Cohen

The following tape, complete in itself, was probably made during Ivy's stay in England in 1960–1. The transcript has been revised in Ivy's hand with the clear intention of including it at some point in her memoirs.

Rose Cohen was a London Jewish girl, very beautiful, a sort of *jüdische* rose. I think she was a member of the Party in the days of long, long, long ago. Somehow she was in Paris and she met there a Jewish Party member, Petrovsky, a Ukrainian Jew. He was the ugliest man you ever saw but very charming. He had one of those great drooping noses and he was a great hulking man, very much older than she was, about twenty years perhaps. And here was this radiant young girl with whom Harry Pollitt remained in love all his life. He married but he said, 'Rose, all my life is yours at any moment, whenever you want it.' Why she married Petrovsky I don't know. I liked him, he was a darling, but why she should . . . but anyway she did, she was fascinated by him and he took her back to Russia. She was quite a little celebrity in Moscow. She worked on the *Moscow Daily News* in those days. They had a lovely apartment and they had a little boy and we all became great friends. I was great friends with Rose. And whenever I was alone with Petrovsky he used to make a pass at me. I don't know to what extent Rose knew about it. He hinted that Rose was so terribly pure, perhaps frigid, that he didn't love her. But there it was, and I didn't think he was too good either.

I knew their little boy very well. He was a very unattractive but sweet little boy—ears sticking out and drooping nose like Petrovsky; and like some people did in Moscow, they dressed him terribly, in plus fours and cloth caps. But he was a charming little boy and Rose and I were great friends in a way. She was always very gay.

She never gave up her English citizenship. She was asked not to, for convenience. It was very nice to have a Party member who could go to and fro. It was good for them in every way, and I suppose she liked it too. Then the arrests began. Whenever we spoke about them she was always rather smug—'well, I suppose they know what they're doing, don't you?'— 'They-don't-take-me' sort of attitude. And if we talked about over-crowding she would say, 'Well, I think everybody has got a flat now, don't you?' I said, 'Well I don't, Rose, I don't think so just because you and I have.' She had that sort of smugness and complacency, the cowardice that comes from shutting your eyes. She lived among Americans and had to keep the flag flying, and she didn't want to know, I think.

Just a little digression to show what a man Borodin was. Borodin was the editor of the *Moscow Daily News,* and when my book on Basic English came out, Borodin calmly handed it to me and said, 'I don't want to give it to somebody who doesn't understand about it. Write the review yourself. I'll give you a column.' So I did. I wrote what I wanted to be said about it, and I remember Borodin looking at it afterwards and saying, 'Look, look, our people don't understand. That's culture. I gave you this to write and you could have said anything you liked, and there isn't a word of praise for the author. That's the way to do it. Our people don't know.'

I was unhappy at home, very unhappy. I was having trouble with ——, and even trouble with Tanya. She was having all sorts of adolescent difficulties and there was a time of rather painful relations between us. So I went to Petrovsky and said, 'I want to tell you something. I'm unhappy. I want to leave Moscow.' He had in his hands all the institutes of higher learning for industry and he could easily send me to one of them. It would not be so easy now, because now a Russian diploma is essential. Even Christ speaking English would be no good to them, they just want a diploma, and I had no diploma of any sort. But he knew me and I said, 'Supposing I go to Kiev or somewhere like that.' But he said, 'No, that would be foolish because there is another language, another nationalism. Why should you mix yourself up in that? I'll send you to Sverdlovsk where we have a new industrial institute. They teach English there and you shall teach Basic English. I'll just tell them you shall.' And he fixed it all and I went to Sverdlovsk and I taught Basic English in the industrial institute to technical students. And I also taught in the pedagogical institute which was the lowest of the low, because they had their entrance examinations after all the other institutes had had theirs and got the ones who failed everywhere else. Those would be pedagogues. That's what happens, isn't it dreadful? Well, anyway, I was several years there—until Maxim was demoted.

During the Yezhovshchina[1] Petrovsky was arrested, but Rose was still on the *News.* I was away in Sverdlovsk at the time and when I came back the first thing Maxim said to me was: 'I hope you're not going to rush off and see Rose.' I said, 'Maxim, I must.' And he said, 'Well, it would be a terrible thing for you to do.' Then Tanya rushed into the breach and said 'I don't matter.' And she went to see her and brought her back. We had a friend who was taking photographs and I had a photograph of us taken together. He wanted to take my photograph and she was sitting on the bench with me. She said, 'I'll move. I don't want to spoil it.' But she came out beautifully in the photograph and I sent it to her sister in England.

Just before Petrovsky was arrested Rose was asked to give up her English nationality. She was trying to get it back. We spent the day together and she

[1] The terror during the period of office of Yezhov as chief of the security police.

said 'You know, you're the only ones . . . the Americans are all round me but not a single one of my friends has been to see me.' She was utterly lonely and trembling of course. She was left with her little boy. That was the last time I saw Rose.

I hadn't gone to her home because Maxim had told me not to, but Tanya brought her to us and then I took her home. I thought to Hell with it! I thought I wouldn't be followed . . . and anyway you see I'm here.

I asked Maxim what had happened to Rose. There had been a question in Parliament about her and Harry Pollitt went to see Stalin and said, 'You must let her go back to England,' and Stalin said, 'All right' but she had already been shot.

A few years ago I was called up by somebody who said, 'Do you remember Rose Cohen?' I said, 'Of course I do.' He said, 'I am Volodya, the little boy you used to know.' I said, 'Oh Volodya, I'd love to see you.' He said, 'Now that this is all over and my mother's and my father's memory is more or less rehabilitated, I thought perhaps you had some photographs of her or something I could see—I don't know anything about her.' So I said, 'Come and see me.' And so this pathetic, extraordinary, wonderful young man came to see me, looking a terrible physical wreck; a great tall young man, he was a geologist or something like that in an institute, and he told us about his life. How he'd been in various children's homes; but he said with tears in his eyes, 'I've had a very tough time but I met some noble people who were very kind to me.' And then in the end some school friend's parents—no relation at all— just took him and adopted him and loved him as their own child. He had terrible difficulty in getting back to Moscow but at last there he was. He was such an interesting, charming and pure person. He married and brought his wife to see us. He was having awful difficulty because he wasn't supposed to be in Moscow. A scientist, imagine! And such a mature man. I simply adored him. He had no telephone. I could never get in touch with him. He used to ring me up. They had a baby but I don't know to this day if they have a room to live in. He has still got relations in England. I would love to get in touch with them and bring him news. But I don't know if I will ever be able to find him again.

Index

[Index]

[Index]